How to
Become a
Data Analyst

My Low-Cost, No Code Roadmap for Breaking into Tech

Annie Nelson

T0286079

WILEY

To Chris,

For doing all the cooking, cleaning, housework, and anything else that needed to be done so I could focus on changing my life

Contents

Contents

Preface

I've never seen myself as particularly "techy" or "good at math." To be honest, I never enjoyed math, and if you'd asked me even a few years ago if I had any interest in learning how to code, I would've laughed at you. So how in the world did I go from that to writing this book about becoming a data analyst? Perhaps I should start with some context, because I find that the more I connect with others in the data community, the more I see my story reflected in theirs.

In the United States the phrase "What do you want to be when you grow up?" is usually synonymous with both "What do you want your identity to be?" and "What career do you want to have?" I grew up thinking that what I did for work had to be my entire personality. I was never quite sure what I wanted to "be." I was a natural caretaker and wanted to be seen as empathetic, and I've always loved spending time with kids. I also knew that I love spending time outdoors and going on adventures regularly.

This led to the natural conclusion that I should become a teacher or maybe a wilderness therapist. Well, after some time dabbling in teaching I realized that it was not the path for me. So after discovering the joys of nature-based occupational therapy with children, I decided I knew what I wanted to "be," and I signed up for my master's degree a few months later.

Fast-forward a couple of years (and many thousands of dollars later), and I was more burnt out than I'd ever been. Unfortunately, a perfect storm of circumstances had rocked my (our) world(s) in the last few years. In my first year of graduate school (1) we entered a global pandemic (hello, 2020!),

(2) I developed a mysterious autoimmune disorder in my brain, and (3) I was juggling full-time graduate school and being elected president of the student government of my program.

Unfortunately, I didn't have the best graduate school experience. I felt that I was often being asked to ingest and regurgitate information seemingly at the instructor's discretion. I'm someone who genuinely enjoys learning, and being forced to perform under high stakes without the joy of being allowed to truly *learn* was a hard pill to swallow. I poured hours of time (and many tears) into trying to advocate for myself and my peers, only to get chastised for being "unprofessional."

After two years of poor physical health (migraines, brain fog, and overwhelming fatigue) and poor mental health (due to graduate school), I knew that something in my life needed to change. The year 2021 in particular felt like it was grinding me down so hard that all that was left was an emotionless pile of dust. So, in the last semester of school I quit my job and moved out of my apartment to go live with my parents, to try to recover some of the spark I used to have for life.

Why am I telling you all this? None of the individual brush strokes of my story are likely to be relevant to you. But, if we back up a bit and look at the whole picture I've painted, I know it suddenly becomes a familiar picture for many people out there. What's the number one thing people tell me when I ask why they decided to take the leap and switch careers into data? "I was burnt out, unhappy, and wondering if there could be more than the life I was living before."

As I started to recover from burnout, the first thing that returned was my interest in learning. The next thing to come was the acute awareness that I still needed to make it through another nine months before I could get a job as an occupational therapist and start paying off my tens of thousands of dollars in student loans. At first, besides the time I was spending on internships as a part of the end of my Master's Degree, I was reading five books a week and delivering for Instacart. At around the same time, I started to see all these TikToks from people who worked in tech talking about their remote jobs, how flexible they were, and how well they paid.

The idea of working remotely, having autonomy over your schedule, and being paid well enough to be comfortable was fascinating to me, but it felt far out of reach. I wrote it off initially, thinking I wasn't smart enough. "I'm just not a math person" and "I could never enjoy coding" and even "I like having a job where I'm on my feet often" were all mental statements I made to myself.

Sometime about mid-January, I decided to look up "tech jobs you can do without learning to code." To my surprise, it appeared there were many paths into the tech industry, not all of them requiring a computer science degree or any coding. I spent a few hours going down the rabbit hole of different options and finally landed on data analytics. What I gathered about data analytics is that it involves working with data in programs like Microsoft Excel. It can be done remotely or in person. And, crucially, it seemed like it had a pretty low barrier to entry.

I put all those pieces together and decided, "Maybe I could learn data analytics well enough that people would pay me to organize and analyze their spreadsheets as a side hustle." It had all the markings of a perfect plan—I could do it on my own time, make more than minimum wage, and do it without having to drive anywhere. I'd found this Google Certificates course in Data Analytics that seemed to have the roadmap laid out for me to prepare for a job or side gig.

I was lucky enough at that point to have already prepared for the time I would be in various occupational therapy clinics full-time to complete the requirements for my degree (kind of like student teaching), unable to have a steady source of income. I had some free time to spend learning, as long as it was cheap. Looking back, what was most exciting to me about signing up for and beginning that Google Certificates course was the ability to finally get to *learn* again.

I'll continue sharing the story of what happened next in the chapters to come, but the short version is that the random decision to try analyzing spreadsheets as a side hustle became not only the catalyst for eventually deciding to switch careers, but also one of the single most influential and pivotal moments in my life so far. As you can imagine, you don't get to the point of writing a book about how to become a data analyst without it being a life-changing event.

I'm so glad that I put a very small amount of thought into the idea of trying out data analytics. If I'd thought about it and tried picturing myself as a data analyst among other data analysts, I never would've started.

If you'd asked me a year and a half ago what your average "data analyst" looks like, I would've answered something like this:

- Male
- Good at math/statistics
- Into computers
- Has a computer science or math degree

This is far beyond the scope of this book and I am not qualified to talk about it, but as I've discussed this topic with others in the industry, something that often comes up is that most people perceive tech to be dominated by cis straight white men. If I had to choose from a multiple-choice list who would be the best fit for "data analyst" and "cis white male" was one of the options, I would've chosen that.

The point I'm making here is this: I *definitely* did not see myself represented in the tech world. I can't imagine that I would've decided to seek a new career that I knew nothing about, where I wouldn't fit in with anyone, while not having any idea if I would ever be good at it—even if it promised good pay and remote work.

That's part of the reason I'm writing this book: I hope readers can see themselves represented in my story. I am neurodivergent, I have an autoimmune disorder. I am a (white) woman. When I was writing this preface and explaining how I hated calculus in high school, I realized two days later that it was *algebra*. I never even *took* calculus in high school (I did take pre-calc). I love spending my time with children. Three years ago was the first time I ever had a full-time job during the summer, because prior to that I would take my summers off so I could spend afternoons swimming, camping, rock climbing, and generally *not working or sitting in front of a computer*.

I'm not what someone would consider the "ideal candidate" for a data analyst role on paper. But you know what? In just six months I taught myself data analytics for less than $100 and landed a great job. I have loved being a data analyst, and I don't get the "Sunday Scaries" anymore, where I spend most of my Sunday dreading going back to work on Monday. I have also never gotten a less-than-glowing performance review from my manager(s) since I changed careers, and others around me tell me that I am learning fast and doing exceptionally well for someone so new to the industry.

So far I've talked about data analytics from the perspective of what it looks like to be an entry-level data analyst. But how about what comes next? If you launch a data career, what can you expect your roadmap to look like in the future?

The beautiful thing about working in tech in general, and analytics is no exception, is that it is always growing and evolving. Earlier I mentioned how curiosity and a love of learning are a valuable part of the data analyst mindset. There are so many ways you can make a career in data.

The only thing I can say for sure is that you can't get into data analytics and expect that it's always going to stay the same. As you move up the chain of data analytics, the expectations for you in your role will evolve. Additionally, the tools themselves will always be changing and evolving. I heard a story recently about someone who got into a senior data analyst role just by getting really good at Excel. When they decided to try to get another role, they couldn't. They refused to learn SQL, and when they tried to find a senior data analyst role that didn't require any SQL (or Python!), they couldn't find one.

Don't worry if you don't know what SQL and Python are yet; they're tools data analysts use, and you'll learn about them in this book.

Since every industry needs to have data analyzed, and data is such a fast-growing field, the possibilities are almost endless. Here are some options and job titles for the future career path you could take once you get into data:

- Data quality analyst
- Senior data analyst
- Senior research analyst
- Senior financial analyst
- Analytics manager
- Director of analytics
- Data scientist
- Data engineer
- Analytics engineer
- Chief data officer
- Data project manager
- Project manager
- Product manager

- Data governance specialist
- Data quality engineer
- Data steward
- Data evangelist
- Head of data analytics

When I decided to get into data analytics, I did it because of the seemingly infinite possibility for growth. I thought that I'd spend a few years as a data analyst, and then look into transitioning into a data scientist role. Now that I have gotten into not only data analytics but also consulting, I've realized I'm very interested in data strategy and quality. I enjoy thinking about the big picture and understanding how each piece of the data puzzle fits with the rest.

In the future I see myself potentially going in the direction of data/analytics engineering, data strategy, or even head of analytics or chief data officer. Who knows where my career will go—not me! It does seem to be pretty common that people think data analytics will be their stepping stone to data science, and then they discover some other path along the way that interests them. I don't want to become a data scientist, but it is a popular transition.

One big benefit of data analytics, at least in 2023, is that it has a fairly low barrier to entry. I often see people who had no prior tech or data experience getting their first data jobs. It happened to me! Many of the other roles I listed require previous experience. Fortunately, becoming a data analyst could be the springboard or prior experience you need to access any one of them.

Even though the barrier to entry is low, it still takes work! In this book, I walk you through everything I needed to know to make the leap from my old career into data analytics. This will prepare you to do the work of becoming a data analyst, without all the uncertainty of not knowing where to start or what to focus on.

Introduction

If you've read this far, you're probably interested in jumping into data analytics. Congratulations! It tops the charts as one of the best things I've ever done for myself. In this book I will lay out my story, and along the way I'll relate that to how you, too, can get into data analytics.

In this book, I'll discuss how I got my first data job six months after I began learning this new career, and it cost me less than $100. I've seen hundreds of people go down this same route since I got my job and experience success as well. I've compared my story and struggles with those of many others and identified the things that we all have in common.

There are many different paths to getting a role as a data analyst, and no two journeys will look the same. At the end of the day, job searching often comes down to luck and timing. I'm not going to tell you exactly what to do, and I can't guarantee that at the end of it all you'll get a job. I can't guarantee you a certain salary, or that it will take you a certain length of time.

What I can tell you, though, is what worked for me. I can tell you what felt hard for me and what things I would do differently if I were to do it all over again. I can tell you the things I've seen people do who followed the same path to successfully land a job in data analytics.

How Do I Know If Data Is a Good Fit for Me?

One of the questions I get asked the most often is "Can I get into data analytics if my only experience is in _____?" The answer is yes. Data analytics is a unique career because it has a fairly low barrier to entry. Every industry needs data analysts! I may not be the best "financial data analyst," but I'm working on a project right now with research/survey data, and my research background has given me a leg up. So, toss aside any perceptions that you may have about "who" makes the "perfect" data analyst. If it seems interesting to you, then you might be a good fit!

Who This Is Book For

This book is for you if you want to take what I call the "DIY" approach to getting into data analytics. You are happy to teach yourself and you don't need an instructor to tell you what to do or teach you hands-on. If you take this approach, it will likely be the cheapest; many people, including myself, have done it for less than $100. However, do not pick this approach just because it is the cheapest.

My "DIY" approach is good for people who already have good critical thinking skills—people who already know how to do research on the Internet. (You'd be amazed at the number of questions I get in my inbox like "What is SQL?" You should be able to Google things like that yourself and not have to ask someone else.) This approach is good for the career changers—people who already have professional experience in another field and just need to learn how to translate that into data analytics. This can be just about anything, from waitressing, to teaching, to occupational therapy (I've done all three).

This book will be helpful if you like to solve problems on your own. I'll provide a general roadmap and some sample projects. However, I'll focus on sharing my experiences with you—and it will be up to you to take that information and apply it to your own situation.

I find that the type of people who are curious, passionate, and good at critical thinking tend to have the easiest time making their way into data analytics and enjoy it the most when they get there. If you'd prefer to have someone to walk you through every step of the process—teach you the technical skills, provide you with résumé feedback, stage mock interviews, help you with your LinkedIn profile—know that this book will not do that.

This book walks you through my journey to become a data analyst, and I'll offer advice about selecting courses and learning data skills. I'll share with you my real insights of what it felt like to run a successful query for the first time, as well as my doubts about my abilities when I reached challenging subjects.

I'll talk about building a portfolio, which is the key to any successful transition into data analytics. Building a portfolio was exciting but intimidating for me when I was learning, and so I'm taking the guesswork out for you and will break it down so portfolio building is approachable—and hopefully fun!

I'll also discuss all things job search. I'll share my honest experience of job searching, being rejected, and considering giving up on data analytics. You'll see how I pivoted my strategy and how I landed my first job in data. I'll also share practical tips about networking, résumés, and LinkedIn. There's even a guide for using artificial intelligence (AI) to help you succeed at every step of the job search and interview process.

If you enjoy learning independently and are willing to put in the work to become a data analyst, then this book will be just the guide for you. My goal is to take all the guesswork out of the equation so that you can set yourself up with a roadmap and avoid all the mistakes I made along the way.

Changing careers into data analytics requires persistence and determination—but it's worth it in the end. At least, it was for me!

PART

I

The Fun Part

1

Is Data Analytics Right for Me?

What's Here

- What does a data analyst actually do every day?
- What makes a good data analyst?
- What tools should I learn?
- Which entry-level tech job is right for me?

What does it even mean to be a data analyst? Before you can dive into data, you probably have a lot of questions about what it would really look like to be a data analyst. If you are in a completely different career (like I was before I transitioned into data), you may want to know about the day-to-day and what would make you a good analyst.

Once you understand what it looks like to be a data analyst, you can make a more informed decision about whether it will be the right fit for you. At the start of my journey, I was unsure if I would enjoy the work of data analytics, but I knew that the idea of remote, flexible work was appealing. Fortunately, I ended up loving everything about being a data analyst once I dove in. It turned out it is the right fit for me!

Since data analytics is a broad and diverse career path, there are many different options for what this career path can look like. In this chapter

I will share with you the basics of what it's like to be an entry-level data analyst, as well as career progression options.

What Does a Data Analyst Do Every Day?

Later in this book, I will talk about what my day-to-day looks like, and share some stories from other data analysts I know whose jobs are vastly different from mine. For now, let's just talk generally about what data analysts do day to day.

Something that I love about the field of data analytics is that it is incredibly diverse. I don't know two people in data who do the same thing. The thing is, unlike other career paths, there is no one "area" that data analytics belongs to. If you're a nurse then it's fairly predictable that you are going to be working with the human body. Real estate agents pretty predictably sell houses and properties. But every industry out there has data, doesn't it?

That means if you become a data analyst you might need to know about

- Banking
- Healthcare
- Stocks
- Insurance
- Auctions
- Manufacturing
- Research
- Sales
- Marketing
- Human resources (HR)
- Construction

The list goes on and on. Although there is a core set of tools and skills that most data analysts will need, the day-to-day of the job is going to be heavily influenced by the demands and culture of the industry and company that the role exists within.

I have found that generally there are two primary divisions to "data analytics," but almost all roles mix and match from both. Data analytics tends to represent the technical aspects of the job—which means utilizing things like Microsoft Excel and SQL to analyze data and draw conclusions. However, almost all analyst roles also incorporate "business analytics," which involves taking what you learn from your technical data explorations and applying it to the real problems and challenges facing the business.

A common phrase in the data sphere is "heads-down work." That refers to when you are doing a deep dive into the data/project. Heads-down work tends to be pure analysis/building, so it doesn't involve emails, meetings, or presentations. A role that leans more heavily toward the "data" side of analytics tends to have more heads-down work. When there are meetings, they are often an internal review of the work that has been done and planning for future work.

Roles that lean more toward the "business" side of analytics, on the other hand, will involve a lot more face-to-face time—internally and externally. This might mean spending some time doing heads-down analyses but then presenting that information to internal executives or external stakeholders or people this analysis affects. It may also involve observing and taking part in processes within a business—I find this to be especially common in small businesses/start-ups that are still defining how they will collect and organize their data.

As I have gotten deeper into the data space, I have realized that oftentimes the most valuable part of an entire data project is the meetings that happen at the beginning—before anyone has even looked at any of the data. These meetings are more than just requirement-gathering sessions; it is the time when knowing how to ask the *right* questions will determine not only how successful a project is, but also how long it takes. As a data analyst, it's your job to have a clear understanding of what the business problem is that you are trying to solve (using data), and how what you are doing is going to directly impact the mission/bottom line of the business.

As a note, I'm not sure why, but I don't know if I have ever actually heard someone use the counterpart "heads-up work." I think I used it in one of my interviews and now I look back and wonder if they thought it was a weird thing for me to say!

Although I think it is possible to get a role that is strictly a "business analyst" role where you hardly even touch any of the technical tools, or conversely to get a purely "data analyst" role where you do not have to go to any meetings or gather any business requirements, that is incredibly rare.

Additionally, it is short-sighted. That could work for someone who is entry-level, but even a mid-level analyst generally needs to know how to do both.

Most analyst roles are going to end up being a mix of gathering requirements, heads-down work, meetings, the occasional presentation, and more generally, spending time thinking about a project plan. For example, in my role as a consultant I spend about 5–10 hours a week meeting with clients to plan, validate my work, and show them what I have been working on. Another fiveish hours a week go to internal meetings, many of which are with my boss to check in about my projects and get support where I need it. The remaining hours I spend getting connected to data, analyzing it, and visualizing it.

Hours / Time

One of the biggest selling points for me when it came to switching careers into data analytics was that I could work remotely. Not every data analyst role is remote; I think about one-third of the entry-level analysts I know work in person (in an office) or hybrid (a mixture of both). Lucky for me, my role is 100 percent remote. In fact, my company doesn't even *have* an office. We do have a subscription to coworking spaces, though, should I need that option.

The day-to-day of someone who works from home is naturally going to look different to someone who works in an office. All of the analysts I know who work in an office have told me that it is the standard schedule of commuting to work, packing their lunches, and working fairly normal office hours. Everyone I have talked with who works in the office has said that instead of tracking their time, their progress is monitored based on their progress toward their projects/goals and that they are generally expected to just be there during normal hours.

When I changed careers and got this (fully remote) job, I was so curious about what that was going to look like. Would I still be expected to work a normal 9 to 5? How would they track my time? Although I am technically a "consultant," I do work for my company full time, I get benefits, and so forth. So I'm not a "freelancer."

I cannot stress enough how much I have loved working remotely. My company has a good culture, which is part of the equation. I am generally expected to be available during standard working hours. I have multiple clients at a time, so I'm also expected to be scheduling meetings with my clients during normal working hours and attending internal meetings during the workweek. Which is normal and completely reasonable.

However, is my boss tracking if I am in my seat by a certain time? Or if I am working my hours at a certain time of the day/day of the week? Absolutely not. On a normal day I will wake up (without an alarm!) and start working by about 9 a.m. Sometimes during the day I will step out to go grocery shopping, do some laundry, or go for a walk. If I am not feeling well I will sleep in, or I will log off early (if I don't have meetings to attend).

I do have to bill a certain number of client-facing hours (working on a client's project or meeting with them) as well as internal hours (working on internal projects or participating in learning, research, and skill development). Since I generally prefer to be flexible in my daily routines, I will often work a few hours on the weekends to make up for time during the week when I was busy with other things (like grocery shopping).

This works for me, but it isn't expected! My coworkers tend to work their full workweeks during standard weekday hours, and then they log off for the entire weekend. The point here is that since we work remotely, we are allowed more control over our schedules and flexibility with them than we would if we worked in an office.

As someone who was about to go into healthcare, this kind of flexibility is mind-blowing to me. I have friends from graduate school who have told me that they needed to use some of their (very limited) paid time-off (PTO) time just for doctor appointments. And, when they did use their PTO to go to the doctor, their boss made them feel guilty about it the entire time because things could not run as smoothly without them there.

I have talked with many other data analysts who work remotely, and not everyone has had the same experience as I have. A handful of people have told me that although they work remotely, they are expected to be at their desks from 9 to 5 as they would at an office job. If their boss were to call them on Microsoft Teams (a common app that businesses use for communications) and they did not pick up, that could lead to them getting in trouble if it happened a few times. Coincidentally, those are also the people who tell me they are actively upskilling so they can look for a new job.

A middle point between their experience and mine is what I see as the most common set of expectations for a remote data analyst role. Most people I talk to who work remotely generally are expected to work a normal 9 to 5. However, if they had a doctor's appointment during the day or needed to take a short break to go for a walk, they would just have to talk to their managers about it, and it would be fine.

I have talked to several transitioned teachers/healthcare workers who have remote jobs that are like the third option I talked about. We marvel together at how much of a relief it is to be able to take care of things like doctor appointments during the day without spending every minute of it worrying about work—and having to use PTO to do it. This is especially relevant to my friends who have children, pets, and more responsibilities than just a few cacti (like me).

This may be unique to me, but another perk of working from home is that I am working from . . . home! This means that I never have to change out of sweatpants, I completely control the temperature, I can play whatever weird music I want to (or have it be completely silent when I am feeling overstimulated!), and I have access to my full kitchen and refrigerator.

I don't know about you, but one of the hardest things about being an adult is having to feed myself every day. Now that I work from home I can stick some food in the oven mid-morning, and it's ready by lunch time. When I need a movement break in between meetings in the afternoon, I can get up and do the dishes left over from my lunch. Not having to pack my lunch every day saves me a lot of headache and a lot of money. I almost never eat out anymore because it's so much easier to just make something in my own kitchen.

One final point on the general workday of a data analyst—especially one who works remotely—is the topic of the workspace setup. Many people take a lot of joy in setting up a workspace that they love, whether it be plants, a cool second monitor, or funky lighting. A hot topic on LinkedIn right now is standing desks + under-desk treadmills.

When I worked as a nanny and later in occupational therapy clinics, I had a pretty physical job. I was walking around a lot! Many people tell me, "Oh, I could never get a computer job, I couldn't stand sitting all day!" Enter the under-desk treadmill—or just walks. I live in New England, so it gets pretty cold here in the winter time. So, I invested in an under-desk treadmill. Once I got used to it, I can pretty much do any kind of work while walking, although I don't take client meetings from the treadmill.

In a standard week, I walk 10–20 miles on my little treadmill while I am working. It is pretty common in the data space to hear people talking about getting out to take walks during the day when the weather is nice. Yes, as data analysts we do have desk jobs. But to think of it as completely sedentary is a big misunderstanding! I also have found that working at a job that I genuinely enjoy, where my boundaries are respected and I am not having to deal with unhappy people all day, leaves me feeling energized. At the end of the day I am perfectly happy to go to the gym, get chores done around the house, or meet up with friends to socialize because I am not completely wiped out from whatever I did at work.

In-Person Data Jobs

To add some context to the conversation of what it is like to work remotely, I talked to some of my data friends who work hybrid/in-person jobs. All of them still do enjoy their jobs! They all said in their own way that in-person data jobs have a similar structure to a lot of the other (non-data) jobs they have had.

They follow a fairly normal 9–5 schedule for in-office work, and then fit in going to the gym or the grocery store after they leave work. Each of them told me that they do have good flexibility to leave work to go to the doctor if they need to but that it is an unusual occurrence to cut time out of their workday.

Some people I talked to feel like they need to be in the office for 8–9 hours a day, 5 days a week. Others told me that they feel comfortable leaving once they finish their work, and possibly shifting their work schedule to be earlier or later if needed.

I have only one friend whose job is fully in-person (with occasional days from home); the other five I talked to all have a hybrid schedule of a few days in the office and a few days out each week.

I asked my friends who have a hybrid job if their days looked different on the days they work from home from the days they come into the office— and they all said yes. In fact, they all said that they still have meetings over Zoom when they go into the office, and they would prefer to have even more days from home each week if it were up to them.

On the days that they work from home they feel that their time is more flexible. They are more likely to take a walk or go to the gym in the middle of the day. Since they do not have to commute, they are very aware and appreciative of the additional time they get back in their day on the days where they work from home.

My friends with hybrid jobs said that a lot of their job could be done remotely. On the days that they are in the office, their employers make sure to schedule team meetings and planning sessions—meetings that benefit from being able to get people in a room together. Two of my six friends who have in-person/hybrid jobs expressed to me that they enjoy getting to go into the office and socialize with their peers and prefer that option.

The other four people I talked with said that, although in-person co-working can be nice sometimes, they prefer the days when they work from home, and that when they search for their next job they will be looking for a fully remote role.

I may have some self-selection bias going on with the people I picked—I am a huge advocate of remote work, so the people who make friends with me may be more likely to also be lovers of the freedom that remote work brings. This means that I am likely not representing the portion of data analysts who prefer in-person work very well!

Many of the employers who embraced remote work during the pandemic are now requiring employees to return to the office at least some days of the week. That means people who are okay with hybrid jobs will likely have an easier time finding a job than people who are committed to remote work (like me).

I can say from experience that for every one job that recruiters reach out to me about on LinkedIn that is fully remote, there are four to five that are at least hybrid. It seems like fully in-person jobs are rare—and from what I have seen they are more common in industries that are not "techy"—and all of their other employees are in-person full time as well.

I wonder if employers are finding it significantly harder to fill fully in-person data jobs with good candidates than roles that are at least hybrid, because the dominant sentiment I see from my many connections on LinkedIn is that most people prefer to work at least hybrid.

Once you are introduced to the benefits of eliminating your commute and being able to spend more time at home, with family, and on other activities besides driving (for at least a few days a week), it is hard to go back.

What Makes a Good Analyst?

If you're still reading, then it means you have decided that maybe data analytics is the right choice for you! Congratulations! When I made that decision it changed my entire life. So let's talk about what makes a good data analyst and what it looks like to be in the career. I find the following information to be exciting; I love that I have found a career where these things are valuable!

When I started learning about data analysts, all I had available to reference to understand what makes a good data analyst was a Google search. The results were mixed. Lucky for you, I have leveraged my 50k+ network and over a year of being in the data space to ask the question, "What makes a good data analyst?"

I talked to senior data analysts, random people on LinkedIn and TikTok, data scientists, data engineers, a few heads of operations, vice presidents, chief data officers (CDOs), chief operating officers (COOs), recruiters, and many random people with unknown titles on LinkedIn and TikTok about what makes a good data analyst. Oftentimes these people are the ones responsible for hiring, mentoring, and promoting data analysts. Here is what I learned from them, plus some of my own thoughts thrown into the mix.

So what makes a good data analyst? Critical thinking. This was the number one response that I got. When you are an entry-level data analyst, you might be able to get away with just clocking in, clocking out, and doing what is asked of you. But in the majority of data analyst roles the most valuable thing you can bring to the table is your ability to engage with problems and business needs and draw your own conclusions.

Think about it this way. Do you need to know how to swing a hammer and use a saw to be a good carpenter? Absolutely. But is it the ability to use a specific tool that makes a good carpenter? Definitely not! Data analytics is the same way. SQL, Excel, Tableau . . . At the end of the day they're all just tools. A good data analyst needs to know how to think like an analyst.

I've put together a list of the nontechnical skills that have been critical to my success in my role lately, and they are planning, organization, critical thinking/strategy, and communication/collaboration. I will explain each of them in the paragraphs to come. Before I elaborate on the list, though, I do want to mention one thing. Since I am a consultant, my role seems to be different from the roles of the other entry-level data analysts I know.

If you encounter terms in this chapter you are not entirely familiar with yet, do not worry about it! Any terms you need to use as a data analyst will be introduced to you later on in the book, but I am going to give some examples in this chapter to make a point.

It seems to me that many entry-level data analyst roles exist within just one company. Usually, these roles report to a senior-level data analyst/analytics manager. Their manager is in charge of planning, cross-department collaboration, and overseeing and assigning project tasks, whereas the entry-level data analysts are the ones who are assigned specific analytical tasks and report their work back to their manager. From what I have seen, entry-level analysts gradually take on more collaboration, planning, and strategy as they gain more experience in their roles.

Planning

Data does not exist on an island in any business. You are never going to find a data project that is *just* "crunching the numbers." Data analysts (especially in more senior positions) have to plan carefully with all of the parties involved. At the beginning of every data project, the analyst in charge needs to meet with stakeholders—which could be managers, executives, or clients. They need to gather requirements for the project and set the scope, which often involves a series of meetings, emails, and the creation of planning documents.

While scoping and planning the project, the analyst in charge also needs to take a look at the data and determine if they have the access they need, and if the data that they have available to them is what they need for the project. Connecting to and digging around in the data often has different technical requirements than what you would see in the actual project.

Once the planning stages are over, the project begins. For any data project that takes more than a few hours, the analyst working on the project may need to be sending emails back and forth, hosting meetings, or even working in collaborative documents to ask questions and check in with the stakeholders.

Once a project is finished, the analyst in charge often needs to do some kind of a presentation. Junior-level analysts may just send their work off to their boss, but senior analysts will often be presenting the insights of their work to managers, executives, or clients.

For example, I recently worked on a project with a fairly small company. When we got together to gather requirements at the beginning, we met with the chief financial officer (CFO), as well as two people heavily involved with marketing.

In that meeting, as we discussed how this project was going to benefit their organization and simplify each of their roles individually, it became clear that the work I would be doing would benefit each of them differently. We needed to have separate follow-up meetings with the CFO and people in marketing, because their roles in the project were different.

In the meeting with the CFO, I got connected with their database and existing Excel spreadsheets, and we went through and defined different columns in their data and how their reporting is built. When I met with marketing, we did not talk about individual fields in the data at all and instead did a whiteboard session to plan out the different dashboards I would be building. We also reviewed which metrics they send out in their newsletter every month to make sure those metrics would be front and center and easily accessible to them.

After those meetings, I got connected to the data and started re-creating fields from their Excel spreadsheet in Tableau (to automate their reporting). But I had to check in regularly with both marketing and the CFO, because the names of columns in the database did not match the names of columns in the Excel spreadsheet, which also did not match the language that they were using for those fields in the newsletter.

Organization

Have I experienced data analysts who are not very organized? Yes. But do I think it is a critical part of my success? Also yes. As a data analyst, I am usually an intermediary, or interpreter. I am receiving information that has been put into the system by other people, and I am analyzing and visualizing it so that other people can take that information and use it to make business decisions.

This opens up a huge need for organization. Here are some of the things I need to have a system of organization for every day:

Files At the start of the project I usually get a lot of files, and they all need to be well labeled and stored together so anyone can easily access them later. **Documentation** For every project I do, I need to keep track of all kinds of things. For example, what does the column "Gains" mean? Is this profit after the cost of goods is taken out? Or before? Additionally, I have to document what I am building and how it is all interrelated. The goal is that once I finish a project, anyone can use that work without having to refer back to me to explain how things are built.

Workload   It is rare for analysts to have just one project that they are working on at a time, that has only one stream of work related to it. Each person has to learn how to organize their own day so that they are making all the meetings they are required to go to and still completing all their tasks and projects on time.

Communication   If you have worked an office-type job before (or really, most jobs), you have already encountered the phenomenon of the never-ending emails. You start your day with a list of things you need to get done, and throughout the day you're likely going to get a steady trickle of emails adding to that list. It may sound trivial, but on top of making sure everything else about a project is well organized and documented, adding on the need to keep track of emails and perform ad hoc organization of whatever comes your way in an email will rely on you already having good organization systems in place.

Critical Thinking/Strategy

It's hard for me to say enough about this skill—it's the most valuable skill I bring to every project. The thing about working with data is that there is never just one way to do something. Even if there is one "right" answer (which there rarely is), there are many different ways to get there. This is where critical thinking comes in.

Let's take a SQL query, for example. Many times there are at least 10 different ways you could write a query and get the exact same table as an output. But, five of those ways are going to take the database three times as long to run the query, two of those ways are going to be long and difficult for anyone else to read and understand, and of the other three, two of them will be better aligned with the way your boss writes their queries.

It is up to you to understand not only how to use SQL, but how to piece together different tables, columns, and functions to achieve the end result you want. The next day you might come back to write a similar query, but just a few things about the data have changed and you have to think through the best way to do it all over again.

Not only is critical thinking necessary for individual tasks, but it also relates back to what I was saying in the "Planning" section. Working on a project is like completing a puzzle. You are taking all the business requirements for the project, combining them with the needs and preferences of the person you are delivering the work to, nesting that within your knowledge of the way the business is organized and its priorities, and needing to fit your individual analyses and uses of the analytical tools within that—like one big puzzle.

At the end you either get something that is messy, over budget, and not quite usable by the intended audience, or you get a piece of work that your intended end user will rely on to make business decisions. For example, let's go back to the marketing dashboard. If you take 60 hours to build a marketing dashboard that doesn't quite do what your client needs it to do, in business terms that means that they just paid you for 60 hours of work and, in the end, they still have to go back to their original Excel spread-sheet every month to pull all the numbers they need to include in their newsletter.

Although that picture is quite grim, let me cast this in a different light. This skill of applying my critical thinking skills and solving puzzles every day is my favorite part of my job! I am the type of person who loves to always have their brain engaged. My brain rarely "shuts off." In the past I have had a hard time staying with jobs long term, because I have had jobs that, although they required a lot of physical effort, were not intellectually stimulating. After a few months I would get bored, and then every Sunday I would dread going into work the next day.

Now, I get my Sundays back. I do not have to dread Monday rolling around, because I genuinely enjoy my job. Of course, every job has its stress-ors. However, I would say that for at least 75 percent of my day every day I am using my "puzzle-solving" brain. Every project I work on brings new challenges, new things to learn, and a new way to analyze data. Most of the data analysts I know also express how critical thinking is not only the most important part of their role, but also the reason that they love being a data analyst.

Collaboration / Communication

Data analysts are not the ones who create the data, nor are they the ones who use the data. Data is created by salespeople, skilled workers, electric bills, property taxes, online reviews . . . you get the point. Data is used by executives and managers—people who pay bills, hire and fire new employ-ees, change their businesses' marketing strategies to run more ads on a well-performing platform, and meet with investors to make more money. So who is the data analyst in all of this? The intermediary.

This means that data analysts are rarely ever going to be working in isolation. For every project, data analysts will likely have to work with people in multiple areas and at multiple levels of the business. For example, when I worked on that marketing dashboard, I was communicating with executives. However, I found the CFO to be a very easy-going guy and we worked best with a less "formal" communication style. I did not need to include a formal introduction to every email, and he was comfortable with us getting right to the point of the task at hand.

I wanted to maintain a friendly yet effective tone in my emails, and I remember that at the beginning of the project we ended up needing to send some emails back and forth that were quite dense, as I tried to understand how different columns from different tables and data sources related to each other. At one point I believe we ended up tacking smiley faces onto the ends of these particularly tricky emails to communicate something along the lines of "I know this material is quite dense and I do not want you to think I am judging you or that I am lecturing you."

On the other hand, when I was emailing the marketing department at around the same time it was usually just me clarifying things like, "I took 'Sold Amount' and added 'Shipping Cost' to it; does that accurately capture that 'Price' field you referenced in the newsletter?" To which I would get a response like "Yes, that is correct. Thank you. [Insert standard signature here]."

At the same time, I was checking in with my boss several times a day via Slack messages to ask him things like, "Hey, can you look at this calculated field for me? Here is the formula I used. Does this look right to you?" or "I could not fit all six of these charts on the top line of the dashboard, so I did it this way instead. What do you think of the grid format?"

This is just one example of a day when I had several very different lines of communication open. I couldn't just plug into a data source and start analyzing. Even after we did our initial planning sessions, I still had to be touching base often with the people involved in the project.

Every data analyst's job looks different, but everyone I have talked to agrees that they are communicating and collaborating with other people daily. When I speak to people who came out of teaching and healthcare they often express how they are glad to have developed their "soft skills" so much in their previous profession, because they feel it makes them a better data analyst to be able to effectively change their communication style to match the collaboration needs of the project they are on.

What Tools Should I Learn?

If you were to poll 50 data analysts on what tools they need to use at their jobs and how, each of them would have a slightly different answer. If you go on LinkedIn and scroll through entry-level data analyst roles, you might feel overwhelmed at the number of tools and skills you see listed. I sure did!

I am glad that I found data analytics with the sole intention of analyzing spreadsheets, and then signing up for the first course that came up online. If I had decided "Okay, I want to try to change careers to become a data analyst; what are all of the things I need to do and learn?" I imagine that I may have been so overwhelmed with what I found that I might have given up altogether.

Luckily, I stumbled my way into it, fell in love, and then decided to try to make the switch. Then, I did it the hard way and spent hours and hours online researching and scrolling through job descriptions. Now, I have taken all of that research and hard-earned experience and compiled it into this book so that you don't have to feel overwhelmed!

There are a few core tools that pretty much anyone who is getting into data analytics will need to get familiar with. As I mentioned before, the most important thing that a data analyst brings to the table is their ability to think. Many entry-level roles are looking to hire someone who is a good fit at their company and shows the right interpersonal and critical thinking skills—the technical tools are often just a complement to that.

That is why I can tell you about the core tools that anyone trying to get into data analytics will need to learn, without having to compile a list of exactly which tools you might see on a given job application or a list of the specific levels of mastery you must achieve with each of these tools. That being said, this section explores the tools with a brief overview of what they do.

Excel / Google Sheets

There is a joke in the analytics world that all of corporate America is built on Excel, and there is a lot of truth to that. It is very likely that as a data analyst you will be handed an organization's spreadsheets and asked to perform analyses on them in either Excel or another tool. The easiest way to understand how to analyze data is by starting in Excel. This is because all the data is right there for you to see!

When you perform a function in a spreadsheet, all the cells of data that are being operated on are highlighted. This means that you can visualize what different functions look like. Being able to actually see what is happening to data as you perform different analyses on it is a great foundation and will help you to learn the basics of the other tools more easily.

Did you know you can do some pretty complex things in an Excel document? Before I got into data analytics, all I knew how to do was understand a table and perform simple calculations, like adding up all values in a column (SUM) or subtracting one cell from another. As it turns out, there is a whole lot more you can do in a spreadsheet!

As more organizations develop more complicated data systems with huge amounts of data, they are moving their data into databases. But as a data analyst it will not be uncommon for you to be handed a spreadsheet with all kinds of complicated things in it, like pivot tables and the VLOOKUP function, and be asked to either help bring all that data into a database for the first time and perform the calculations in there, or automate pulling data from a database and into a visualization software and perform all those calculations there.

Although Excel is the foundational skill of data analytics, I only know a couple of people who actually use Excel or Google Sheets regularly at their jobs. When I was job searching, I was asked a lot of questions about my ability to use the tools that are to follow on this list. I had Excel/Spreadsheets listed as a skill on my résumé, but out of the 30+ companies that I spoke with about a job, only one asked me about my skill level in Excel. It is for this reason that a good number of data influencers on social media will advise people not to waste their time taking any courses that go over using Excel or doing projects that incorporate steps in a spreadsheet.

I disagree with that advice. In my opinion, everyone should start their data analytics journey in Excel. Even if you decide to exclude jobs from your search that primarily use spreadsheets as the tool in which you do your analyses, being able to understand the structure of an Excel document and perform all the basic functions and calculations will be a solid foundation on which you can build all your analytical skills.

SQL

SQL can be pronounced "S-Q-L" or "sequel." One of my first semi-viral TikToks was one where I said, "Today I learned it's actually pronounced 'sequel' and not 'S-Q-L,'" because I had just heard someone say it out loud for the first time and felt like an idiot for pronouncing it "S-Q-L" in my head. In just a few hours I had gotten over 100s comments from people voicing their opinions and support. Sometimes I see people debate how you should pronounce it, but for the most part nobody in the industry really cares which way you say it.

While Excel is data analytics' most foundational tool, I would argue that SQL is the core tool of data analytics. Trying to picture what SQL is for the first time is a little tricky. It is easy to understand how Excel relates to data—all you have to do is open up your spreadsheet, and there is all your data.

Now, imagine you own a large department store that has 10,000 locations across the country. Where do you store your data? It would be ridiculous to store all of your data in spreadsheets—what's more, it would be incredibly inefficient. What if the VP in Washington needs to access the records from a store in New York? How would they even know which one of the 10,000 spreadsheets to open up?

Instead of keeping it all in spreadsheets, companies turn to using a database. The database contains all the tables and information for every store and every department, all combined into their own tables and structure of organization. For example, you are likely going to have just one Orders table, and that is going to contain information on the orders from all 10,000 stores.

The thing about using a database like this is that it is not structured the same way it would be if it was just spreadsheets on your computer. There is not one common file folder that everyone in an organization can access and just search around folder by folder and then double-click to open the spreadsheet they want. Not to mention how impractical it would be to try to open a spreadsheet with 5 billion rows! Your computer would crash.

This is where SQL comes in. SQL is the language that we humans use to chat with databases in order to get the information that we want.

SQL is not a tool itself, like Excel. You can open an Excel file. With SQL, however, there is no "SQL file" on your computer. You do not need

to worry yet about the specifics of what programs you need to use to communicate with a database or what that looks like—it is just important to
know that SQL is the language you use to talk to the database.

When you want to go into a database and get some information, you
need to write something called a *query*. SQL queries look a little bit like
code, but SQL is not a full-on coding language like Python, Java, or other
programming language that developers use. I refer to SQL as "pseudocode."
It isn't quite English, because it follows a specific structure. An example of a
simple SQL query looks like this:

```
SELECT
    order_id,
    store_location,
    price,
    date
FROM orders
WHERE date > 01-01-2023
```

After you "run" this query, it is going to give you back a table that
might look like this:

order_id	store_location	price	date
1	Montana Central	5.99	01-01-2023
2	New York City	4.52	01-01-2023
3	Southern Idaho	100.45	01-01-2023
4	Las Vegas	50.55	02-01-2023
5	Florida North	513.45	02-01-2023

In this query, the SELECT statement told the database which columns
we wanted. The FROM statement told us which table we are pulling from
(we want to look in Orders, and not Returns). Finally, the WHERE statement
filters the data based on the condition that we do not want any orders older
than 2023.

This may look quite simple, but there are hundreds of different functions in SQL! SELECT and WHERE are just two functions. Now imagine that
in these queries we are potentially doing all kinds of analyses, like more fil-
tering or joining information from one table to another and then subtracting columns from each other, and more. It can take years of working in SQL
regularly to "master" it.

Entry-level data analysts are not expected to be SQL masters (thank goodness!). Usually, entry-level positions that require SQL skills are only looking for people to have the basics down.

When I took that course so I could try to get a data analytics side hustle, I didn't even know what SQL was. I was just taking the course for the Excel portion, but then I was enjoying it so much that I stuck around. After the Excel part of the course, it dove right into SQL. I probably would not have independently sought out learning SQL, because it looked intimidating and at that point in time I did not think I was ever going to need it (I still just wanted to analyze spreadsheets for some extra cash).

So color me surprised when I started the SQL portion of the course and realized "hey . . . this is actually pretty fun!" I realized that learning to write SQL queries was intellectually stimulating but not too hard. It gave me just the right balance of structure combined with a more normal "English" way of writing, so learning how to write queries felt like a game. Each time I ran a query successfully it gave my brain a hit of feel-good chemicals (specifically one called dopamine, which is the chemical that is released in your brain when you do something interesting or rewarding).

Before I knew it I was coming home from work every day just obsessed with getting back on my computer so I could learn more SQL.

I have talked to a lot of data analysts in the last year and looked through a lot of job postings. SQL is the skill that I see come up the most. Not only that, but SQL is a skill that is worth paying for. I noticed (and this is just my own personal observation) that most of the jobs I applied for that ended up being mostly Excel-focused jobs tended to have a starting salary about 10k–15k less than jobs that listed SQL as the primary tool. You can get by as an entry-level data analyst without using SQL, but pretty much any mid-level role and above is going to require a good knowledge of working in SQL.

Tableau/Power BI

The third and final tool that you need to have in your entry-level data analyst tool kit is some kind of visualization tool. Tableau and Microsoft Power BI are the two most commonly listed tools, and it seems to come down to a company's individual preference which one they use. They are both tools with which you can connect to a database or a spreadsheet, and then perform analyses and create visuals of the data.

People ask me often if they should learn Tableau or Power BI, and honestly, I do not have an answer to this. It seems like the tools can both do roughly the same thing. I am a Tableau consultant, so I only know how to use Tableau. However, the real skill that I have developed in my role is the ability to create effective visualizations and use this tool to do complex analyses. So, if I needed to switch over and learn to use Power BI someday I would just have to learn the differences in the user interface, and then I would be able to make an easy transition into Power BI.

When data analysts are using Tableau, they are typically using it to create something called a *dashboard*. A dashboard is typically a set of visualizations that have all been brought together with a specific purpose in mind.

For example, Figure 1.1 shows a sample dashboard that I made using publicly available data a few months into my job as a Tableau consultant.

This dashboard is designed for an executive at a superstore called Basic. Someone like a CEO or a CFO could look at this dashboard and get a quick understanding of how their business is performing this quarter as

Figure 1.1 A sample dashboard that I created after a few months as a Tableau consultant to show off my skills.

compared to last quarter. When we look at the bar charts with the line charts overlaid on them, it gives us a week-by-week breakdown of the quarters.

Whether you are using Tableau or Power BI, dashboards are always interactive. The labels you see in the top-right corner are actually filters, and changing them will affect every number and chart on the dashboard. Additionally, if you click any of the regions in the bottom right (for example, West), then the entire dashboard will filter to only show you data from the West region.

If you hover your cursor over any of the visualizations on this dashboard, a small box will pop up with more information. For example, if you hover over one of the bars, the little box might say "Week 3, Sales: $8,644." This is how you can get a lot of information into a dashboard without overwhelming the end user with too much ink on the screen.

That is just one example of an overview dashboard, but there are thousands of ways that a dashboard could go. When developing a Tableau dashboard, you have to get a clear understanding of the following:

- What problem is this dashboard trying to solve?
- How will the end user use this dashboard? In other words, how is the person I'm making this for going to use it? Will they use it in Tableau? Export to PowerPoint? Do they have a good understanding of data terms?
- How does this fit into the workflow of the people who are using it? If I am designing a dashboard for a marketing department so they can use it to make their newsletter, am I using the same terms they use in the newsletter? Am I reporting on everything they want to put in the newsletter so they do not have to look elsewhere? Could we make this dashboard exportable so they can put it right in the newsletter?

This means that creating a dashboard is both an art and a science. You need to pull elements from many skills to create dashboards, including design, psychology, basic statistics, business, and actual analytics.

When I design a dashboard, I spend no more than 50 percent of the time writing calculations and designing the technical and analytical components. The other 50 percent of the time is spent in the beginning and end of the project—whiteboarding design ideas, discussing with the end user how each piece of the dashboard is going to solve their business problems, and then once the dashboard is made, actually going in and formatting and designing it.

I think that some people see the design portion of the work as trivial, and I have gotten some comments from people who think that Tableau is "easy." I don't take offense at this, but it does make it clear to me they do not have much experience with the tool. Creating an analytically rigorous yet also simple, clean, and well-designed dashboard is a labor of love. And a skill people will pay quite nicely for.

Python

Knowing Python is *not* one of the core skills you will need as an entry-level data analyst. So why am I including it in this list? Well, a few things. First of all, when I decided to go for it and learn data analytics so that I could switch careers, I saw Python in a lot of places. So I thought I had to learn it. I spent a month taking a Python course. It was a fun course, and I don't necessarily regret it! But it turned out to be no more than a fun detour.

I listed "introductory Python" on my résumé. I talked to over 30 companies when I was applying for jobs (those are just the ones I got a call back from), and not a *single one of them* even asked about Python. You can find an exception to everything I say in this book, but for the most part, entry-level data analysts do not need to know how to use Python.

Whenever I say "The core tools you need to know to get an entry-level data analyst job are Excel, SQL, and a visualization tool," there will inevitably be at least one person who brings up how knowing Python is a great nice-to-have skill as a data analyst. In addition, if you do get into data analytics, you will likely need to learn at least basic Python to progress higher than an entry/mid-level data analyst role.

I have talked to hundreds of entry-level data analysts, and I only know one who told me they use Python in their role—and it's just because they like it, not because it is required.

So what is Python? Python is a coding language. Fun fact, it is apparently not named after the snake but after the British comedy troupe Monty Python! You can do all kinds of things using Python, like "web-scraping," which is getting a bunch of information from the Internet in an automated way, or designing apps and games that people can use on their computers.

You can also use it to program little devices. Something I am working on right now as a personal project is a little sensor with just a bit of code that I can hook up to my stove, which is linked to the Wi-Fi in my house so that no matter where I am I can check my phone and see whether I remembered to turn off my electric stove when I left the house.

However, none of this is relevant to data analytics. So what would you use Python for as a data analyst? The simple answer is analyzing data. You could take a bunch of data, put it into Python, and ask Python to delete any completely blank rows, delete duplicate data, and replace every 0 with Null. Then you could pick specific columns or rows in the data and find out how they are correlated, and ask it to also visualize the data on a simple scatter plot.

In summary, there are a lot of things that you could use Python for. As a data analyst, most of them have to do with analyzing or changing data. However, if you do decide to get into data analytics, you do not have to worry about any of that now. You should know what Python is, and if you would like to learn the basics, go ahead! It is a nice-to-have skill. But if just learning Excel, SQL, and a visualization tool is enough for you and you just want to go and get your hands on data in your first entry-level role, you likely will not need to dive into Python.

R R is a coding language that is very similar to Python, but you see Python much more often in data analyst job descriptions. Everything I said earlier about Python applies to R. I find that R is more commonly used in research-related positions.

My mom is a scientist; she has a PhD in biology and she works in a lab doing research on stem cells. In her lab, they use R to do in-depth statistical analyses on their data. If you wanted to go into analytics with a biology focus, you would likely need to learn R!

Which Entry-Level Tech Job Is Right for Me?

Before I decided on data analytics, I needed to know what other options I had for entry-level jobs in technology. Data analytics is not the only path into entry-level tech jobs! This section will guide you through the options I found while researching my options.

If you Google **no-coding tech jobs**, you may be frustrated that a lot of the articles will include roles like "System Administrator." For jobs like that, you have to have already been *in* tech for a few years to even be considered for interviews. What I wanted to find when I was deciding if data analytics was right for me was jobs that *anyone* could get into.

As I did my research on different possible tech paths that were code free, here are some of the options I found, along with my perception of what would make someone a good fit for them. As you read through the list, think about your strengths, passions, and what kind of work environment would suit you best.

Graphic Designer   Graphic designers craft eye-catching visuals for items like products, promotional content, websites, and beyond. If you have a flair for design and enjoy working together with others, this role might be the perfect match for you.

Business Analyst   Business analysts improve business processes by aligning technology with company goals. If you're a strategic thinker with strong analytical skills, this role might be for you.

UI Specialist   User interface (UI) specialists design visually appealing and intuitive interfaces for digital platforms. If you're creative and enjoy problem-solving, consider this path.

UX Specialist   User experience (UX) specialists focus on how users feel when interacting with digital platforms. If you're interested in psychology, marketing, and technology, this could be a great choice.

Technical Writer   Technical writers create user manuals, design specifications, and other documentation. If you're skilled in writing and enjoy learning about technology, this role might suit you.

Marketing and Sales   Non-coding tech jobs in marketing and sales revolve around promoting products and managing the ways they reach customers, such as through online stores, physical retail locations, or direct sales. If you have strong communication skills and enjoy business administration, this career path might be a good fit for you.

Project Manager   IT project managers oversee the development, launch, and improvement of software, systems, and devices. If you're organized, detail-oriented, and enjoy managing resources, this role might be a good fit. (As a caveat, it seems like getting into project management from zero experience can be really hard, but I have seen it done by people who have relevant experience in the same industry that the product serves.)

Game, Website, and App Testing Testers ensure the quality and functionality of games, websites, and apps. If you enjoy exploring digital platforms and have a keen eye for detail, this could be a great fit. (This requires having a strong background in one of these domains already, but it could be personal, not professional, from what I can tell.)

Digital Marketing Digital marketing encompasses search engine optimization, search engine marketing, and other fields aimed at enhancing a brand's online visibility. If you enjoy planning strategies and engaging with web technologies, this career path could be a great choice for you.

Cybersecurity Some cybersecurity jobs don't entail coding and instead concentrate on overseeing systems, addressing breaches, and handling user permissions. If you're keen on safeguarding digital assets and have a penchant for problem-solving, critical thinking, or a curiosity for understanding human behavior, this career path could be an excellent choice for you.

Data Analyst Data analysts collect, analyze, and interpret data to help businesses make informed decisions. If you have a strong analytical mind and enjoy working with data, this role could be a great fit.

Tech Recruiter Technical recruiters help companies find and hire skilled tech professionals. If you enjoy connecting people with job opportunities and have strong communication skills, consider this path.

Tech Journalist/Blogger Tech journalists and bloggers cover technology news and trends. If you enjoy researching, interviewing, and writing about the latest advancements, this could be the perfect role for you.

Skills/interests that relate to each of the above careers:

- Creativity and collaboration
  - Graphic designer
  - UI specialist
  - UX specialist
  - Tech journalist/blogger
  - Visualization-focused data analyst roles
- Strategic thinking and analytical skills
  - Business analyst
  - Data analyst
  - Digital marketing
  - Project manager

- Problem-solving
  - UI specialist
  - UX specialist
  - Cybersecurity
  - Data analyst
  - Game, website, and app testing
  - Project manager
- Design
  - Graphic designer
  - UI specialist
  - Visualization-focused data analyst
- Psychology and human behavior
  - UX specialist
  - Cybersecurity
  - Tech recruiter
  - Data analyst consultant
- Marketing and promotion
  - UX specialist
  - Digital marketing
  - Marketing and sales
- Technology
  - Technical writer
  - Digital marketing
  - Cybersecurity
  - Tech journalist/blogger
- Communication skills
  - Business analyst
  - Technical writer
  - Marketing and sales
  - Project manager
  - Tech recruiter
  - Tech journalist/blogger
- Business administration and management
  - Marketing and sales
  - Project manager
- Organization and planning
  - Project manager
  - Cybersecurity

- Keen eye for detail and exploration
  - Game, website, and app testing
  - Data analyst
- Helping people be their best selves
  - Tech recruiter
- Research, interviewing, and writing
  - Tech journalist/blogger
  - Technical writer

What's Next

In this chapter we covered all the big questions that I had when I was thinking about becoming a data analyst. Now that you know the basics, it is time to learn how you might go about becoming a data analyst and what my experience was like. The rest of Part I will be dedicated to learning data analytics.

Learning how to become a data analyst was the most fun and exciting part of my journey. I enjoyed the courses and learning about all the different ways I could get my hands on data and work with it. I did not expect to enjoy all the data tools as much as I did!

The goal of Part I is to help guide you to make the best choices about what to learn and when, from where. There are so many options on the Internet for free, cheap, and expensive paths to learning data analytics. It is my hope that hearing about how I did it (for less than $100!), you can make the best choices for you, your learning style, and your bank account.

2 | Understanding the Paths into Data

What's Here

- How hard is it to become a data analyst?
- What are the different ways to become a data analyst?
- How did I decide on taking the DIY approach?

If you want to become a data analyst, you need a game plan. Having a clear roadmap to follow takes the guesswork out of the process, which saves time and energy. Without a clear plan, many people end up spending too much money on courses they don't need and getting discouraged by a lack of direction.

I know people from so many different backgrounds who have changed careers to get into data analytics! Everyone's story is different, but the key themes can be boiled down to a few different approaches. I decided to take the cheapest and most independent route into data analytics, and that is what this book will focus on. But first I will present you with each of the options so that you can make the right decision for your situation.

How Hard Is It to Become a Data Analyst?

This was one of my number-one questions when I was still on the fence about whether I was going to uproot all my life plans and go into data. I cannot tell you how hard anything along the way is going to be for *you*. However, I can share with you my story and how hard it was for me, and tell you what I have observed from hundreds of other people who have made their way into their first data analyst role.

Becoming a data analyst is *work*. Anybody who tells you otherwise is trying to sell you a course or gain you as a follower. It took me six months of hard work and less than $100 to become a data analyst. I have seen others who read every piece of content I put out, took all of my advice, and did it in less than three months for about the same cost. I have also seen people who took six months to get through the course that I finished in one month, and others who applied to hundreds of jobs for four or more months without getting a job. My first data course that I took in a month? I was spending 20 or more hours *every week,* in addition to the other things I was doing full time. And I am generally a fast learner!

I found that the first four months of my journey were the most fun—because that time was mostly focused on learning all the tools. I loved learning SQL, Excel, and Tableau. I even greatly enjoyed the Python course that I took (which turned out to be basically a fun waste of time, which I mentioned in Chapter 1, "Is Data Analytics Right for Me?" in more detail), as well as a brief dip into R (which was also a fun waste of time). My first step along the way was the Google Certificates course in Data Analytics. By the time I finished that, I was positively ecstatic to finish the course and start working with "real" data in my own projects for the first time.

Were there times along the way when I second-guessed myself? Absolutely. I was running my queries and getting error after error, no matter how much I reviewed my notes and Googled around for an answer. I had to suspend any fear of failure and go and fail over and over because at the end of the day, I found the great puzzle of working with data to be fun. Even when it drove me crazy.

Once I finished my courses and got into the next steps, I was completely overwhelmed. I had no idea where to start, where to get free data, what to focus on, anything! That is why I am writing this book so that you will not have to hit all those roadblocks that I did. But figuring out all the stuff that was not neatly outlined in a course was hard work.

You know what the hardest part of learning data analytics and getting a job was? For me, it wasn't any of the technical skills. It wasn't building a portfolio, or even making my own website to host my portfolio. It was the gray space between "I have learned the data skills" and "I am a great candidate for a job."

To get a data job, I had to dive full time into being a job seeker. I had to figure out on my own how to use LinkedIn and how to optimize my LinkedIn so that recruiters would find me. I had to learn as I went along how to give good answers to recruiters when they called me about jobs, and I had to learn why I was hardly getting any responses to the dozens of job applications I had sent out. If this sounds intimidating, don't worry— Part III of this book is dedicated to job searching! I can't tell you how to become a data analyst without also sharing everything I learned about job searching.

Job searching in data is difficult for everyone. I see it on my LinkedIn feed again and again, every day. Everyone finds the gray zone between learning data skills and getting a job to be uncomfortable, difficult, and for many people, bad for their mental health. It makes sense, though—none of us signed up to be job seekers. We didn't decide, "Hey, you know what I would like? I would like to go to a whole bunch of interviews for a job I am not sure I am qualified for and expend my time and emotional energy just to get rejected." We decided to become data analysts! But unfortunately, unless you get *really* lucky or have good connections, the job search kind of sucks.

I do not tell you this to discourage you. I just want to give you a realistic picture of what this all looks like. Additionally, the fact that so many people struggle with the job search is actually a little bit of good news. If the job search is usually the toughest part, then you know what that means? Learning the data tools is not the hardest part. In fact, the overwhelming majority of people I talk to say that although learning SQL, Excel, Tableau, and Power BI felt hard at the moment, looking back, it wasn't that hard!

I know people from all kinds of backgrounds who have transitioned into data analytics. Nurses, teachers, doctors, truck drivers, waitresses . . . I was a nanny and an occupational therapist! All kinds of people are learning these skills every day. So, is it easy? No. But is it as difficult as something like a web developer job where you have to know math and coding and all kinds of crazy and hard-to-learn things? No! Most people I know who get into data can learn to do it in half a year or less.

What Are My Options for Getting into Data Analytics?

Although every person's path into data analytics is unique, we can broadly separate every story I have heard into four main paths:

- Transitioning into data analytics from an analyst-adjacent role, one where you are already using a lot of the tools that data analysts use every day (Excel, SQL, or Tableau, for example). This option is free but (obviously) requires experience.
- Getting a degree in data analytics or something related, like computer science, data science, or IT. This can cost at a minimum $10,000 or up to $50,000 or more depending on what level of degree and type of college you attend. No experience required.
- Attending a boot camp where you have an instructor teaching live or asynchronously all the data skills and (if the boot camp is any good) also preparing you for interviews, providing portfolio support, and helping you optimize your LinkedIn. These seem to vary from $5,000 to $15,000 on average. Some boot camps are offered on a "pay later" basis where you do not pay until you get a job, and then you're required to give them a certain percentage of your paycheck until you have paid it off. No prior experience or specific degree is required.
- The "DIY" (Do-It-Yourself) route where you create your own learning path, teaching yourself the skills with the help of self-guided courses and a whole lot of Googling. This could be done for free, but more realistically it will cost at most a few hundred dollars. This is the approach I took, and it cost me less than $100. No experience or specific degree is required.

When I started learning how to analyze spreadsheets just to see what would happen, I never could have predicted that it would lead to me switching careers. One of the things that caught me off guard the most about data was when I realized that you *do not need a degree in data* to get a data analyst job. I hope that by reading this book you will be encouraged to learn that unlike a lot of other jobs in the United States, data analytics has a fairly low barrier to entry and you do *not* need a specific degree or certification to get your first job.

As a side note, it was not until I decided to get into data analytics that I began to see the verb "Googling" as a real word. Trust me when I say this, if you gave any data analyst a list of data skills and asked them to pick their most important skill and "Googling" was on there, it would win every time.

Transitioning from an Analyst–Adjacent Role

Whenever I talk to someone who wants to get into data analytics and they tell me they've already used SQL, Excel, or Tableau heavily in their current role, I always get excited for them. One of the biggest hurdles I had to overcome when I was job seeking was that a lot of the recruiters I spoke to were looking for someone who already had professional experience using a certain tool. I had many phone calls in which I could tell that the energy from their side of the phone trailed off when I said I did not have any professional experience in the tools on their list. We will talk in Part III about how to get around the issue of not having the experience, but if you *do*, then that puts you ahead of a lot of other applicants.

I won't spend any more time talking about this path into data because it is not the path I followed. However, all the tips that I am going to give throughout this book can still absolutely apply to you if you already have the advantage of experience with certain analytics tools. When I talk about optimizing your LinkedIn and résumé and building a portfolio to showcase your skills, these will be good additions to the experience you already have and can help you land a great first data analyst role.

Getting a Degree

Admittedly, I do not have much to say about this path into the field of data analytics. I think that at least as of this writing, getting a degree in data analytics is overkill for landing an entry-level data analyst role. If I see a lot of people get data analyst roles after just spending a few hundred bucks on courses and building a portfolio, I can't find a good reason to recommend to most people that they get a degree.

From what I can tell, a degree might be the right path for you if:

- You are around 20 years old (post-high school) and although you know you want to go into data, you also want to get a traditional degree.

- You do not have any degree and would like the experience and credential you would gain from higher education.
- You have an employer who will pay for your education.
- You can find a way to get the cost of an advanced degree covered for you (scholarships, fellowships, etc.).
- You are already a data analyst and want to take your career to the next level and believe a degree (typically a master's) will do that for you.
- You are interested in starting in data analytics but would like to use that as a foundation to move into another field, like data engineering or data science, and you want to leverage the status and knowledge of a degree to help propel you there.

I have a master's degree (in occupational therapy), and so I can tell you with certainty that I never even considered a degree in data when I was getting into this field. In fact, the ability to just learn all the skills online without having to attend another lecture or spend any more money on tuition was one of the things that drew me to data.

There are not many programs out there dedicated to data analytics specifically. It is more common to see degrees offered in data science, computer science, and other disciplines that require true coding. Other degrees that could be beneficial to someone who wants to be a well-rounded data analyst are business degrees, statistics, and even psychology.

Boot Camps

Since I did not get a degree in data and I did not have any prior related experience, my content online and in this book is for people who are looking to get into data in less traditional ways. As a result, I end up talking to a lot of people who are in or have been through boot camps. Data analytics is a fast-growing field, and it seems like the number of boot camps out there (or very expensive course/program offerings that look a lot like a boot camp) are growing at least as fast.

I never wanted to go the route of enrolling in a boot camp, because they are expensive and require a huge time commitment. A lot of boot camps I researched cost about $15,000 and demanded a six-month commitment. Even after I decided to switch careers into data, I had no interest in that kind of commitment! However, there are a lot of boot camps out there, and they can be a good option for some people.

Boot camps come in a few different formats. Some are full time; others are part time and in the evenings or on the weekends. Some boot camps have an in-person component, and many are fully virtual. Every boot camp is going to address the same fundamental skills, but each one will differ in how many "extras" they offer, such as courses in statistics or business, and in their requirements about independent projects and capstones.

I have seen some people who went through boot camps and loved them. I have also had people comment on my posts that they did a boot camp three months ago and still have not gotten a job. When I talked with them more, I could not believe that they had spent over $10,000 on a boot camp and nobody had helped them prepare for interviews—at all. So next I'll focus on two things: when a boot camp may be right for you and how to choose a good boot camp.

When a Boot Camp May Be the Right Option for You If you decide to become a data analyst, you need to sit down with yourself and have a serious conversation. What are your motivations for getting into data? Are you doing it for the paycheck? (No shame in that—we all have our own motivations.) Are you doing it because you want to be able to work remotely? Or are you doing it because you have found a love of working with data and are excited about pursuing that as a career? I find that if people are more interested in the benefits of working in data and maybe not as psyched about the actual data learning/work, they may benefit from the more structured and hands-on education you get in a boot camp.

For the first six months that I was learning data analytics, I was *obsessed* with it. I kid you not; every day I had to get up and go to my occupational therapy internships as part of finishing my master's degree (in occupational therapy). But you know what was in the back of my mind all day? Data. I would literally come home, change out of my scrubs, and sit down with my computer to keep learning and creating projects. It was not hard for me to stay committed to learning or to overcome the difficulties of solving problems on my own because I loved every minute of it.

When people tell me that the "data stuff" is "cool enough" but they are not very motivated by learning it, that is when I suggest that they consider whether a formal course or boot camp, where they have instructors and other peers to help motivate them and keep them on track, might be in their best interest.

Another situation in which a boot camp might be a good fit for you is if you have already tried learning the data tools and concepts (like SQL) on your own and struggled with it. The beauty of a boot camp is that although they teach you and allow you to work on things on your own, there is (or at least should be) someone on staff who can help you when you hit a roadblock. Additionally, the hardest part about getting a data job for someone with no prior experience is often the job search. A good boot camp will not only teach you the data skills with the support you need to learn SQL, but they will also help get you interview and job ready.

Is "job ready" different from "interview ready"? Absolutely. In order to get a data analyst job you are likely going to need to do the following: learn the data analyst interview process (it was like nothing I had experienced before), get your résumé ready, optimize your LinkedIn, and prepare for technical and behavioral interviews.

A good boot camp will have tips for all of these steps, and they should be able to help you prepare for it all. Plus, they should give you insights into the kind of work you would be doing as a data analyst, and help present different options for avenues you can take once in the field—basically, everything I am covering in this book, but coming live from instructors who (hopefully) have years of experience in analytics.

How to Pick a Good Boot Camp   Not all boot camps are created equal. I am not an expert on choosing a boot camp, but I can reflect on the things that came up as most important to me as a job seeker, and the things I have heard from people who have been through boot camps. When you are considering a boot camp, here are the things I would look for:

- They give you a good foundation in all the necessary data tools (SQL, Excel, Tableau, and Power BI). It wouldn't hurt to do a general overview of Python and R either—but I would avoid boot camps that spend a majority of time and energy on either Python or R because they are not requirements for most data analyst entry-level roles. Hybrid data analytics/data science boot camps will likely focus more on Python.
- They give you exposure to people who are actually data analysts so you can see what it is like to be a data analyst. I think that it is quite difficult for someone who is overwhelmed with learning SQL for

the first time to take a step back and understand that this is just a tool in the analysts' tool kit that is going to help them solve business problems. It took me a while to figure this out in my job search. A good boot camp should help its students understand how data analytics is about so much more than the ability to make a dashboard or write a complicated formula.

- Projects. Projects, projects, projects. Any boot camp worth paying for should require that you build a portfolio of data projects and help you to do so. If you do not have any professional experience using SQL, Excel, Tableau, and Power BI, then how are you going to show employers that you have the skills? With a portfolio of data projects! You should exit any boot camp with a portfolio that showcases your ability to use each of the core tools I listed earlier.

- Career services. Like I said before, the hardest part of getting into data analytics is usually not learning the tools—it is job searching. A good boot camp should provide you with support and resources for résumés, interviews, and networking on LinkedIn.

I don't have a good answer for the following questions, but I get asked them often: "Is doing a boot camp going to increase my chances of getting a data job just from having a boot camp on my résumé? Will they have resources to get me connected with jobs that otherwise would not be available to me?"

To be honest, my answer is pretty much "I'm not sure." Whether it will make your résumé look better will probably depend on the hiring manager. A hiring manager who is old school may prefer a candidate who has a degree or at least has attended a boot camp, because that is the mental model they have for successful people.

All I know is that I did not have boot camp experiencer or a data degree, and I still found numerous companies that were interested in me as a candidate because I found other ways to demonstrate my skills (a portfolio, carefully crafted résumé, optimized LinkedIn profile, and good interview skills). Having a boot camp on your résumé certainly would not hurt! But I cannot say for sure how much of a competitive edge it will give you. And if you ask people who run a boot camp, of course they will say "Yes, it would!"

When it comes to referrals to jobs, I imagine that for every boot camp this depends on the circumstances. If a boot camp had direct connections that could guarantee every graduate would get a job with a company they were connected with, I assure you that you would see it in their marketing material. So, if they are not advertising that, then it is probably questionable. If a boot camp is sending through hundreds of students, I find it hard to believe that they would have the connections to get all of them jobs, regardless of their skills at the end of the program.

Here's the bottom line:

- Boot camps are expensive.
- They could be the right choice for you if you prefer detailed instruction or someone else holding you accountable to a schedule.
- You do not need to do a boot camp to get a job in data.
- The right boot camp should provide you with an excellent foundation to get into the data field, so make sure you choose your boot camp wisely.

DIY Approach

If you are reading this book, I imagine you are the most curious about my DIY approach to getting into data analytics. I was too. First, let me define for you what this approach involves:

- Taking free or cheap courses to learn the tools you need to use as a data analyst (such as SQL, Excel, and a visualization tool).
- Does not require prior experience in data or any "related" fields.
- Will almost certainly require you to build your own data portfolio (collection of projects on freely available data) in order to get a job.
- Requires you to do a lot of work and research on your own—not only do you have to learn the data tools, but you also have to build a portfolio, learn how to job search, write a good résumé, optimize your LinkedIn, and figure out how to interview well on your own.
- This approach is good for people who like to learn at their own pace, on their own time, and in their own space. You need to be able to set your own deadlines, keep yourself motivated and on track, and chart your own path. For people who do especially well at the DIY approach, the idea of being the master of their own path is exciting.

- It generally costs about $100 if you are efficient about taking courses and don't take courses just for the satisfaction of having another course under your belt. It can cost less if you can learn from YouTube.

Taking the DIY approach to data can be incredibly rewarding. As a warning, if you successfully chart the course for yourself to change careers and change your entire life and do it without relying on someone else to tell you how to do it, that can be revolutionary. I personally will never look at myself in the same way now that I know *I can learn hard things.*

The typical DIY approach follows the same path as you would while earning a degree or going through a boot camp, but it requires more research on your part to pick the right courses, find free data, figure out where to start your job search, and so forth. It may take less time than some of the six-month part-time boot camps out there from start to finish, but you will spend considerably more time on the "not data analytics" things, like writing your résumé. Writing your résumé is not data analytics, but it is essential to becoming a data analyst.

The rest of this book will be dedicated to explaining to you all the steps I took, how I felt along the way, what was the best use of my time, and what things were a waste of time. Essentially, I am writing this book so that I can give you the "big sister" advice that I wish I'd had when I decided to switch careers into data analytics.

How I Decided on the DIY Approach

I was lucky to have started out with data analytics with a completely unrealistic plan (getting the Google Certificate in Data Analytics and using that to get a freelance position analyzing spreadsheets . . . that was a bad plan and I now know that positions like that don't really exist). If I had sat down right from the start with the desire to get a data analytics job, I probably would've felt like I needed to do a boot camp or get a degree.

However, I lucked my way into realizing that did not have to be the case. When I started my data journey, I did not know a single person who was in data. I didn't even know what data analytics was. For the first two months or so, I was just having a great time learning how to use the data tools. I really love playing board games and solving puzzles, and data analytics felt like one big, fun puzzle. I wasn't focused on what I needed to do to get a job, or at what point I could call myself an "official data analyst." I was just having a good time.

By the time I realized that maybe I should consider switching careers to become a data analyst, I had already heard the stories of dozens of data analysts and data professionals. Slowly I realized that there were loads of people who had transitioned into data analytics from completely different fields like teaching or healthcare, and there was no formal barrier to entry such as a specific certification or exam you had to pass. I also realized at that point that there are thousands of resources out there for learning data analytics for free, and when I looked at the curriculum for boot camps, it was all just things that I was already doing.

So, that's how I decided on the DIY approach for myself. I saw it as an experiment. I was enjoying learning data analytics, and I had the time and availability to do so. So, I decided, "Why not? I'll give this a shot, see if I can continue to keep my costs low, learn on my own, and try to get a full-time data analyst position. If it doesn't work out, I will be graduating with my master's degree soon, so I will just continue to be an occupational therapist like I originally intended."

Here is a short summary of my learning and job searching journey into data analytics:

- January: I did not know what data analytics was.
- February: Spent taking the Google Certificates course in Data Analytics learning SQL, Tableau, Excel, and R.
- March: Building a website, getting active on LinkedIn, working on some portfolio projects.
- April: Taking a course in Python, deciding to try to switch careers, and getting my résumé and portfolio ready.
- May: A month of rejections. I applied to over 50 jobs and did not get very far with any of them.
- June: A strategy pivot. I spent June focused on building a portfolio, leveling up my skills, and talking about my skills and what I was learning on LinkedIn.
- July: The month I got my job, and did several other successful end-stage interviews.

If you would like to read a more in-depth version of my month-by-month journey into data analytics, you can find it in Appendix A.

I am very grateful that I decided to take a chance and tackle getting a data job with no experience, no fancy degree, no boot camp—just me and my passion. Being a great data analyst requires independent learning, curiosity, and a love of working with data to solve problems. Taking the DIY route into data was a learning exercise in all those things.

My manager has consistently told me that he is impressed and happy with my performance and my learning since I started my job. This week he told me that I am tackling things at month 9 that he did not attempt until year 3 of his data career! I am sure that I would have succeeded no matter which route I had taken, but I believe that doing it my way is part of the reason I have been able to jump in head-first and launch my data career so holistically.

As an added benefit to you, since I took the DIY route and it worked for me, I now spend at least an hour a day most days creating content about getting into and being in data so that thousands of other people can follow in my footsteps, skip the boot camp, and get into data without breaking the bank. I have been told by some people to keep to myself how approachable it can be to get into data analytics, to gate-keep that information.

In response to that, I invite you to join me in the next chapter of this book, where I will help you come up with your own DIY plan for breaking into data analytics—and share all the details of my story with you along the way.

3

Designing Your Data Analyst Roadmap

What's Here

- Can you show me your data analyst roadmap?
- How do I choose the best course?
- How do I avoid the "course-hopping" problem?

If you have decided to take the DIY approach to becoming a data analyst, the first step is building your roadmap. Many people struggle to figure out what path to take—there is a lot of conflicting information on the Internet about how to do it. I did not have a plan, which led to me feeling lost and discouraged at times.

If you can make a plan and stick to it, you will thank yourself later! I will share with you the path I took, the insights I learned about picking the "best" courses, and how to avoid the trap that many career changers fall into—something called "course hopping." This chapter will help you design your own roadmap into data analytics.

Can You Shows Me Your Data Analyst Roadmap?

Deciding to get into data analytics on your own, without a boot camp or a degree to guide you, is both exciting and intimidating. When I took my first course, I was just having a good time learning and messing around with data. If I had thought I was embarking on a journey where I would have to create an entire roadmap into a new career I didn't even know existed a month before, I almost certainly would have felt differently about it (and I may not have ever even started).

Time is money, and so most people understandably want to take the fastest path into data they can, while also still maximizing the value of the learning that they are doing, which will set them up for the next steps in their career. I have seen many people who hit walls of frustration and borderline despair because they did not know what to do next and felt like they were aimlessly wasting time, trying to move forward in their journey and not knowing how.

There are a lot of questions you have to ask yourself when you are coming up with a roadmap for yourself. What is my preferred learning style? What is my budget? How many hours a week will I be able to devote to this? Should I take multiple courses? Which course is the best course? The list goes on and on. Although it is overwhelming, asking yourself these questions from the start can save you time, money, and a lot of headaches down the road.

Building Your Roadmap

If you take an approach like mine and fling yourself into learning data analytics without making a plan, you will come out of your first course and be hit with a lot of decisions that you need to make. The problem with this is that every decision you have to make is consuming your time and energy. Many books are dedicated to the subject of decision-making and how in modern society we suffer from decision fatigue.

I have heard that people like Mark Zuckerberg and Steve Jobs wear the same outfits every day to reserve their mental energy for big decisions. Learning data analytics is tricky enough without also juggling the mental load of having to decide what you need to do or learn next.

After I finished my first course, I wanted to work on some projects with data from the Internet. I was so excited to give it a try! After the first few datasets I had opened up, I realized that taking a course was far more straight-forward than trying to find and work with real datasets. I had so many con-flicting priorities racing around in my head at that point: my LinkedIn presence, portfolio projects, and the other skills I might need to learn.

I ended up being so overwhelmed by all the choices that when I real-ized how vague creating portfolio projects felt, I considered giving up. It was hard for me to figure out where I could find data to analyze and what analysis to do on it. In Chapter 6, "Portfolio Project FAQ," and Chapter 7, "Portfolio Project Handbook," I will explore this subject at length and pro-vide sample projects so you don't have to hit the same walls that I did. But there are a few steps before we get there.

My solution to feeling overwhelmed was to hit pause on doing projects on my own and jump into another course! Looking back, this was not the right choice. I had fun taking the course, but taking it was a detour from the otherwise straight line into data analytics that I had been on.

Now that I know what it takes to get from start to finish, let me tell you what my roadmap looked like and how yours should be similar, and different.

Step 1: Skill Development

The first thing you need to do is learn the foundational skills. You can refer back to Chapter 1, "Is Data Analytics Right for Me?" where I discussed the tools in greater detail. The tools you will need to learn include Excel, SQL, and either Tableau or Power BI.

In theory you could skip taking any courses at all and go right into learning these skills hands-on by doing projects, but taking that route would be tricky, and I do not recommend it. Instead, this first part of the journey is exactly the right time to take a course. If you are changing careers to become a data analyst, you have likely never learned anything like any of the tools you need to use to be a data analyst. That makes it challenging to pick up those skills on your own without clear guidance.

There are many good courses that will teach you the skills you need to become a data analyst. Data analytics courses are designed to walk you through everything you need to know about the fundamentals—and then you will be ready to take what you have learned and apply it hands-on.

The most common criticism I hear about data analytics courses is that they only teach the fundamentals—they do not get you a job! However, if you come into it looking to learn and expecting an end-to-end solution (which doesn't exist for less than at least a few thousand dollars), then you can be satisfied with your course experience.

Hundreds of courses are available, and which one you choose depends on your budget and preferred learning style.

You can mix and match courses if they do not teach you all the tools in one course, but I recommend sticking to one course per topic. Some people think that they need to take multiple courses on the same tool to enhance their learning, but in my opinion the main function of a course is to teach you the foundational skills so that you can apply that learning on your own to datasets.

It does not matter tremendously in which order you learn the technical skills, but if I were suggesting an order I'd recommend starting with Excel, then learning the basics of SQL, and then moving on to a visualization tool.

When I took the Google Certificates course in Data Analytics, I loved it. Working through a course is easy and can feel like a game when you are watching your progress bar as you go through the course. When I say working through a course is *easy*, I mean that you do not have to make any decisions. There are certainly going to be pieces of any course that will feel hard and even leave you stumped, but at no point are you ever going to have to make a decision about what you are going to do next.

If you have never encountered anything related to data analytics before, I suggest finding a course that covers not only the technical skills needed to be a data analyst but also the soft skills and ways of thinking that make a successful analyst. Maven Analytics (a data analytics course platform) currently has a course available called "Thinking Like an Analyst," and they have assured me that they will always offer a course of this nature, even if they change the one they currently offer.

Starting with a course like that is a great way to dip your toes in and think about whether data feels like a good fit for you. I ended up browsing through Maven's course only a few weeks before I got my job, and I wished that I had seen it sooner.

Aside from helping you decide if you can truly see yourself enjoying being a data analyst, I think that starting with a course that talks about the soft skills (communication, problem-solving, curiosity) is incredibly valuable because it sets the stage for the rest of the journey. I did not start with a course like this, so I saw data analytics as only a few steps removed from coding. I pictured it being a relatively technical and introverted profession. It was not until a few months of job searching, reading LinkedIn, and taking that "Thinking Like an Analyst" course that I realized being a data analyst is more about solving problems than it is about technical skills. If I had known that from the start, it would have changed the ways I approached learning the tools, doing portfolio projects, and job searching.

Step 2: Building a Portfolio

What is a portfolio? This is a question I get asked a lot. In short, a portfolio is likely what is going to get you a job.

When you hear the word *portfolio* you may think of art or investments. A data analytics portfolio is not unlike an art portfolio—it is a collection of your work that you can show employers to demonstrate your data skills. Building a portfolio simply means using free data from the Internet and doing analyses on it using tools like Excel, SQL, Tableau, or Power BI and then putting those projects together on a website so that people can look through what you have done.

For example, let's say you decide to do an analysis using a dataset about pizza (which you can find in Chapter 7). The data contains information about a fictional pizza place—their sales for the year, the pizzas they sell, and the prices. When analyzing this data, you might be looking for insights on their best- and worst-selling pizzas, and trying to help them identify what days and times are the busiest at their shop.

For your portfolio project on this data, you might bring the data into SQL and ask these questions of it, and get single answers such as a list of the popularity of each pizza, or a small grid with the average number of customers each day and time during the week.

Another option would be to bring the data into Tableau. You could build a dashboard with different graphs on it, such as a line graph that shows the average number of customers at certain times of each day of the week, and a bar graph that shows the total sales of each type of pizza.

This analysis would give the owner of the pizza shop insights beyond just a "gut feeling" about their pizzas and customers. They could then use these insights to make business decisions, such as when to have more staff on duty or how to prepare their inventory. This is an overly simplistic example, and a real analysis would likely have many more variables, but this is an example of a good, straightforward portfolio project for new data analysts to get the hang of using SQL and Tableau.

Once you have a solid foundation in what data analytics is and how to use the basic tools, it is time to apply that knowledge to some projects, which you will put in your portfolio. If you take a course that teaches you all the data skills back to back, you can save this step for after you finish the course (especially if you are paying a monthly subscription). However, if you are taking courses to learn the skills one at a time, I suggest waiting to take any further courses in a new skill until after you have completed at least two projects of your own.

For example, if you take an Excel course as your first step, take a break after the course. Come straight to Step 2, and start working on your own project, applying the things you've learned. The best way to learn is to do it hands-on. If you jump right into another course without practicing the skills you've just learned in the Excel course, you're wasting your own time! You will forget a lot of the things you learned, and by the time you come back to the tool to do a portfolio project on it, you will have to go back and relearn the things you forgot.

Even if you are not ready to make an official portfolio landing page yet or do any of the steps I'm about to list when you've just finished your first course, at least complete the projects and save them to your computer. This will reinforce your learning, boost your confidence, get you some projects to put in your portfolio when you are ready, and leave you with a reference to come back to when you return to this skill later.

Once you complete a few projects in your newly learned skill, you can either go back to Step 1 to start the process over with a new skill, or you can move on to the rest of Step 2.

Creating a data portfolio is more than just running some queries or analyzing a spreadsheet on your local computer. In order to be able to share your work publicly, you will need to find a place to host your projects so that others can see them. There are a lot of options for this, which I will discuss later in this book, but for now you need to know that at this step of the roadmap you need to plan for doing projects and putting them into one central location.

This is not essential, but it is my recommendation that at this stage you also take time to reflect on what you have learned so far, and share it publicly. Some places that you can share and reflect on your learning at this stage are LinkedIn, TikTok, blogging, and various Discord and Slack groups that have been created for aspiring data professionals. Each platform has its own uses and benefits, but the most important thing here is just taking the time to share your learning. I made my own portfolio website on Wix and added a section for my blog. I do not think the blog was helpful in getting me a job, but having somewhere to reflect on my learning helped me organize my thoughts. I was also still making TikToks as well as posting on LinkedIn at this point, so that was another avenue for me to discuss my learning.

I did not realize until after I got my job that having my TikTok, LinkedIn, and blog were all incredibly valuable assets for helping me find a job, but not for the reasons you may think. If you remember the start of my story, I was not even remotely a data analyst before I started this journey. Not only was I not a "data person" but I also did not know anyone who worked in tech. All of my friends are in healthcare, childcare, or adventure sports!

Creating content about what I was learning forced me to slow down, think about what I was doing, and put words to it. Being on various social media platforms gave me the chance to interact with other people and talk about data and my data projects. When I got to my first interviews I was clunky and awkward, and fumbling for words to describe my data skills and projects. By the time I got my job, however, I had learned how to put words to what I was doing. When interviewers asked me about my SQL skills, I was no longer fumbling to find the words for what I could do, which allowed me the mental space to focus on answering questions and showcasing my skills.

This is why I am advocating that as a part of Step 2, as you are building your portfolio projects, you take the time to slow down, think about what you are doing, and share it with others. You will thank yourself later if you do it in the moment, instead of waiting until the end or, even worse, weeks later.

Another aspect of building a portfolio is that it allows you to see where your natural strengths and weaknesses are. When I returned to building a portfolio after I took my Python course detour, I focused on getting some SQL and Tableau projects into my portfolio. I found that I was able to upskill myself and learn new SQL functions by just searching around on the Internet for common interview questions and functions used by data analysts.

When it came to Tableau, on the other hand, I realized that I had hit a wall. I felt like I had brought myself as far as I could in self-teaching Tableau skills, but my projects seemed to be lacking *something* but I did not know what *something* was, or how to get there. So, I decided to go back to Maven Analytics and take a course in Tableau. I identified a specific skill gap (Tableau dashboards) and made a plan for addressing it.

Step 3: Getting Yourself Ready to Job Search

The final preparation step of the roadmap is preparing for the job search. For me, this took about a month and a half. Once I decided I would like to try switching careers and getting a job in data, I knew that I had some serious work to do. I had seen online that getting your first data job could take months. Sometimes, interviews could last for "weeks." As someone who had never encountered more than one round of interviews, I did not understand what that could possibly mean.

Everyone has a unique job search, depending on their history, the time of year, and the current market conditions. Many times, getting a data job comes down to luck. I got my job in part because I was in the right place at the right time (online). However, the "preparing to job search" step has a few common elements for most. In no particular order, they are:

- Writing your résumé
- Optimizing your LinkedIn profile
- Discovering and understanding the various other non-LinkedIn job boards
- Ensuring your portfolio and other public-facing works are cleaned up and ready to go
- Networking
- Preparing for the different types of analytics interviews
- Picking some industries you are interested in/may be a good fit for

This part of the process was by far the hardest part for me. I felt like a leaf blowing in the wind; I had no purpose, no direction, and no idea what I was doing. When I decided, "Hey, maybe I will get a job in data," I was hit with this wall of things I needed to do that I had never done before.

"Optimizing your LinkedIn"? I remember thinking to myself, "What the heck does that mean?" It was all so foreign to me. Even if it feels unfamiliar and strange to you, you do not need to feel so lost and alone on this step of the journey. If you know it is coming and plan to work job search into your roadmap, it will not be so overwhelming when you get to that stage.

I would argue that the best roadmap is one that is not segmented into Steps 1–3 sequentially. The best plan for getting into data analytics would be sprinkling all of these Step 3 items into your entire journey. For example, you're reading this book now. If you're still at the beginning of your journey, then the tips I have for your LinkedIn, résumé, and interviews will put you far ahead of where I was when I got started.

I will not talk about networking until Part III of this book, but for now I recommend you start this as soon as possible and stick with it at every step of the way. If you can begin by following people who talk about data on LinkedIn and other platforms, watching videos on YouTube, and connecting with a few people already in the field to hear about their stories, then you will be setting yourself up to gain invaluable advice and knowledge that you will never get from a course.

Later in this book I will dive deeper into what job searching will look like and how to best prepare yourself. What you need to know for now is that this is Step 3 of our roadmap into data analytics. Most people I know who have gotten into data have danced their way through these three steps. I say *dance* because many of us have not followed this process in a linear fashion. As I said earlier, the best roadmap is one that contains all three of these components but includes a lot of switching around from courses, to networking, to doing projects, back to your course, and so on.

How Do I Choose the Best Course?

One of the most commonly asked questions I see in the data space is "I am thinking about taking _____ course. Will this course get me a job, or is _____ better?" The thing is, no course is going to get you a job. Not even a combination of courses will get you a job. I will say it again: *there is no course that will get you your first data job.* Do not mistake good marketing for reality. Of course, it is in the best interests of many courses/course platforms to sell themselves as containing everything you will need to know to get a job in data. If they told you that, actually, they were just laying the foundation and the real work is up to you, they wouldn't sell anything!

I absolutely fell for this marketing. In January 2022 when I thought I could get a side hustle in data analytics, the first course I found was the Google Certificates course in Data Analytics. They essentially promised that in about six months they would have me job ready, and they even said that they had a special jobs portal I would get access to at the end.

It seemed to me after browsing the curriculum that I could finish it way sooner than six months. If I am being perfectly honest, the course had eight modules and I had just browsed the first module and thought that was the entire course. So there I was, thinking that I could take this single module course and, *poof*, I would have access to some kind of side hustle job at the end of it. So I signed up for the free trial. I bought that marketing hook, line, and sinker.

I also thought that the promise of finishing with a certificate would help me stand out and get a job. Since I was just finishing my master's degree, the idea of having an official certificate seemed important to me. I learned later that "certifications" that you get at the end of finishing a data analytics course hold very little weight in the job market. The market is completely saturated with courses, and there is no standard that they are held to. Getting a certificate at the end of the course is a good marketing tactic for selling more courses, but it is not a good indicator to a recruiter or a hiring manager that you have a certain set of skills.

Something a bit different from certificates are "certifications" that are issued by software companies that own analytics tools. I have heard from numerous hiring managers that they will pay attention to, or even look for, certifications in tools that their company uses. An example of this is Tableau: you can spend a few hundred dollars to get a certification in Tableau, and that will provide employers with a benchmarked standard for what your skills are. Although these can help you stand out, I do not recommend spending hundreds of dollars on them unless you are sure that you want a specific job that is looking for that certification—which is not usually something you will encounter for entry-level roles.

You may find it challenging to distinguish between a certificate and a certification. The way to tell them apart is that a certification is usually offered by the company directly (such as Tableau Software), and costs a good amount of money. Certificates usually come at the end of independently offered courses and boot camps.

Although the promise that the course would get me job ready ended up falling flat, I am still glad that I took the course. It was my gateway into analytics. The Google course turned out to be very well designed, and it made learning fun! If I had started with a dense course that actually provided a higher value, I likely would have been bored or overwhelmed, and checked out.

After I took the Google Certificates course I went on to take two other courses. Now that I have made my way through earning a master's degree (in which I largely disagreed with the instructional methods my professors used), one course that I enjoyed but ended up not finding relevant, and two courses that I enjoyed and found well worth my time, I have reflected on my opinions of what separates the courses that are worth your time from the ones that are a detour (at best).

What Makes a Good Course

If you do a Google search and look for courses in data analytics, SQL, Tableau, Excel, or Power BI, you will likely find yourself overwhelmed. The market is absolutely saturated with courses, and costs range from free to a few hundred dollars per course.

Generally, a good course will cover one or more of the core skills that I listed for data analysts. If you see a course that covers a range of data analytics topics and also covers topics like Python, machine learning, or advanced statistics, then those courses are probably not designed for someone learning data analytics for the first time.

When you are deciding on the right course for you, think about your learning style, budget, support, interests, and time constraints. Let's look at some examples of how these affected me.

Learning Styles   I am a visual learner, and I am *not* an auditory learner. When I watch movies and shows, I always turn the subtitles on. I personally cannot succeed in a course without subtitles or captions. It especially helps me if courses have subtitles on screen and a transcript that I can just read. I especially love when the transcript is interactive so I can click a point in the transcript and the video scrolls to that point.

On the other hand, I have friends who do not like to read information and much prefer to hear it. Some of my friends in graduate school had the "listening" learning style, which turned out well for me because I would read my notes to them and try to teach back what I had learned, and they would just listen. Think about what learning styles may or may not work well for you, and look for courses that can match that.

I see learning styles as more of a preference than a rule. There have been a number of studies that have come out in recent years debunking the classical theory of "learning styles" in which someone is more dominant in visual, auditory, or kinesthetic learning. One such study came out in 2016 (https://pubmed.ncbi.nlm.nih.gov/27620075), and their findings are consistent with many other similar studies in showing that, although people perceived their learning to improve when it matched their preferred learning style, that was not reflected in their actual learning.

The best way to truly retain information is hands-on practice and, if possible, the opportunity to teach others. So do not get too stressed about finding your specific learning style and matching a course to it. I find that it helps to match a course to your preferred way of learning (if you have one), because it makes it more fun.

Of course, if you (like me) have specific reasons why one learning style is more challenging for you–such as auditory processing disorder, dyslexia, or other related learning barriers—considering the type of content of your courses may fall higher on your priority list. In my opinion, the best courses out there are ones that provide content in all different forms—courses that provide you with learning materials, lectures, audio, pictures, and hands-on practice will give you the best chance to get familiar with data in a variety of formats.

Budget   I had no interest in taking a course that was more than $50. I made it my mission to find resources for myself that were free, because I was a broke graduate student who was not making any money! There are plenty of free courses for learning the basics out there, and I have heard good things about them! I have also browsed the marketing materials of $100+ courses before, and they seem like they offer a pretty comprehensive and interesting course experience.

When I took the Google Certificates course, it was $45. I probably would not have spent much more than that on it. I also pushed myself to get through it as fast as possible, because I was paying for a subscription to

Coursera to take the course. I managed to finish the course in one month (four weeks, plus the extra week that I had gotten from the free trial).

The next course I took was a Python course. I am not sure what its original cost was, but I got it when Udemy had a sale, and it was only $8 for lifetime access. At the time of purchasing it I remember thinking, "It's so cheap that even if I do not end up needing it, I will not regret this purchase."

When I got into my job search and identified some specific upskilling I needed to do, I turned to Maven Analytics because I had recently discovered them through social media and loved their platform. They were often putting out great content about learning and breaking into data analytics on LinkedIn and TikTok, so I knew I could trust their courses. At the time that I took their courses a Maven Analytics subscription was $45, and I finished the courses I took with them after a few weeks.

For me, signing up for a monthly subscription in order to learn the basic skills and then canceling my memberships once I was finished was a good option. It was not too expensive, so I could afford them. But, as part of building your roadmap you need to be honest with yourself about your budget. If you know you are not a fast learner, or you will not be able to dedicate 20 or more hours to learning every week, you should keep your subscription past that first month.

Support   When I got my job, one of the first things my boyfriend said to me was, "So are you going to be able to spend time with me again?" When people hear my story, they are often amazed I was able to learn so quickly and stay on track for that long. An important part of that story is to understand the other things happening in my life at the time.

When I was learning data analytics, I was also finishing graduate school. This meant that I was working full time but not getting paid to do so. However, I was not doing anything else on the side. I do not have kids or pets. The only things I am growing is mint (which is nearly impossible to kill) and cacti (which I have managed to kill before). I have/had very few responsibilities apart from work/school and making sure that I eat every day and do basic things like my laundry.

While I was learning data, my boyfriend was getting ready to open a business. A year prior we had moved to a new area so that he could be the general manager of a brand-new rock-climbing gym. For the previous year the gym was being built, and it was finally scheduled to open in August 2022.

Fortunately for me, the gym not being open yet meant he had a bit of extra time on his hands during the winter and spring of that year. He was going to the gym to help oversee the build on most weekdays, but any work he had to do from his computer had to be done at home. This meant my boyfriend was around often.

The thing you have to know about my boyfriend is that he is the best cook I know, and he likes a clean house. So, while I was pouring myself into learning two careers at once, spending over 20 hours a week on learning, he was there to pick up the slack. He would cook for me and usually wash the dishes too. My partner is the type of person who, when I wake up on Sunday morning, has already finished his first cup of coffee and says, "Oh good, you're up," and starts sweeping the carpet in our bedroom.

I cannot overstate how important having his support, and the emotional support of my family and friends, was during this time. If I had more responsibilities (like kids) or did not have as much support from the people around me, I may have had to make different choices about purchasing course subscriptions or even the types of courses that I was enrolling in.

Another thing to consider is whether you know people who are in data already. If you have people in your life who know SQL, Tableau, Power BI, or Excel, then you may not need to spend money to take a course on the subjects.

Interests   Although data analytics may sound like its own field/career, it is not like other professions that stand on their own. If you are in real estate, banking, or archaeology, then you have a fairly well-defined path of the subjects you need to know and be interested in. But every profession creates data. That means that you can analyze all kinds of data—financial data, climate data, operations data, and so on.

As you consider a switch into data analytics, remember that being able to solve business problems is a huge part of the job. When you look for a data analyst position, it is in your best interests to match it to your own interests and backgrounds. This benefits you by keeping the role interesting, but it also makes you stand out as a candidate. I have seen people get data analyst jobs after just a few months of learning and job searching because they had prior experience in that industry in another non-data role, and so they were already a subject matter expert.

Why am I telling you this? Well, when I started my data journey there was not even a thought in my mind about leveraging my background and current skills to get a data job. I never considered that maybe I could do certain projects or take certain courses that may prepare me better for roles that I may be interested in or a good fit for. But it's not too late for you!

One particular area of specialty I see a lot is financial data. If you know already that you like numbers and working with money, you may want to consider focusing on courses that have a heavy financial focus. When you are thinking about buying a course, you can usually read through the syllabus and the reviews. This is your chance to look for courses that will help you prepare your candidate profile for specific industries.

If you do not have a specific industry in mind or cannot find courses that cover that topic, that's okay! This is not an essential step. It is simply something I thought was worth mentioning while we are on this topic.

Time Constraints This last one I considered taking off the list altogether, but I decided to leave it on. At the beginning of your data journey, you have no way of knowing how long it will take you, how fast you will learn, or how much time you are going to *want* to spend on learning every week. This is why I break down the journey into actions you must take and milestones you want to meet, instead of chunking things by lengths of time.

However, I decided to keep time constraints in here because I realize that some people have tighter schedules than I did and need to wrap their heads around some kind of a timeline. For example, my friend Matt Mike was out on parental leave for a month or so, and he knew that he wanted to make the most of that time so he could get a new job as close to coming off his leave as possible.

Matt had seen my content on LinkedIn along with some other creators, and he pored through every free piece of content we had out there before he went on leave. While he was at home with his new baby, he poured himself into learning, and in less than two months, Matt had accepted his first job as a data analyst. He is one of the people I know who managed to find a position as a data analyst that was related to his previous job, which gave him a leg up in the hiring manager's eyes since he had transferable experience.

If I had told Matt about a course that could take several months that had a lot of great material about soft skills and technical skills, he probably would have said thank you, but no thanks. He did not have the time for that! Stories like his are the reason I decided to keep this section about time constraints.

Many courses on the market today will give you a general idea of how long they may take. As a data analyst, arguably your most valuable skill is being able to query the Internet. When you are looking at courses that interest you, look up their reviews! People will often include how long the course took them in their reviews.

I think that it is valuable to take courses that spend time exploring such things as what it's like to give data presentations and the thinking skills you need to be a data analyst. However, some people see that as "just fluff." It will inevitably take you longer to take a course that spends time talking about the full picture of what it's like to be a data analyst than one that just exists to teach you a new technical skill.

Both of those course types have their place. When you are picking a course, think about how long you are able to spend on it, and how long you *want* to spend on it. Look over the syllabus carefully and read the reviews from previous participants so that the time it takes to complete the course does not catch you off guard.

Getting Started for Free

If you would like to learn all of the fundamentals you need to become a data analyst as well as get some support on creating portfolio projects, writing your résumé, and networking on LinkedIn—*for free*—I recommend you check out Alex The Analyst's "Data Analytics Boot Camp" playlist. It is on his YouTube channel and 100 percent free. You can find it here: www .youtube.com/playlist?list=PLUaB-1hjhk8FE_XZ87vPP SfHqb6OcM0cF.

His boot camp did not exist when I was learning data analytics, but I looked over the videos since he has created them and I am very impressed. He covers SQL, Excel, Power BI, and even Python in the boot camp, as well as projects and job search topics. I love his calm and practical educational style, and he breaks concepts down so anyone can follow along.

The thing about free resources is that we tend to place less value on them than paid resources. So do not fall into the trap of getting lazy or writing off the material just because it is free on YouTube. Alex covers everything you need to know (and more) in the boot camp, and on his page in general.

If you can stay motivated to follow a free roadmap with no subscription deadline looming over you to keep you on track, then this truly is an excellent option.

Despite what the marketing materials are going to tell you, the basics of data analytics are pretty standard, and most people can learn them. You truly build your data skills through doing—the most important learning you do will come from the hands-on projects you do once you master the foundational skills.

When Not to Pick a Course: How to Avoid Course Hopping

For those of us who do not have a background in data analytics, when we sit down with a blank page to write our résumés and look at the abysmally short prior experience sections, it is only natural to feel like having courses or certificates to add into this section may make us a better candidate. Especially if you have grown up with an understanding that degrees are important, the thought of trying to get into a career that could one day in the not-too-distant future lead to a six-figure salary without any official proof of your "merit" is mind-boggling.

This need to prove ourselves on a résumé has led me, and many others, to feel like we need to get certifications or courses into our résumé, just to say that we have them. Not only that, but taking courses is fun! It is so rewarding to see yourself progressing through a course, and to look back on everything you have accomplished. Having a clearly laid-out learning path can light up your brain in all the right ways.

Don't fall into the trap! I've spoken with dozens of people in the last year who admitted that they fell victim to "course hopping." As I mentioned earlier, the first thing you should do after learning a new skill is to find some data and practice the skill. If you did your research before selecting a course, then you picked a good one! It may be hard to start a vague, intimidating new data project and stick to that project instead of jumping into another well-defined data course, so make sure you put completing projects into the roadmap to hold yourself accountable to it.

Once you have decided on your roadmap, it is time to fully commit to it and start learning. Print it out, put it on a whiteboard, whatever you need to stay accountable! For the last chapter in Part I, I will tell you about my personal experience with taking courses, learning data skills, and changing careers. You will hear about how I *felt* along the way—not just the skills that I learned.

4

My Experience with Data Analytics Courses

What's Here

- My first data course (The Google Certificates course)
- Finishing and working on portfolio projects
- Changing careers
- Evaluating the usefulness of taking a different course

Before learning your first new data skill, you might be wondering: How hard is it going to be? What is it going to feel like? Am I going to have to do a lot of math? Will there be things that I can't find an answer to?

I wanted to take a break from giving advice to tell you what it was like for me to learn data analytics. In this chapter I'm going to focus on taking courses and learning the fundamentals—I will talk about the learning I did while building my portfolio in Part II, and at my eventual job later on in Part IV of this book.

The Beginning

To begin with, I can say that learning Excel was the easiest skill to pick up because I already had casual experience with Excel. Python and R were tied for the most difficult—they are actually coding languages! Tableau was easier to learn than Python and R but felt the most vague. SQL was the most exciting tool to learn, but part of that was because it was the first thing I learned after Excel, and I did not go into it thinking I was going to like it.

Here is my story about learning the skills I needed to get my first job, starting with the Google Certificates course in Data Analytics.

The Google Certificates Course

My data journey started with the Google Certificates course in Data Analytics. It is an eight-module course, and it covers Excel, SQL, Tableau, and R. It also discusses the soft skills you need to be a data analyst, and what it's like to be a data analyst. At the end of the course, it briefly discusses writing your résumé and job searching, before setting you up with a portfolio project or two (called a "capstone"). It was all prerecorded; nothing needed to be done live. Everyone who takes that course does the exact same thing.

If you are reading this book, you are putting a lot more thought into learning data analytics than I did to begin with. I am normally a very organized person who plans everything out in advance. So, it was pretty out of character that I did not even look past what the course would cover other than Excel, and that I did not realize the course had eight modules.

The first module had almost eight sections to it, so I just assumed that it was the entire course. I had not paid for the course yet—I was still on a free trial—so I felt I had little to lose. After I finished the first few sections of the first module, I realized that not only was the course far more interesting than I'd anticipated, but it was also fairly easy, and I felt like I was making fast progress. I decided that I could easily finish the course by the end of my weeklong free trial.

A few hours later, I finished the course. That's when I realized—I had just finished the first module! There were seven left, and the first one was just an easy introduction. I talk often in this book and on my social media platforms about how data is so much more than just knowing how to use some tools. It's really about soft skills, working with businesses, and critical thinking. The Google course did cover a lot of those topics, especially in the first two modules. At the time, though, I did not want to become a data analyst as a career. I did not think I would need to think about data cleaning and data quality—I just wanted to learn some new tools, get my certificate, and get out.

I sped through the first few modules of the course. Anything that felt like "fluff" to me I listened to, but not in depth. We had the option to make posts in forums to absorb what we were learning, but after the first few I stopped writing in them altogether. I was so excited to just get into it!

Finally, after a module or two, I started learning some neat things in Excel. I still remember how amazed I was when I realized that you could pull down the header bar of the spreadsheet to "freeze" it so that no matter where you scrolled to, you would still be able to see the top- or leftmost header row of the sheet.

I did not struggle with anything the course covered in Excel. Even when I had to start writing formulas and tackling multistep logic, I found the material interesting but not challenging.

The first doubt I had while taking the course was that I was never going to be able to remember everything I was learning in the course. So, I started a Google Drive folder, with subfolders and files. Every time I came across a section that was particularly good (especially if it was a graphic), I would put it into its own document. I also started a running document of every function that I was learning (like SUM), so I could have it to refer back to.

Once the course picked up on technical content, I loved it. It would present new material in the form of a video/lecture (with a transcript), and the teachers would usually show examples of themselves walking through the actual work they were teaching us. Google would often pair these videos with a long, detailed page with visuals—kind of like a section from a textbook.

Then, it would give in-course options for practice, such as short, ungraded quizzes between sections; formal quizzes that had hands-on exercises; and one test at the end of every module. Getting the chance to mix up the learning methods and then apply everything to tricky but doable hands-on exercises was perfect for me as a learner.

Working through the first three modules of the course—which were mainly introductory content, fluff, and the foundations of Excel—went fast. I had never seen myself as someone who would be particularly "techy," so I was surprised to realize that I was enjoying taking a course in data analytics, of all things.

Learning SQL   When the course introduced me to SQL for the first time, I remember thinking, "I won't need to know this." In fact, I considered stopping the course after I finished the Excel section because I thought the other "stuff" was only for people who wanted to do this as a career. But I was enjoying myself in the course so I decided to give SQL a shot.

I didn't want to like SQL. I wanted to just breeze past it. At that point I was beginning to struggle with my internalized feelings that my career, the thing I loved to do, was working with children, not data. But after just a few lessons, I knew I loved writing SQL.

The interesting thing about SQL is that it has a specific structure that reads like something halfway between code and written English. It has rules that need to be followed, and if you get even just a period out of place you will run into an error. But it's not code. Once you learn to structure your thinking the way SQL is structured, it's like moving around puzzle pieces until you get the right fit.

I remember the first time I wrote a full query of my own and it returned data. I was so excited I squealed. Out loud. Fortunately, I was alone, but it was an exciting moment for me. I had solved the puzzle and unlocked the data behind it!

Then came the hard parts. The third through fifth modules of the course covered SQL, which gave me plenty of time to get stumped. As much as I loved taking a completely online course with no live instruction, it meant that any time I hit a wall I had to go and figure it out for myself.

By the time I got to the harder SQL in the course, I was already starting to burn myself out. I knew I wanted to finish the course before my subscription renewed for a second month. I had also started my TikTok and gained a solid following of at least 5,000 followers at this point. On top of the course, my job/internship, and keeping up with all of the comments and questions on my TikTok account, I was constantly rushing.

The whole month of February felt like a whirlwind to me. Every time I finished a module I would dive right into the next one without even taking a breath in between. Thinking back on that time I can feel the excitement, but I can almost feel a tightness in my chest from how out of breath it made me feel sprinting through the month.

Running through the course worked for me for the first few modules, but learning SQL is not something you can do in a hurry. So when I hit challenging puzzles that required learning how to think in a whole new way, I hit that wall hard.

When I hit the wall of challenges, it came with self-doubt as well. What was I really doing? Could I do this? I've never been someone who is good at "this stuff." What makes me think I could suddenly do it now? I also felt the pressure of having shared my journey with so many people at this point. Failing in front of everyone felt like a pretty bad option.

Each time I encountered a new concept I did not understand, I would try to take a step back. I had continued my practice of keeping a running document of all the functions I had learned, so I would refer back to that and look at my notes and examples of how to use that function.

Sometimes I could tear myself away to take a break, walk around, and maybe have a cup of tea (I should have done more of this). Walking around and getting my blood flowing always helped me get some mental clarity. But I am the type of person who likes to hyperfocus. When I can get myself into the zone, if I just stay in it and don't take a break, even to get a glass of water, I can power through and get so much done.

The first few challenges I came up against that I didn't get right away, I was able to Google and figure out the answer with a relatively cool head. But I didn't take enough of a break, or spend any time reflecting after I solved them. So by the fourth or fifth challenge, I was out of patience with myself.

I have a clear memory of working through something called a "subquery" for the first time. I spent a few hours on it and just kept getting error after error. Subqueries are tricky because there are a few layers of logic that you need to keep track of, and everything needs to be separated appropriately with commas and parentheses.

I finally gave up and looked at the solution. The worst part was that when I compared them side by side, it still took me about 20 minutes to notice the difference. You know what the difference was? I had used "front ticks" instead of `back ticks` on one of the lines where I named the table I was pulling information from.

I closed my computer and took a break and told myself that after I finished this module (I was very close to the end), I needed to take a break. I did take several days off from the course in between those modules, because the next thing up was a new tool called Tableau.

The next day after I had cooled down from my inward-facing exasperation, I posted a TikTok about how I was struggling. I felt nervous about being that vulnerable online, but I am also a big believer in being real and honest and not just posting the highlight reel of my life.

Very quickly a bunch of data people spoke up in the comment section to let me know that this is normal, and it happens to everyone! I thought that being a data analyst was about having the answers and being good at using the tools. It was around then that I learned that even people who have been in the field for a decade still have to Google things all the time.

It was also around then that I learned that you do not have to memorize everything! There are no "closed book" tests when you're a data analyst. Although you need to learn what all the functions do and how to use them, you don't need to have any of it memorized. You can always look things up, and copy and paste is a normal thing.

This didn't exist yet (publicly) while I was learning, but as of this writing, there has been a huge increase in the availability and adoption of the use of AI for the "average person" like you and me. It's easier than ever now to write SQL and all kinds of code, and as long as you have access to the Internet or a document with your notes, you will never have to remember any of the exact details.

Learning Tableau and R   In my few days off from the Google course, I did not actually take a break from data analytics. I took the time to make some content on TikTok, start a LinkedIn, and start a blog to keep track of my learning. I probably should have taken a real break and done some activity outdoors, but it was February and the weather was awful.

The next module of the course focused on Tableau. I was skeptical of Tableau at first—I didn't see how creating visualizations would belong in the same course as all the SQL I had just finished. I had some basic experience creating graphs in Excel, so I was not sure how Tableau would offer more than that.

Boy, was I wrong. The course had me download Tableau and do a small guided project right away. The first time I dragged some columns of data out onto the screen and it magically turned them into charts and maps, my eyes just about popped out of my head. Somehow the course had done it again! I had underestimated something and then been happily surprised to realize how much I enjoyed using it—and how much it could do!

That module of the course went by pretty quickly. The course only skimmed Tableau; I did not feel like I learned much about it. The biggest issue I had while in that module was that the web browser version of

Tableau had a lot of bugs. At first I thought that I was just doing something wrong, but after a lot of searching around on the Internet I learned that the sizing of the different containers was preventing me from taking the actions that the course was prompting me to take.

After seeing what Tableau could do with the sample data from the course, my mind was spinning with ideas. I was starting to get impatient with taking the course—part of me wanted to finish it so that I could do some projects with real data. Looking back, the best thing to do at that point would have been to take a break and work on some projects. In fact, I should have done that after the SQL modules! But I kept racing on.

Now that I have the perspective of being a Tableau consultant, I can say with confidence that I didn't squeeze any of the juice that the course had to offer around Tableau at all. It was more of an "ohh, this is a possibility!" than any real learning.

The final skill to learn in the Google course was how to use R. R is a programming language that is mainly used to write code related to statistics and crunching data, from what I understand of it. I was nervous about this module, because the whole point of the data analytics thing was that there was no coding required.

I found getting set up with using R to be difficult and discouraging. In the other modules, I got a soft introduction to the tool by getting to practice in the module and then taking the learning out of the course to a browser or Excel. This time, I had to jump right into using it in the browser.

The first hour or so of trying to use R was just a whole bunch of "wow, that's a lot of buttons and things I don't know how to use." On the flip side of that, the course did have good instructions. I still did not know what to think of it all, until I ran my first line of code.

The first thing that I did was not analyzing any data—it was just installing "packages," which are sets of functions R has for analyzing code that do not come preinstalled. I ran one line of code and then my screen filled with hundreds of lines of information about all the packages that were being installed within a matter of seconds. I felt like a hacker from a movie. It was so cool. It's funny to look back on because I was not doing anything except a simple installation, but that didn't matter to me; I was hooked. Again.

After that I took the rest of the module much more seriously. While I was in graduate school I did research that involved running my own statistics on my data. When I got going in R and realized how seamlessly and powerfully it could perform analyses that took me hours to do on my own,

I couldn't believe this tool had existed, for free, and I had never found it before.

I made quick work of the R module, but I was careful not to rush through it. I could see a real-world application of the tool, unlike when I was learning SQL. It was interesting to learn SQL, but abstract. It felt different to learn and use R, because I had ideas in the back of my mind about what I would use it to do, given the chance. Plus, it was harder than SQL! That also kept me from rushing.

Finishing the Course   The last and final module of the course was the capstone, as well as some tips about résumés and interviews. I did not find much of that information to be very exciting or helpful; many of the creators I had found on LinkedIn and TikTok were giving out great advice on résumés and interviews that made the Google course information feel watered down. Once again, I sped through this module to get to the end—the capstone. I could not wait to get my hands on some data in a real project.

Since I was paying a monthly subscription, I wrapped up all the content in the last module, downloaded what I needed, and ended my subscription. I was relieved; I was a few days early from when my subscription would renew and I would be charged for a second month.

When it came time to get the data fired up and create my first project, I fired up BigQuery (which I used for SQL), and quickly hit writer's block. While working through the course, it had set me up with "what" and all I had to do was come up with a "how." But as I looked at several huge files' worth of a wall of text, I felt like I had not learned a single thing.

In the course, they had told me to "consider the business problem" and "try and give answers" in my project. That made sense at the time, but I looked at the dataset and realized, "I have no business experience. I don't know what they're looking for!" I sat there stumped for a while, and then decided to go back to my notes.

If you'll remember, I kept a handy list of notes about every function I learned in the course and how to use it. When I looked back over the functions, I felt like I knew them and was ready to try using them. I made a choice that instead of trying to be perfect and amazing at analytics right away, I would take things one step at a time. And right then, the step I was on was just getting practice using the things I had learned.

I decided to forget the idea of trying to solve business problems for my end user in my first projects, because I could always redo it later, once I was more comfortable with the skills. To begin with, I was solely focused on applying as many of the things I had learned in the course as possible to the datasets available to me.

It was still slow going at first, and I had to spend plenty of time researching various errors I ran into and questions that came up. But, slowly and surely it started to work! I was doing it—I was analyzing actual data, without a course setting me up with the exact questions to answer! It was exciting, and even though it started slow, it put the wind back in my sails and made me want to keep going.

After trying a bunch of things out, I realized that I had not considered saving anything I was doing. I was just running queries and then writing back over them when I wrote the next one. That brought me to the next issue: "If I'm going to keep track of this, how do I do that? What would employers want to see?" I had no answers to any of these questions, and no good reference material for figuring that out. My solution was just to copy and paste everything I was doing into a Google doc, often along with the table that this resulted in.

I still do not have a perfect answer of how to keep track of your queries, but I have a better idea now. If I were to go back and do that part of the experience again, I would keep track of what question I had that I was trying to answer (how many people came to the event?) and then my query in its own code block. If there were any problems with this, I would record that, and then continue. That would be a good place to start. No data pasted in—it was not necessary.

I spent about two weeks in total bringing data into Tableau, SQL, and R and trying out different things I had learned. I was extra busy with my internship at that time, so that did slow me down, and I worked through the projects in pieces. I kept feeling like I needed to keep refining my work, making changes, and trying to add more. At some point I realized that I just needed to share my work and move forward—it would never feel perfect! I had accomplished my mission of using all of the little skills I had been building throughout the course, and I felt proud of myself for having come that far in such a short time.

I will talk more about true portfolio building in Chapter 6, "Portfolio Project FAQ," and Chapter 7, "Portfolio Project Handbook," but I wanted to include the capstone in my write-up of my course experience, because I still mentally consider that project more of a review of the course concepts with some new learning added on, rather than part of my portfolio-building phase.

What Came Next

I was relieved to finish. I had raced through the course and all of the learning as quickly as I could handle, and it had taken up all my free time. Once I finished, I took a few days to unplug, go camping, clean the apartment, and generally catch up on everything I had been neglecting.

When I tried to figure out what to do next, I felt lost. I had not intended to start something so big when I began the Google course, but by the time I finished I knew I was hooked and wanted to see it all through. I also knew I probably was not job ready—despite Google boasting that the certificate would get you job ready. The first thing I did was look around at job postings, and as I looked, I kept seeing Python come up. It seemed to me like I would need to know at least a little Python in order to become a data analyst.

Without thinking whether that was truly what I wanted, I decided I would need to take another course, this one on Python specifically. After a little bit of research, I found a highly rated Python course on Udemy that was on sale for around $10 that gave me lifetime access, so I signed up and dove in.

I ended up enjoying the course, but I'm not going to go into detail about what taking that course was like. As it turned out, it was not a good use of my time. I did not need to learn Python to get a job as an analyst. I now refer to it as a "fun detour."

There are two things that are important about this chapter. The first thing was that I decided to officially commit to a career change.

Changing Careers

While I was taking this course I went to Austin, Texas, to visit a friend. Austin is a fun city to be in. There was all kinds of music, good restaurants, and outdoor activities to explore (it was April). While I was there, I could not help but think about how cool it was that I was learning this whole new skill without ever having to attend a lecture.

At this point I had started to realize that data analytics jobs were a pretty good deal. Many of them could be done remotely, and the pay seemed surprisingly good for something that does not require a specific degree. From what I was seeing, entry-level analysts could start at around \$65k–\$85k per year, and then make their way up to a six-figure salary within a few years. Senior-level positions seemed to range anywhere from \$110k to \$160k, depending on the company and location (these numbers were just things I found looking around on Glassdoor and TikTok in spring 2022).

Being away from my home environment gave me the space and clarity I needed to think about my future. I had just spent years and lots of money to get a degree! Yet from what I was seeing from being in clinics and hearing from my friends, being an occupational therapist would often involve being treated poorly by patients and the medical system, having a salary that is likely capped by what insurance companies decide to pay for services, and needing to be at work in person every day in order to get paid. I knew I would love the work, but the conditions were a drawback.

On the other hand, if I got a remote job as a data analyst, I would potentially be able to leave the American healthcare system, get a job that afforded me good work–life balance, and travel the world, all while getting a good salary and doing something that I had also come to love. But it would mean I spent all that time getting a degree I did not even use!

I felt like I was maybe going a little crazy, but that week is when I truly decided to switch careers into data analytics. Once I pictured a future for myself that involved taking trips like the one I was on whenever I wanted, I could not unsee it.

Course Hopping: When Is Taking Another Course Worth It?

The second thing that happened as a result of my Python course was that when I finished, I realized that I had gotten rusty with all of the SQL that I had just gotten comfortable with a month before. In order to prepare myself for job searching I had taken a look at my portfolio and realized that the SQL portion of it was woefully small.

There is an important lesson here besides "Don't learn Python because you think you need it to get an entry-level position." It's that, although course hopping can be tempting, it is the wrong choice. Course hopping means going from one course to the next, some to repeat a skill you've already learned, others to go after a new skill.

The thing is, course hopping is damn tempting. When you scroll through Indeed and LinkedIn jobs boards, it seems like there are so many

things you need to know. It is easy to feel overwhelmed and start this infinite checklist of "must-dos." The other appealing thing about courses is that
they provide a clear path and structure. You get to work your way through
it like a game, track your progress, and you do not have to constantly think,
"What's next?"

The other alluring and problematic thing about courses is that they are
often supported by great marketing strategies. The Google Certificates
course all but promises you that you'll get a job after completing the course.
Many courses have discovered that people like to take courses where they
get a badge or certificate at the end that they can display on their résumé
or LinkedIn.

There is nothing inherently wrong with these courses having great
marketing, and some of them are truly good courses. But that might lead to
you thinking there's more value in the courses than there truly is.

Think about this scenario—let's say you're given the choice to (a)
follow a structured path to learning a new skill with a badge at the end, or
(b) practice the skills you just learned, *and* spend time and effort sourcing
data, analyzing it, and (somehow) publishing your work. The second option
seems like a lot more work! It's not unreasonable to expect you would
choose to take a course instead.

I have talked with so many people who look back at their journey of
learning data analytics and they confirm that they did course hop, and it was
a detour along the way. One thing we can all agree on is that you should
consider the courses as a foundation or a jumping-off point, and then you
should stop taking courses and go out and use the skills you have learned.

The reason for this is twofold. One, most hiring managers and recruiters do not care about any specific course. There is no gold standard for
courses, and the market is flooded with them. I was expecting that coming
out of the Google Certificates course in Data Analytics and being able to
show the certificate and badge would be impressive and demonstrate a certain skill level or dedication, but it did not seem to leave an impression on
anyone I talked to.

Second, just as a hammer does not make a carpenter, SQL does not
make a data analyst. The real skills that make you a valuable data analyst can
only be truly learned by going out and doing the hard work of researching
to find data, figuring out how you are going to analyze it, and debugging
your errors. Courses try to help you do that, but with significant training

wheels. Take off the training wheels, and do not fall for the course hopping trap! That may be intimidating and take a lot more discipline, but it is necessary.

This rule is not hard and fast. When I took that Python course, it was kind of course hopping. I got out of the Google course and went right into Python. But after that I started building my portfolio and applying to jobs. That's when I realized I needed a little extra help pushing my Tableau skills to the next level, so I found a good course on it by Maven Analytics and dove in. That was not course hopping; it was learning with a specific purpose.

Before you sign up for a course, ask yourself the following:

- Do I need to learn this skill to get the type of job I am looking for?
- Have I already learned this skill? If so, have I already practiced it on my own?
- What will this course enable me to do that I cannot do right now?

If you do not have a good, clear reason to take that course, the next step is to keep going on your portfolio (or start one). Hopefully, if you follow the roadmap I have laid out for you in this book, you will come out of it thinking "Annie, I don't know what you're talking about with this course hopping thing. It wasn't tempting to me at all!"

PART

II

The Scary Part

5 Introduction to Portfolios

What's Here

- What is a data analytics portfolio?
- Can I see an example?
- Why do I need a portfolio?
- If I have experience from another job, do I still need a portfolio?

If I had to narrow down all my advice on my various social media pages to one thing, it would be "build a portfolio." Often when I make that statement, people will respond with "A portfolio? Like an art portfolio? What is that?" I had no idea what a portfolio was until I was already almost finished with the Google course, so I know what it's like to feel a little uncomfortable with the idea of figuring out what it is and how to create your own.

What Is a Data Analytics Portfolio?

Essentially, a portfolio is just like it sounds—a way to show off your work. Creating a portfolio means finding data that you can use, and then bringing it into your tool(s) of choice—SQL, Excel, Tableau, or Power BI—and analyzing it. You keep track of your work and final product, and then put it in a central location where you will also keep your other projects.

Where you put the projects is up to personal choice. I will get more into this in the chapters to come, but generally you can make your own website using a free website builder (no code). There are several common spots for different types of projects such as Tableau Public, a website built by Tableau for publishing dashboards so that anyone can see them.

The act of building a portfolio is at least as important as having one. When you take the time to work on projects, it reinforces your learning, teaches you new skills, and gives you the opportunity to get comfortable analyzing data.

Can I See an Example?

There are many places where you can find examples of people's portfolios. If you go onto LinkedIn and start connecting with people who are new to the data analytics field, many of them have a portfolio and would love to show it to you. Additionally, Maven Analytics is a website for transitioning data analysts. They have courses, a boot camp, and a free portfolio-hosting platform. All the portfolios on there are public, and they often feature the portfolio of a current job seeker. We will discuss some of Maven's other free resources in the next few chapters, but for now you just need to know that they will host your data portfolio for free.

When I was building a portfolio, I made my own website using Wix, a free site where you can customize your own pages without any coding—it is all drag and drop. I wanted to have a comprehensive landing page for myself and my whole journey. My website has a home page, my blog, and a page for my projects. I also added a page for a place to store files related to this big post I had made on GitHub that highlighted all the resources I'd found and tips I loved from early in my analyst journey.

I decided I'm going to retain the site exactly as it was when I got hired at my first job back in July 2022 so that you can use it for reference. You can find it at https://anniesanalytics.wixsite.com/annie-nelson. Funnily enough, I am job searching right now as I write this book, so I have a new portfolio, which you can find at https://anniesanalytics.carrd.co. For transparency, the only thing that changed in the first portfolio on the Wix site is that it links to my GitHub and Tableau Public profiles, which I have updated with my new projects as I have gone along in my career. I have left notes on my original portfolio website about where to look for my old projects.

If you want an example of someone who has a top-notch portfolio on Maven Analytics, check out Gerard Duggan, a strong user of their portfolio platform, at `https://mavenanalytics.io/profile/Gerard-Duggan/44421347`. Gerard, who lives in Australia, has been building dashboards for quite a while. He is active in the Maven Analytics community and has won a few of their challenges. His work was inspiring to me when I was starting out.

Why Do I Need a Portfolio?

I could talk about why you need a portfolio for hours! And if you want to absorb all the content I've created on why you need a portfolio, it might take you hours. Let's start with the value it is going to bring you as an analyst, and then we will move on to what it will do for you as a job seeker.

As an Analyst

As I have talked about many times in this book, building a portfolio is your chance to practice all the skills you have learned. This is critical to becoming a good analyst—putting the hours in will pay off, even if they feel like slow hours at times.

When you go out and search around, you grow in your ability to research and use that research to form a plan. It also teaches you how to search the Internet to get unblocked from a technical problem you are having. Your boss won't be there every day to help you through things at work, so the better you can get at independently solving technical problems, the better off you will be in the long run.

Another benefit to building a portfolio is that it gives you the chance to get hands on with data analytics before making any life-changing decisions. When I was an undergraduate, I thought I wanted to be an elementary school teacher. I love working with kids! Fortunately for me, I got some experience in the classroom early on. I had somewhat of an existential crisis one day when I realized I actually *didn't* want to be a teacher.

As it turns out, I love working with children. But once I realized that teaching would mean dealing with a lot of school politics, creating lesson plans that must comply with state legislation, and managing parent expectations—as well as forcing kids to go against their natural instincts and sit still and learn things they did not really want to all day—I came to the conclusion that it was not a good fit for me. I ended up redirecting, and to this day I still babysit, but I'm glad I didn't waste anymore time or money going down a path I would've ended up leaving.

The same thing applies to building a portfolio. You get hands-on experience working with data and seeing how you like it. Just remember, you are allowed to feel intimidated! It will be hard at times, and you will have moments of doubt. But if you complete your projects (or can't finish them) and realize that you did not get any joy out of them, then that's a red flag! We all have different reasons for wanting to go into data, but it would cause me to pause and think hard about what I want if I did not enjoy portfolio building.

On the flip side, many people find building a portfolio to be quite energizing! They work hard, produce something they are proud of, and come out on the other side feeling happy and like they have gained some confidence. I know I did!

As a Job Seeker

If you don't have any data analytics experience, creating a portfolio is the best thing you can do for yourself as a job seeker. It is the only way you can demonstrate that you can actually do it! If you remember, I said earlier that employers do not seem to care very much about data analytics courses because it does not tell them about your skills. But a portfolio? That is a clear demonstration that yes, you can do the job they need you to do.

I found that many of the places where I applied or interviewed for a job did not seem to look at my portfolio—at least not until the later rounds of interviews. When I started my job search I had a very weak portfolio, but when I started investing in my portfolio the number of responses and interviews I got started going up! You know what the difference was? It was this: spending time building my portfolio showed me what it would be like to be a data analyst. It gave me ideas for what I could put into my résumé and gave me all kinds of new things to talk about in my phone screens and interviews.

Something that I realized when I looked back at my job search was that I was fortunate to have been making TikToks, sharing on LinkedIn, writing a few blog posts, and generally sharing my learning as I went through the process of building my portfolio. It felt like a lot of work at the time (because it was!), but I have concluded that my ability to talk like a data analyst was improving as I went along.

If you're learning data analytics remotely, on your own, from a course, and nobody else in your life is in data analytics (that was me at the time), you do not have any opportunities to talk about data analytics. If you are in a boot camp or in college, you have the chance to talk to peers and professors and learn what it is like to talk with other data analysts. You have to present your work and learn how to articulate how and why you did things. From the safety of your home computer screen, you never have to do any of that.

However, I think you should talk about your work. Find your own way to talk about the projects you are working on. You could do so through a channel on Discord, Slack, or Reddit (there are spaces to talk about data in all those forums). You could start a blog. Another option is to post on LinkedIn and network with other aspiring analysts to share your work and even set up coffee chats to talk about your stories and projects so far.

It does not matter what forum you use; it just matters that you are building up the ability to talk about your data analytics projects. This gives you practice and experience in talking about data, which is different from "doing" data. You learn scripts and gain familiarity with talking about what you have done—an ability that pays off in your interviews.

Interviews are hard to begin with. Many people find that their brain goes into "survival mode" when they are in an interview, and it is nearly impossible to come up with a smooth answer for something new that you have not talked about yet. If you have practiced talking about your projects and skills, then that "content" and comfort with data is stored in your head, making it easier to think of what to say in an analytics project.

If you look up any creator in the "transition into data analytics for very little money" space, we all talk about the need for a portfolio. It is intimidating, and hard work, but it is what makes the difference for career changers.

If I Have Experience from Another Job, Do I Still Need a Portfolio?

Yes, probably.

If you have some experience using Excel, Tableau, Power BI, or SQL from your current/previous job, congratulations! It will likely be easier to get a data analyst job. If you get lucky and do some networking on LinkedIn, you could possibly get away with not having a public portfolio.

However, I maintain that the best way to get experience as a data analyst and show people you can truly do the work is to have a data portfolio. If you want to get a job in data because you enjoy working with data, why not do a few projects? All it is going to cost you is time, and you will be better for it.

Building a portfolio is important for your data-learning journey for so many reasons. It builds your skills, allows you to speak well in your interviews, and shows employers that you are serious about data.

The rest of Part II is a practical and approachable guide for building your data portfolio so you can feel confident and ready to apply to entry-level data analytics jobs.

6 | Portfolio Project FAQ

What's Here

- Where do I find free data?
- Can you tell me more about completing projects?
- Should I share my work publicly?

Finally getting to the point where you are ready to jump into portfolio projects is both exciting and intimidating! You may have a lot of nontechnical questions—I know I did. If I'd just had a FAQ page to help me get started, it would've saved me hours of research and uncertainty.

The tricky part of building a portfolio is that when you take courses, you just learn the skills themselves. But knowing how to write an inner join versus a left join is not very helpful until you have figured out a lot of the contextual things you need to know in order to complete portfolio projects, such as where to find usable data and whether you can use any data you find on the Internet, or if it must be limited to certain industries.

In this chapter I will answer the questions that I had, and you'll hear from career changers on social media, which will take a lot of the guesswork out of it for you.

How Do I Find Free Data?

"There is data everywhere! Just look on the Internet or use data in your own life!" I hear this a lot, both from people who are experienced data analysts or scientists and from people who had a more "traditional" education in tech. The website I hear these people direct new analysts to the most often is Kaggle.

Kaggle is a website where anyone can upload free datasets, so you can search for data in an industry that is interesting to you for use in your data projects (www.kaggle.com). Although this is not bad advice, I don't recommend it. I got this advice when I was starting out, and I can tell you exactly what happened. I went on Kaggle, spent over an hour searching around the different datasets on there, felt completely overwhelmed because I had no idea what industry I wanted to get into or what I was looking for in a dataset, and then gave up.

The next day I tried again with renewed energy looking for datasets. I ended up finding a couple that I thought could be interesting and downloaded them. I think that two of the three datasets I found originally ended up being way too difficult for me to work with as a beginner. There were tons of columns that didn't make sense as well as missing data. Looking back now, I see that it was just dirty data.

Now is a good time to define dirty data for you. "Dirty data" is data that is not suited for analysis. There are different ways data can be "dirty." Some of the most common ones you hear about as a beginner are:

- Duplicate data, which will affect counts and totals.
- Nulls when the value should be 0 or something else entirely.
- Misspellings or inaccuracies that would affect your analyses. For example, if you want to count the number of Toys in a dataset but sometimes the term Toy is used instead, you would miss counting the rows that used Toy instead of Toys.
- Columns without a helpful label, so you do not know what the data means.
- Mismatched ID fields. Your ID in one table might be 711 but then in another table it is AN, so when you try to use those tables together your data cannot be linked from one table to another.

When I was trying to use data I found on the Internet I was encountering some of the issues listed here, as well as dealing with a lot of confusing columns that I did not know what to do with. It was all too overwhelming for me to get started working with it.

The third dataset ended up being workable, but then I got it into both SQL and Tableau and realized that I had no idea what I was doing. I remember just looking at this blank screen and thinking, "What the heck? I'm supposed to be asking business questions and finding answers to them, but what does that even look like? In SQL am I supposed to be exporting a table of the results that I find? Or am I supposed to be finding and reporting on single answers such as the number of sales last month?"

What I needed at that point were *beginner* datasets. It took me a while to find any, and I'll be honest, that held me back from working on my portfolio. I instead focused on my content, my website, or a course. Now that I'm on the other side of things, I never tell people who are starting out in data to go look on Kaggle. I cringe when I see other people do it, because I know what it is like to struggle with it as a beginner.

Instead of Kaggle, I can recommend a couple places where you can find data that is good for beginner projects. First of all, most courses that you take will provide you with some data. That is a good place to start, especially if you took my advice and you are doing projects after finishing a course, instead of jumping into a new skill in a different course. Since you're already familiar with that data from the course, why not think of other ways to analyze it?

Maven Analytics

The number one resource that I most often send people to is Maven Analytics. I've mentioned them before in this book, and you'll probably see me talk about them again. I love Maven Analytics because they have the same mission that I have. They genuinely want to help people get into data, and they offer a lot of great resources for free. Maven Analytics is an all-in-one "transition into data analytics" platform. Their entire platform is dedicated to helping people transition into data analytics. As part of their platform, they have something called a *data playground*.

> *I do not get any money from Maven Analytics for promoting them—I just really love what they do. Their site is a great resource and I wish I had found it sooner in my journey. I have a friend who works at Maven, and she told me that when they ask people how they heard about the company, they hear a lot of referral sources such as LinkedIn, Google, and "Annie." Yes, I am in my own referral category because I send so many aspiring analysts their way.*

The Maven Analytics data playground is a place where you can find free data to do projects on. They've worked with thousands of people who are trying to get into data analytics, and everyone who puts together their courses and data playground are or were data analysts. This means that the data in their data playground is perfectly suited for beginners. It's not like Kaggle, where the data can be difficult to work with. I feel totally comfortable sending everyone to Maven to find data for portfolio projects, because they have a good range of data and I know that every single dataset on there is usable for beginners.

Another thing I like about Maven's data playground is that every dataset comes with some guiding questions. You could choose not to read those guiding questions if you want and just jump into the data and the project yourself. But if you are new to data and this is one of your first projects, I recommend reading their case study and going one by one and answering the questions that they ask in the case study. There is no need to do everything in every project, and using their guided case studies is a perfect way to give yourself some support for thinking of business questions.

Another thing I like is that Maven Analytics has published many challenges using the various datasets in the data playground. This means that if you are doing one of your first projects and feeling stuck, you can search on LinkedIn or YouTube for Maven Analytics and the name of the dataset and challenge that is associated with it, and you can see the projects that other people have done using that same dataset.

Many of the people who submit entries to the challenges use Tableau or Power BI. At the end of every month, Maven posts the top entries on their page. They also have YouTube videos where they review the top 10 submissions and give feedback on what the person did well and what they could use improvement on. This is an excellent learning tool for beginners to help them come up with ideas and learn from feedback.

If you are looking for inspiration or guidance on what single projects might look like, you can look at other people's SQL portfolios on Maven's free portfolio-hosting website to see what they're doing with the dataset that you want to work with.

Real World Fake Data

Recently I found a source for free data called Real World Fake Data (#rwfd) created by Mark Brabourne. Essentially, it is a collection of datasets that are not real, but closely resemble (clean) data from the real world. For example, they have a call center dataset and a help desk dataset. They have been generated by a computer (probably using a Python script), and so they are very "clean." What this means is that the data is quite easy to work with; it is clean and clear.

My friend who has been in the Tableau world for a while told me about the Real World Fake Data project when I mentioned I was looking for a job. He told me that this data is popular on Tableau Public; if you look on Tableau Public by searching **#rwfd** you will find a whole bunch of projects on these datasets, which you can download for free.

Just remember that if you do browse these projects, you're not expected to be an expert. Some of the projects that you're going to see on there are very beautiful, but complex, and it's okay if you are not at that level yet. I am just suggesting browsing other people's projects because it might give you ideas and inspiration.

Your Data

I am also hesitantly suggesting that you can use your own data for your projects. I am hesitant to share this with you because I don't want this to be overwhelming, like Kaggle. The data you might have on yourself, such as data from a smartwatch, probably has not been optimized for beginner projects. So, it could be a cool project, and I imagine employers would be interested to see it in your portfolio. However, again, the most important thing is that you don't get so overwhelmed when you're starting out that you stop altogether.

Sources of your own data that you might be able to use include data from your smartwatch or a smart ring, your monthly finances, or a food journal. You can also download your own data from sites like Spotify, but I caution you on that one because when I looked it up and tried downloading my own, it was in JavaScript Object Notation (JSON) instead of a format that you can use easily, like an Excel spreadsheet. If you are interested in this idea, think about your own life and the people around you and what data you might be creating or able to use.

A cool project example I have seen is that a friend of mine (on LinkedIn) who had been diagnosed with diabetes kept track of his own daily blood sugar and eating habits, and then presented this data to his doctors in a dashboard. I thought this was cool, and more than that, it demonstrated that he had experience using data to answer real questions. If I was a hiring manager and saw that, I would definitely ask about it, and it would give the candidate the chance to showcase their analytical skills.

Data from Me!

When I started authoring this book, I considered the resources that have been most helpful to me when I was starting out. As you learned from my story about how much I struggled with Kaggle, finding data to practice on was a large hurdle for me to overcome. I love the resources that I have pointed you to already, but I wanted to do something extra, something personalized. So, I decided to create some of my own datasets.

I used OpenAI's ChatGPT, an artificial intelligence–powered language model, to help me write Python code that would generate Excel files of realistic (but fake) data. My first project was creating an operations dataset that had a couple of different tables for products, sales, and shipping. This data is all clean and formatted nicely so that beginners can use it.

Recently I had an idea that I haven't seen anywhere else on the Internet. I saw a few data influencers complaining about the Google Certificates course because the data that you learn on and practice with in that course is all clean. However, real data analysts rarely work with clean data. A lot of my time is spent cleaning data and exploring data that doesn't quite make sense to me the first time I look at it. I might have columns of data that just have random names and numbers on them, but then I find out the next time I meet with the client that a particular column actually represents discounts, and I have been calculating profit wrong for the past week.

So, I decided to just make a few dirty datasets and then put them out there so that anybody could use them for free. I went to my favorite places to get data and grabbed some datasets that looked like they would be good for making dirty. I thought about the most common "dirt" that I see in my work as a Tableau consultant and what that would look like if I were to apply it to the clean data I'd downloaded.

I used a Python script again to make the data dirty and then published not only the resulting dirty data, but also the Python script that I used to create it. You do not need to worry about the Python script, but I thought that some people might be interested to see it.

I wouldn't recommend starting with the dirty data. For your first couple of projects, you should explore either Maven Analytics or the Real World Fake Data project for some simple datasets. However, once you get more comfortable and have done a couple of projects in both SQL and Tableau or Power BI, I think it is worth checking out my dirty datasets and doing a project end to end on one of them.

What I mean by end to end is exploring the data yourself to see what errors you can catch, without looking at my notes on how I made it dirty. Then, with or without the help of my notes, clean the data. You can do this in Excel, SQL, Power BI, or Tableau. I recommend not cleaning it manually in Excel. That is the easiest way to do it, but it doesn't allow you to show off any analytical skill or practice anything tricky.

Then, once you do have clean data once again, you can bring that into either Tableau or Power BI and visualize it in a dashboard. Then you'll have a portfolio project that involves data exploration, data cleaning, and a visualization of what you have found.

SQL Practice

This is not quite free data, but it belongs in this section. There are a few places online where you can practice SQL for free, and you could even put those queries into their own project file in your portfolio. Here are the top ones that I know about:

Data Lemur   A site where you can practice real, known SQL interview questions for free (`https://datalemur.com`).

HackerRank   Another site with practice SQL interview questions. You might encounter some odd questions. Sometimes companies use a

customized feature of HackerRank to give technical interviews (`www
.hackerrank.com`).

SQL Murder Mystery   A fun online investigation where you use SQL to
solve a murder mystery puzzle (`https://mystery.knightlab.com`).

SQL Island   Another fun online game where you use SQL to get off a
deserted island. You may have to switch the language to English when you
open it (`https://sql-island.informatik.uni-kl.de`).

There are other sites where you can practice SQL for free, but these are
my favorites.

Other Places

There are so many places on the Internet where you can get data, I could
not possibly list them all. For example, there is weather data everywhere in
the world, every day. Lots of nonprofits and government agencies have to
publish their data, like water quality. If you are looking to do a unique project on data that is interesting to you, you could find it online.

If you go on LinkedIn, you might see a content creator suggest that you
use your own LinkedIn data to do a project. You can download your data
from LinkedIn, including your followers and information on some of your
posts. I think that this advice is not only bad, but tacky. Many people who
are trying to transition into data have never used LinkedIn socially in their
life. They may have a couple of posts and a few hundred connections. When
I was getting into data, I got the advice to use my LinkedIn data to do a
project. You know what happened? I downloaded my own data and was hit
with a whole lot of nothing. I did not have enough data to make any kind
of an interesting project. I ended up just floundering around, wasting my
time, and feeling like an idiot for not being able to do anything with my
own data. But I realized it wasn't because of anything I did wrong.

Usually when a content creator gives you the advice to use your own
data to do a project, they will then post a dashboard of their own data visualized. To me, they are just flexing their follower count. They want you to
know that they have a lot of followers who interact with their posts a lot.
So, they disguise it as a portfolio project and post about their following.
Unless you have been creating content on LinkedIn for a while and have a
good number of followers, it's not worth it to do a project on your own

LinkedIn data. In most cases there will be so little data that creating any kind of a meaningful analysis out of it will be challenging.

Can You Tell Me More about Completing Projects?

Completing projects requires three stages: planning, completing, and publishing. Sometimes the planning stage can be the hardest part! I can tell you what I learned about all three stages.

How Do I Get Started on Projects?

I gave a lot of suggestions for how to get started in the previous section. For many people, the hardest part of doing a data project is figuring out how to start. Here is my advice for getting started.

If you are doing your first project in a skill, forget about the idea of answering any business questions. When you are getting into analytics, you will hear all the time how important it is to make sure that your analysis is answering business questions. The whole point of data analytics is not to use the tools, but to use the tools to answer business questions. However, in your first projects, throw that out the window.

When you are just getting started in a tool, whether it is SQL, Tableau, or anything else, your job is to learn how to use the tool. Nothing else. What you can do is look back at the course you took and review all the functions you learned. Did you learn how to use SUM in SQL? Now see if you can write a query using SUM on your own. Next, see if you can combine that with something else, like WHERE (which basically filters the data).

Your first project in Tableau? Great! Drag and drop data (like Sales or Category) to all the different locations you can possibly think of and see what it does to the view. Try out all the different colors, filters, and visualization types. In future projects you will worry about making sure your color scheme works and you are doing something insightful with the data. But for now, just have fun with it!

I wish that I had gotten this advice when I was starting out. I put so much pressure on myself to create novel and interesting projects when I should have just been exploring and being curious.

Another option when you're just getting started is to do guided projects. I did not do any guided projects; it was simply because I did not have the patience. I don't like watching YouTube videos, I rarely have the patience to listen to podcasts unless I'm driving, and doing a guided project was just too boring for me. However, a lot of people say that doing a guided project gave them the confidence to move on to their own project.

Alex The Analyst is my absolute favorite person to send people to on YouTube. He is a YouTube creator, and he has so many amazing free videos. He has done a bunch of guided projects, and he has made a video on pretty much every data analytics topic you can think of. I really love Alex's content, and if you are the type of person who likes to watch videos you should definitely check his out.

If you do a guided project, after you finish, take some time to think about how you can upgrade the project and do something different yourself. Can you change the color scheme? Are there columns in the data that you didn't address in the project but think you could? Think about how you can make this project your own.

Another place that you can find guided projects is on my YouTube channel. I typically do not create any content that I would not consume, so I was hesitant to get into YouTube because, like I said, I don't like watching YouTube videos. However, when I knew that I was going to be authoring this book I decided that I would do a few guided projects because I have heard time and time again how helpful they are for some beginners.

I have done a couple of different things on my YouTube channel, including a few guided projects as well as some reviews of projects that I have done to point out the distinctive features that I think differentiate beginner projects from more advanced projects. You can find my videos on https://youtube.com/@anniesanalytics.

Once you get going with projects, you will become more comfortable with the idea of creating projects. After your first few, you might get more comfortable with the idea of trying to ask business questions of a dataset. For example, you might go over to Maven Analytics and look at one of the case studies in their data playground and try to answer the questions they ask in the case study.

I advise you to keep some kind of record of your thought process when it comes to trying to use the data to answer business questions. When you get to your interviews, it will help you be more successful as a candidate if you can talk this way: "In my Pizza Parlor project, I wanted to figure out for the owner which pizzas were costing them the most money, and which days of the week, month, or year they might want to have extra staff in because they tend to make more sales on those days."

Does My Project Need to Be Original and Industry Specific?

Some people on LinkedIn claim that the only way to get a job as a data analyst is to create "original projects"—projects on uncommon datasets. I think that some people just like to make big statements to get a reaction out of their followers. My opinion on this subject is much more nuanced than this bold statement.

On the one hand, it catches your attention when you see someone do a project on a dataset that is truly interesting or meaningful to them and come up with a unique analysis that has not been done before. I imagine that if you were trying to get a job at Google or some other big tech company, you might need to have some original and interesting projects out there.

However, do I think this is a requirement to get a job as a data analyst? No. Many of the hiring managers and recruiters that you will encounter as an entry-level data analyst are not looking for you to reinvent the wheel. They know that when they bring you on board, they will have to train you. That's why you're entry level. In my experience, interviewers were just interested in seeing whether I could use the tools.

I have seen plenty of people get jobs in data with portfolios using exclusively datasets like the ones I have suggested in this chapter. Stick to those resources and try a project or two with dirty data as well. Once you become familiar with data projects *and* you have already started applying to jobs, then you can begin targeting the next-level portfolio projects, such as ones using data that is specific to the industry you want to go into.

I have given this advice to people who told me that it helped take a lot of the mental load off and enabled them to get started. They said that, once they built the "harder" projects into the roadmap, they felt free to learn and just enjoy analyzing data for fun. Most of them ended up getting jobs as data analysts while still building their portfolios, so they did not even get around to creating those harder, intimidating projects before accepting a job! They were glad they had taken the approach of job searching while continuing to build their skills past the foundations.

How Do I Know When a Project Is Ready?

Once you get going on a project, you might be tempted to just keep working on it for weeks until it is "perfect." I hate to break it to you, but there's no such thing as a perfect project. I can't give you a set endpoint for any project, but I will give you the advice that if you get to a point where it seems as if you're just making a lot of little edits, you might be done. Don't second-guess yourself because you are nervous or being a perfectionist.

If you have gone out there, done your best, and practiced your new skills, then your project is probably ready to be published in your portfolio. It also helps to remind yourself that just because you publish a project to your portfolio doesn't mean that you can never change it. In a couple of weeks, if you learn something new or get a new inspiration, you can always go back to edit the project and republish it. You are your own harshest critic.

Where Do I Publish and Store My Work?

There are a few different answers to this question. If you have created a Tableau project, you can publish it to Tableau Public. This means that anybody can come and interact with your dashboard, and you have a profile with Tableau Public that anybody can click on and view all your projects.

If you have created a SQL project, you can keep track of all the queries that you write and then put them into a GitHub repository. GitHub is a website that people in the tech world use to store code and queries. You can make something called a repository, which is essentially just like a separate page for each project or group of projects.

A friend of mine who is a Power BI consultant told me that he uses a website called Novy Pro for publishing his public projects. It is similar to Tableau Public, except it's for Power BI.

I very rarely see anyone posting Excel portfolio projects. If you are new to Excel, I still recommend that you do some projects in Excel. I don't think you need to find somewhere to post them publicly like you do with the other tools—just save them to a folder on your computer in case you need to refer to them later. There is no straightforward way to quickly glance at an Excel project and see what functions have been used, so employers are not expecting to see Excel projects in portfolios.

All of these different locations for uploading projects are good to know about, but what if you had one central location that could be a landing page for all your projects and you could include a link to it on your résumé and LinkedIn pages? This is where the idea of a portfolio-hosting platform or a portfolio website comes in.

It seems like every day there are more portfolio options coming out. When I started my journey to become a data analyst, I hadn't found any resources for a portfolio-hosting website. So I made my own website using Wix, as I mentioned before. Making my own website took a lot of time and effort. It didn't require any coding, but I did have to figure out where to put containers, what color scheme to use, what font to use, how I was going to structure things, and so on.

In autumn 2022, Maven Analytics came out with a free portfolio-hosting platform. They took care of designing everything and figuring out how people could bring in images of their projects. This means that all you have to do is create your project, upload it, and leave a description.

You can use the Maven Analytics platform (or another similar portfolio-hosting site) as a central location to showcase your projects, but you may have to store the project elsewhere. For example, if it is a Tableau project, you will initially publish the project to Tableau Public, and then provide a link to the dashboard so that Maven can embed the project right there onto your portfolio page.

On the other hand, for SQL projects you can choose to just upload a summary and pictures to the project page. You can't embed the SQL code as you would a Tableau dashboard because SQL is formatted differently. Although it might feel like duplicating work, I suggest also publishing this project to your GitHub portfolio page and having a SQL portfolio on GitHub.

On GitHub you should store your SQL code as files, as well as adding at least a basic description of the project and the functions you used. Chapter 7, "Portfolio Project Handbook," goes into greater detail about formatting your GitHub portfolio. But the point I'm making here is that you should publish your projects to both the base location where it would normally go (GitHub, Tableau Public, etc.) *and* your portfolio page. Your central portfolio landing page is where you can spend the most time and effort on formatting and explanations.

I make this recommendation because hiring managers are almost definitely familiar with Tableau Public and GitHub, and they will be used to viewing portfolios on these sites. Going the extra mile to have your projects in a central location will streamline the process and help you stand out as a candidate. But you still want to show that you know how to use the sites they are familiar with, and give them the opportunity to benchmark you against others using the same sites they are expecting.

I know that there are other portfolio-hosting platforms out there, but I'm not going to list a bunch of them because I'm happy with the one that Maven has available for free. However, I'm sure that you can Google **portfolio-hosting platforms** and find other options if you are interested.

People have asked me whether it's better to have their own website made for their portfolio instead of just using a portfolio-hosting platform like Maven Analytics. I tell them that for the purposes of getting an entry-level analyst role, it is totally fine to use a portfolio-hosting platform. Again, ask yourself what hiring managers have in mind. Are they looking for a graphic designer or a website designer? No, they just want to know that you can use the tools required for that job in their company.

Using a portfolio-hosting platform can save you a lot of stress and time and allow you to focus on building your actual projects. However, there's no harm in creating your own website, besides the extra time and stress it's going to take. Now that I am job searching again, I did make my own website using a site called Carrd (`https://carrd.co`). I did this because I am not only a data analyst and job seeker, but also a content creator. So for me it is helpful to have a landing page to send people to from my LinkedIn, whether they are a potential employer, fellow data analyst, or aspiring data analyst.

How Many Projects Do I Need?

As with many other things in this book, there is no one answer to this question. I have seen people get hired with almost no projects in their portfolios, and I have seen people struggle to get hired with eight or more projects in their portfolios. As I've said before, getting hired as a data analyst often comes down to luck, people skills, and the state of the market at the time that you are looking.

I would get a project or two into your portfolio before expecting much interest from interviewers. Some people say to start applying as early as possible, because you're going to get a bunch of rejections in the beginning of the application process anyway. But in my experience, until people get a project or two into their portfolios, they're not ready to be a candidate for jobs.

After that, take a combined approach of working on a portfolio while beginning to job search. A solid portfolio has at least two projects that you are proud of in each skill you've listed on your résumé. So, if you list SQL, Tableau, and Power BI, then you should have six projects in your portfolio.

If you do end up taking a course in R or Python and you want to list that on your résumé, do so in a way that makes it clear that you are familiar with them but not proficient, unless you have some projects in your portfolio using that skill. As I have mentioned previously, it's not important to get Excel projects into your portfolio, as companies do not seem to be looking for them. However, if you want to do an Excel project or two, it certainly wouldn't hurt.

Once your resume includes two solid projects for each skill you listed on your résumé, take a breather, reflect on everything you've done, and take a moment to be proud of yourself. It might be a good idea to invest a little more time and effort in your job search than in actual analytics until you get a job.

That does not mean that you need to stop doing any analytics until you get a job just because you have projects in your portfolio. I recommend that, however long it takes you to get a job, continue doing some projects. This keeps the skills top of mind, it gives you something to talk about, and it gives you the opportunity to post on LinkedIn to share your work and your skills.

Should I Share My Work Publicly?

Yes!

I have talked to a lot of people who are hesitant to share their work on LinkedIn or other social platforms. They worry they aren't good enough, that people are going to criticize them or just not going to care.

However, all the people I've talked to who have started posting on these platforms are pleasantly surprised to realize just how supportive everyone is. The biggest demographic of people on LinkedIn are other job searchers. So, the majority of people who are seeing your work when you post about your first projects on LinkedIn are going to be other job seekers who are at about the same stage as you.

I've talked about this in a few other places in this book, but I'd like to stress that there's a lot of value in sharing your work publicly. It gives you an opportunity to talk about it, which is great practice for interviews. It also gives you the opportunity to meet other people who are at the same stage as you, which can be encouraging, especially if you're doing this all remotely. And finally, it gives you an opportunity to show off your work—which might just help you land a job.

Project Time!

Now that you know *how* to go about building a portfolio, it's time to jump in! In the next chapter you will find everything you need to get started on your portfolio, including some guided projects, case studies with optional helpful prompts, and free data that ranges from "super easy to use" to "good for showcasing your analytical skills."

The number one way to change careers into data analytics without any experience is by creating a portfolio (which is essentially creating your own experience), so in the next chapter you will work hard on creating a mini guidebook/workbook that will provide you with a practical and approachable way to get started on building your portfolio.

By the end of Chapter 7, you will understand how to format and present your projects so that they're ready to be published to your portfolio and shown off to the world (and linked to in your résumé!).

7

Portfolio Project Handbook

What's Here:

- Project levels: What separates a beginner from an intermediate project?
- Three guided projects with different difficulty levels
- Getting in the mindset for projects

As I wrote this book, I got the (somewhat ambitious) idea to put out a suite of projects that would show you what portfolio projects would look like at different skill levels, give you the opportunity to create these projects on your own, and offer support from me if you would like it.

The advice in this chapter focuses heavily on Tableau for two reasons. The first is that this is the area where people often need the most help from a guided project—the options for creating dashboards are nearly endless, whereas with SQL you are typically putting together the same functions in different arrangements. The second is that as a Tableau consultant, my strongest skill is Tableau, and I can provide the most value there.

However, since I am providing data and analysis suggestions, you are not limited to creating your projects only in Tableau. In fact, I encourage you to see how you can take this data and work with it in other tools as well.

Each project would also be suitable for SQL, and I have pointed out in the description of projects when they are especially well suited to be completed in SQL first, then continued in a visualization tool.

Before the chapter is over, you will gain insight into what Tableau projects look like at different levels, have access to guided or structured projects that you can complete on your own, and understand how to format your results so that you can publish them to your portfolio.

Project Levels: What Separates a Beginner from an Intermediate Project?

I created a project that displays how Tableau skills might look at all the different levels, using similar styling and the same dataset. You can find that at `https://public.tableau.com/app/profile/annies analytics/viz/Multi-SkillLevelExampleCallCenter DashboardProject/Experienced`. When I got my start using Tableau, I struggled to identify the types of things that might bring my dashboards to the "next level." It would've helped me better see the differences if I'd had a clear comparison between skill levels. I may not have had that when I started, but at least you do now!

I also did a video walkthrough of the project on my YouTube channel at `www.youtube.com/watch?v=Qlaoc1OKVPE`. I knew that explaining what differentiated the levels would be easier if I could show you as I described it. Appendix B covers some Tableau-specific tips and upskilling exercises if you would like to know more about how you can progress between the levels.

It is important to note that real data analytics projects require more analytical work than just Tableau. Perhaps you need to do some data cleaning in Python, or write custom SQL to bring only the data you need into the dashboard. These are not covered in the levels discussion, because I am focusing on Tableau (or otherwise visualization-based) projects.

The projects I've created give you a variety of options for a "choose-your-challenge" kind of adventure. I spent a long time deliberating what to call these levels, but ultimately decided on the following.

First Project

This will be an example of what your first project using Tableau might look like. In my YouTube video at `www.youtube.com/watch?v=rZhDuhI BnG0&t=3s`, I walk through my creation of this dashboard. Along the way,

I offer tips on how I might improve things if this was not a first project, which hopefully gives you some ideas on how to upgrade this dashboard on your own after the tutorial finishes.

Whether you follow the tutorial or just look at the finished product, this dashboard serves as a good example of what a first project looks like. If you follow along with my YouTube video, it also serves as a little "Tableau tour," as I talk through the different elements of Tableau that we are seeing and using.

Beginner Project

The beginner projects that I created or outlined for you later in this chapter are intended to represent somewhere around the level of "someone who has been casually using Tableau for a little while" or "someone who wants to get into data analytics and has taken a course/started creating projects in Tableau but has not yet gotten a job that gives them hands-on training or application of Tableau."

To give you a variety of options, I made a few different examples of beginner projects and some videos related to them. I wanted to give you the chance to create projects with the amount of structure that you are looking for—with the ability to downgrade the level of support you need for the next project.

Intermediate Project

The intermediate projects I created for you are intended to roughly benchmark the skill level of "someone who uses Tableau at work and has received some training but doesn't use it all the time or is still new to using it regularly." From what I have seen, this is as advanced as the "average" data analyst whose job does not have a heavy Tableau focus ever gets. This is because many people are not trying to make beautiful, complex Tableau dashboards that can fit every use case—they just need to build some monthly reports for their department that often pull from similar data.

In the intermediate projects, I looked back at my work from when I had been at my job only a few months (as a Tableau consultant, I use Tableau every day and received excellent training from my boss on how to improve my skills). I also scrolled through Tableau Public for inspiration, to see what other people are doing and creating.

Regular Tableau User

I shied away from using the term "advanced Tableau user" because I do not think that even 11 months into being a Tableau consultant I can call myself "advanced." I also think that in general, it's not useful in a book like this to show see highly advanced and complicated Tableau creations, because even people who have been in the data field for years rarely have a good business use case for something beautiful and complex. Most end users just need to see bar charts, line charts, and tables.

The "regular tableau user" level is what I would consider myself to be now. It is meant to represent someone who can do a lot of interesting and useful things in Tableau, but more important, someone who has figured out how to use Tableau dashboards to tell a story. When businesses come to me to make dashboards for them, it is my responsibility to create work that clearly meets their business needs, allows them to explore their own data, and has a clear "what's next."

What I mean by "what's next" is that they should not just look at the dashboard and think, "Oh, pretty bar chart!" Instead, they should look at the dashboard and then _____. That blank might represent exporting a few select users to send them over to the sales department for a follow-up, or going to another dashboard to dig into why the San Antonio store made 25 percent more in sales but lost 10 percent in profit last month.

Guided Projects

I've collected a few project ideas that you can use for practice or portfolio projects. You have a choice with these projects, which allows you the flexibility of using more or less structure—whatever you're ready for.

I've intentionally created a few projects using different datasets so that if you start with one of my guided projects you have the opportunity to complete another one with less structure. The structure I have provided is centered around Tableau, because Tableau is the place that people tend to need the most support and structure for creating portfolio projects. It is also my area of expertise!

New Year's Eve Resolutions Project

If you'd like to do a guided project, even if you are a true Tableau beginner, this is for you. For this project, I posted a two-part video series on YouTube. The first video is a "Tableau walkthrough" where I informally give you a little tour of Tableau while we create a first project together. In the video, I offer tips on how you could upgrade this dashboard if you want to make it your own. You can find that video at `www.youtube.com/watch?v=rZhDuhIBnG0&t=3s`.

If you start here, you can try pausing after the first video and seeing what edits you could make to this dashboard to use Tableau in different ways or make the dashboard more visually pleasing.

In the second video, we upgrade that first project to a beginner-level project, found here: `www.youtube.com/watch?v=1olyfNFTSaQ`. I add in the use of color, as well as some other Tableau techniques that are good for beginner projects. Again, it would be an excellent idea to take what I've created in this project and make it your own if you follow along.

You can download the data for this project from Maven Analytics at `https://mavenanalytics.io/data-playground?search=new%20y`. If you'd like a little more challenge than a guided project, you have a few options:

- You could download the data yourself, without looking at any case studies, and see what you can analyze and create by yourself.
- Maven Analytics provides their own case study along with the dataset, in the same location where you download the data. In the next paragraphs, I will pretend to be your end user and write up what I would like you to accomplish with this dashboard based on the case study that Maven Analytics provides.
- In case you'd like a little extra support with coming up with ideas for how to answer the end user's questions in a dashboard, I've written some prompts for you so that you can leave the critical thinking to Tableau. You can find these prompts in this chapter, following the case study.

Case Study: New Year's Eve Resolutions Project Hello. I am a student who is doing research on the popularity of self-help-related content on social media. I have obtained a dataset about New Year's Eve Resolutions tweets, and I want to analyze this dataset to see what insights it has for me.

In this project, I'm looking to see a few specific things, but I'm open to your recommendation.

- I'd like to see the New Year's Eve resolutions on a map so I can identify which states had the most and least tweets coming out of them.

- I'm interested in understanding what kinds of resolutions people are tweeting about. If you could show me the most and least popular resolution categories for original tweets, as well as potentially retweets per tweet, that would be insightful for me.
- Can you tell me when people were tweeting? I'd like to know what time of day, as well as which day, the peak number of tweets occurred.
- I'd like you to calculate the number of retweets per tweet in the different categories. Right now, I know the retweet count of individual tweets, but if I look at retweets per category I fear that it will bias the results based on how many total tweets there are in that category.
- I'd like to be able to filter the dashboard using the different categories we see in the data—for example, gender.
- *Optional (this is a little trickier):* I'd like for you to include a table that is normally hidden but that can pop up over the whole dashboard to which I can add filters and see the text of only matching tweets.

Semi-Structured Case Study with Hints   Here are some ideas that might make this case study easier to complete. Stop reading now if you do not want spoilers.

- I recommend putting your title on the top of the dashboard and the filters on the top or left. If you are feeling fancy, use the Add Show/ Hide button to allow users to hide the filters.
- To compare the count of tweets per category to each other, I recommend a bar chart. Do not use a line chart for this, because a line chart should only be used with time-series (or at least sequential) data. I also do not recommend a pie chart—there are too many categories for a pie chart.
  - Your other option for this is a tree map. A tree map would be visually interesting, but it is much harder to draw insights from than a bar chart. This is a primary visualization for your dashboard, so I suggest sticking to the bar chart.
  - Can you figure out how to label the bar chart with percentages of total tweets per category, instead of the number of tweets? You can do this with calculated fields or with table calculations.

- For the timeline of tweets, this is the right time for a line chart.
  - It would be interesting to add a "sheet-swapper" using dynamic zone visibility to allow the end user to switch between two different sheets on the dashboard. This would allow them to either see one line for tweets at certain times or see a different sheet where Gender or Category is placed on Color in the marks card so that you have different lines (of different colors) representing that field. I wrote a blog post on how to use the dynamic zone visibility feature, which you can view at `www.zuar.com/blog/how-to-use-the-new-dynamic-zone-visibility-feature-in-tableau`.
- You'll need a calculated field that counts the number of tweets per category and uses that, plus some simple math with the number of retweets per category, to find the average number of retweets per tweet per category.
- If you're just showing the number of tweets per state on the map, I recommend the map type that fills in color over the whole state instead of using dots to make the map more pleasing visually. You can find your map options by clicking the Show Me button.
  - If you'd like to spice your map up a little bit, though, you could use the dots to show two different numbers at the same time. The color of the dot could represent the number of tweets in that state, and then the size of the dot could represent the average number of retweets per tweet in this state. They may all be the same size, but who knows, maybe one state will be more popular for retweeting.
  - Another option is to use a calculated field to find out which tweet category had the most tweets per state, and then use that calculated field with the "shape" option in the marks card. Have it show you one shape per state—and that shape will represent the category with the most tweets in that state. Tableau will use a legend of categories so each time you see a shape, it represents the same category.
  - Can you figure out how to make Alaska and Hawaii into their own sheets on the dashboard so that you can zoom the main map into just the continental United States, and get rid of all the extra whitespace from Mexico and Canada that is in the default United States view when Alaska and Hawaii are shown on the map?

- Can you try adding color to the background of the dashboard?
- Can you build the dashboard using "tiled" containers? Then format the tiled containers and add some padding to the sides, which gives the different charts room to breathe on the dashboard.
- Try turning off axes and using labels (sparingly) instead, paired with tooltips.
- Format all your tooltips! Maybe try writing them out to use plain English (a sentence) instead of displaying like this: Tweet Category: Fitness.

Final Thoughts   No matter which option you choose, be sure to save the project to Tableau Public. From there, you can export an image of the dashboard to LinkedIn and make a post where you talk about creating the dashboard, add the image, and add the link to Tableau Public in the comments (not the body of the post!).

Please feel free to also tag me, Annie Nelson, in the post so that I can give you a virtual high-five! You can tag me on LinkedIn by using the @ symbol before typing my name like this: **@Annie Nelson**. A drop-down menu should pop up where you can click on my face and my name. Then when it posts I will be notified that you tagged me in a post. I also suggest only using a few relevant hashtags right at the end of the post to give it an algorithm boost, but only a few, and don't tag more than one or two people in your post! Lots of hashtags or tagged profiles will hurt the reach and readability of your post.

Help Desk Project

In Chapter 6, "Portfolio Project FAQ," I mentioned that the Real World Fake Data project (#rwfd) is an excellent way to practice using real-looking data. In our next case study, we're going to dive into the Help Desk dataset, which you can find at `https://data.world/markbradbourne/ rwfd-real-world-fake-data`.

I picked this data because it is straightforward enough for an entry-level Tableau project but there is enough information in the data to showcase your ability to consider the end users' needs and how they may use the dashboard. This one does not have a guided project associated with it, but I'll provide you with a case study as well as semi-structured prompts that you can choose to use—or not! You can also find my beginner and intermediate versions of the project on my Tableau Public at `https://public.tableau.com/app/profile/anniesanalytics/viz/ExampleofaBeginnerIntermediateHelpDeskProject/intermediate`. Your final option for slightly more structure is to purely test your Tableau (or Power BI) skills and remake my dashboards and/or put your own twist on them.

Case Study: Help Desk Project   Your client today is a help desk manager. They check in often on how their team is doing, but the most important review of their data is a once-a-week meeting on Friday afternoons to review how their team performed this week. They are the most concerned with open tickets that need to be addressed, but they also like to keep track of how many tickets their team has closed this week.

Another important metric to them is customer satisfaction. Some of the funding for their team depends on keeping their satisfaction scores up.

When you ask the manager what they will do as a result of what they see on this dashboard and what they will use it for, they tell you the following:

- It will be reference material for their Monday morning review with their manager of how the team performed last week, as well as a monthly and quarterly review.

  They want to know how their team is performing on a weekly basis, but they know there is volatility in the data, so comparisons are best done at the quarterly or monthly level (not weekly).
- This is their sole source for knowing how many open tickets need addressing, especially higher priority tickets that have been open for more than a week.
- They'll check this dashboard regularly to see if their team's satisfaction scores start to drop—and if they do, they'll need to investigate (hint: likely in a separate dashboard; this dataset does not cover this subject well) what could be causing that.

If you do not want any hints, stop reading here!

Semi-Structured Prompts   Let's start by defining a purpose for this dashboard. By looking at what data we have available to us, and the manager's requests, a good purpose could be "To allow a manager to understand the current status tickets in the help desk system, and track customer satisfaction so that they can intervene on open ticket or satisfaction issues." Here are some elements to include:

- Filters that allow the manager to filter to specific departments or ticket issues, or ticket statuses.
- Counts of tickets that are open, in review, and recently closed—*with context of what those numbers mean*. Instead of just "There are 55 open tickets," they may want to know "There are 55 open tickets, which is 15 percent more than the last month's average." Then they know their team might be under stress to resolve all these tickets.
- The ability to see a visual breakdown of departments that are filing tickets, or the issues (reasons) tickets are being filed for.
- A way to link to or view actual tickets that are in the most need of attention (high priority and open the longest), with the ability to filter and export this information.
- Bonus: It would be helpful for this manager to know if some days of the week are busier than others, for staffing purposes.

I am about to give some more hints! If you are happy with the previous guidance, stop reading now before I go to the next level of structure.

Still with me? Okay, so let's talk about how you might want to visualize some of this information:

- Tickets over time: Anything to do with time-series information is a great choice for line charts. This is tricky, but a line chart with two lines—one for the current period and one for the previous—is a good fit for this dashboard.
- The number of open/closed/pending tickets are well suited to be BANs (Big-A★★ Numbers) at the top of the dashboard.
- The issues for which the ticket was filed or the owning department of the ticket would be well visualized with a bar chart.

The manager will likely want a way to export a crosstab (simple spreadsheet) of certain tickets that they have selected and filtered down to. This is a good candidate for a show/hide button as well. One idea is to have one big floating sheet that covers the whole dashboard and contains all the necessary ticket information, which is in a hidden container that has a button at the bottom right of the dashboard to show/hide this container.

The reason I say to put this button at the bottom right is because we read dashboards from left to right, and top to bottom. Exporting a table of tickets would be the last step in the analysis process.

Pizza Sales Project

Are you looking for a bit more of a challenge? Here is an idea for a project that would be a solid addition to your portfolio as one of the projects you showcase while applying to jobs. This project will be done using the Maven Analytics Pizza Sales dataset. You can choose your level of difficulty—I have a few options. From easiest to hardest, we have:

1. A semi-structured project where I give you tips, and you build the dashboard from clean data.
2. A case study and clean dataset for you to build a project from.
3. A dirty dataset of the pizza data that you need to transform and clean before doing a project on it—with hints from me on what cleaning steps you will need to take.
4. Just the dirty data and a case study, no hints!

We will start again from the hardest level and work our way to higher levels of structure and more hints so that you do not read any spoilers if you choose the hardest option.

Before we begin, let's start with the case study.

Case Study: Pizza Sales Project   This time, we are going to use the case study from Maven's challenge at `https://mavenanalytics` `.io/blog/maven-pizza-challenge`, where you can Google and find other applicants' work:

Welcome aboard—we're glad you're here to help!

Things are going okay here at Plato's, but there's room for improvement. We've been collecting transactional data for the past year, but haven't been able to put it to good use. Hoping you can analyze the data and put together a report to help us find opportunities to drive more sales and work more efficiently.

Here are some questions that we'd like to be able to answer:

What days and times do we tend to be busiest?

How many pizzas are we making during peak periods?

What are our best- and worst-selling pizzas?

What's our average order value?

How well are we utilizing our seating capacity? (We have 15 tables and 60 seats.)

That's all I can think of for now, but if you have any other ideas, I'd love to hear them—you're the expert!

Thanks in advance,

Mario Maven (Manager, Plato's Pizza)

   I will warn you that when I talk about purpose-built dashboards, I'm talking about a professional situation where there is updating data. If you look up dashboards from their Pizza Challenge, you will find a lot of "infographic-style" dashboards. Infographic-style dashboards are made to be beautiful, eye-catching, and extra informative. They often contain text summaries on screen and use color choices to highlight specific anomalies in the data. Those design choices would not be relevant on data that updates regularly, because the insights and anomalies would change.

   In this book, I discuss creating dashboards that are intended to be used by businesses with regularly updating data. There's nothing wrong with info-graphic dashboards! But as a professional data analyst, you typically are building exploratory dashboards, not infographic-style. I wanted to warn you about this so that you do not feel confused if you notice a mismatch between the advice I'm giving and the dashboards that made the top 10 for this challenge.

   To see the finalists, visit www.linkedin.com/posts/maven-analytics_pizzafinalists-activity-6994285921554608128-9MDV?utm_source=share&utm_medium=member_desktop.

Dirty Data + Case Study   You can find the dirty dataset at www.wiley.com/go/becomeadataanalyst. Once you do, I encourage you to challenge yourself to clean the data in SQL, visualize the resulting data in Tableau, and then come up with a summary of your findings and an overview of what you did in each tool. This is a good way to showcase your skills and how you can use them together.

For the analysis in SQL, you can query one table at a time to clean them, and use them as independent tables in Tableau (or your BI tool of choice), or you can see how you can use joins plus complex table expressions (CTEs) in SQL to do some cleaning and create metrics that you export to Excel to use with Tableau.

Once the data is clean, use the case study to get going on creating a purpose-built dashboard!

Dirty Data + Case Study + Hints   Are you new to cleaning data? It might help you to understand what you are looking for, and then it is up to you to figure out how to write the functions to clean the data. Here is a list of the changes I made so that you can focus on cleaning:

1. Order Details
   (a) I modified the quantity of each order from 1 for every order to a range from 1 to 5. This means you *must* use the quantity column to calculate profit.
2. Orders
   (a) The order IDs are modified in several ways so that you will have to clean them to be in the same format as the Order ID column in other tables if you want to be able to join them.
   (b) 35 percent of the order IDs have been modified to add the prefix AA.
   (c) 18 percent are prefixed with "_".
   (d) The Time column is modified to replace the colon character, :, with a period, so if you want to read this column as date-time, you need to change it.
   (e) You will have to decide what to do about duplications; otherwise, you will have artificially inflated numbers.
   (f) 28 percent of the orders have been fully duplicated.
   (g) 30 percent of the orders have been duplicated but only order_id is kept; date and time are set to NaN.

3. Pizzas

    (a) The Pizza ID has also been modified to make joins more challenging. You will need to clean the IDs so that they match the other tables.

    (b) 46 percent of the IDs have the first underscore replaced with a space.

    (c) 41 percent have the last underscore replaced with a space.

    (d) Price is modified so that 41 percent of the rows have a $ in front of them. This will change the column from a number to a string, which means that some of the rows will not be able to be used and will either break calculations or create incorrect answers.

4. Pizza Types

    (a) The Ingredients column is split into individual ingredients (from what was once one row with all of them listed), and a new binary column is added for each unique ingredient. Each new column indicates whether the corresponding ingredient is included in the pizza type. You will have to decide how you want to display ingredient information, but figuring out how to create a column that has them combined and separated by commas would be a good problem-solving exercise.

    (b) The Pizza_Type column is renamed Pizza_id. This is an easy adjustment, but if you were not paying attention and tried to join Pizza ID in this table to the same column in another, it would not work and would result in blank data.

Good luck! I recommend practicing each cleaning step individually but eventually getting them into one query (or query with CTEs for each table). In addition, keep track of every function you used for when you do a write-up. If you want to test whether you've done it correctly, check the original dataset.

Clean Data + Case Study   For this tier of the challenge, all you need is the clean data, which you can find at `https://mavenanalytics.io/data-playground?search=pizza`. I've listed the case study earlier—it's called Case Study: Pizza Sales Project. This is representative of what it is like to do one of the Maven Analytics monthly challenges. Good luck! And feel free to tag me when you post your project.

Semi-Structured Case Study with Hints Staring at a sea of data can be intimidating, and I'm here to give you some pointers on this analysis that will help you get over the initial hump of getting started. The first thing we need to do is pull analysis questions out of the case study.

- What days and times do we tend to be busiest?

  You are looking for an Order Date column, which you may also want to multiply by the number of pizzas per order.

- How many pizzas are we making during peak periods?

  This means you need to first find when the busiest times are, and then figure out how many pizzas are being made at these times. This would possibly be helpful to understand on a daily, weekly, and yearly basis (accounting for seasons and holidays).

- Are there are certain pizzas that sell more or less at busy or low times?
- What are our best- and worst-selling pizzas?

  You will want to find a count of each pizza type from the orders, and an additional layer to include would be adding pricing and profit information.

- What's our average order value?

  You will have to find or calculate profit.

- How well are we utilizing our seating capacity? (We have 15 tables and 60 seats.)

  You're going to have to make some assumptions about what percentage of those sales are ordering takeout versus staying to eat, as well as average length of time to stay and eat.

  That's all I can think of for now, but if you have any other ideas I'd love to hear them—you're the expert!

This project is asking for a general overview of their data, which the challenge participants did in one dashboard. There will not be much extra room if you stick to the infographic-style single dashboard. If you decide to develop a set of dashboards with analytical flow from one to the next (maybe a KPI to a top-down), you might be able to find and display extra insights.

What I mean by "analytical flow" here is that the analysis of the end-user follows an intentional path. For example, perhaps they start at a KPI dashboard that is a single-page overview of all of the key KPIs they care about. Then, they say "ok, show me more about sales." Then they go to a "top-down" dashboard, which has the broadest information at the "top," and then as they move "down" the dashboard the information gets more specific and exploratory.

Let's go through some ideas for visualizing each piece of information for this project.

Busy Times   Time series are always done well when visualized on a line. A line chart could make the quick point of when sales are at their busiest and lowest. If you want to add end-user interaction to this, you could allow users to choose their date range. Users could use a parameter and a sheet-swapper to choose whether they want to see a line chart of sales with a date filter to show a month or two at a time, or whether they want to see the aggregated data for the entire time period's busiest days/times of the week. For example, if they chose the second, they may see that Fridays are always the busiest days. But if they chose the first, they may see a huge spike in the data around Thanksgiving.

You'd need to use a sheet-swapper combined with a parameter if you wanted them to be able to swap back and forth between two views.

Another option for this would be a *heatmap*. Using a heatmap, you could show when during the week the busiest days and times occur, and it would be an interesting way to break up the dashboard with a unique chart type. Be careful to use color sparingly on the heat map; I like to choose a color spectrum of just one color.

Be sure that no matter what you choose for this, you format your tooltips!

Pizzas during Peak Periods   The line chart you just created will answer the question of how many pizzas are sold during peak periods. An interesting addition to this in the tooltips is sales information. If you added this, then when you hover over "Fridays at noon" you might see the average profit from sales during that time block.

Best- and Worst-Selling Pizzas   Depending on the style of your dash-board, you could answer this in a few different ways. You could include just a simple text list—one of the finalists of the Maven challenge included a box with the titles "Favourites to Promote" and "Consider to Replace with New Pizzas." Then they included the lists of the favorites and replacement pizzas below. Simple, yet effective.

This data is perfect for a bar chart. You could create separate charts for only the top three and bottom three, or you could make a bar chart with all the pizzas and then add color. You could create a calculated field that will color the pizzas in the middle a neutral color; the top three a bright, positive color; and the bottom three a bright, negative color. Just keep in mind that red/green color blindness is common, so for people who have that condition, red and green look like the same color. Try to find a different color scheme for positive/negative.

You could use a parameter and a measure switcher here to allow the end user to see the top and bottom pizzas by sales ($), or count. This would add simple but interesting interaction.

A twist on the bar chart idea would be to use a stacked bar chart instead of a regular bar chart. I suggest you use that option only if you already have a bar chart or two on the dashboard.

Average Order Value This is a good spot to introduce some BANs to your dashboard. Average order value is one potential BAN, as well as sales ($). Another one would be the average number of pizzas made, or total orders, per time period. You could either display each time period on the dashboard or use a date switcher to allow the end user to switch between time periods and change the date range. This would be more of an exploratory dashboard option, whereas the infographic style would not have filters and would give you an overview of the entire year. Again, either one is fine for a portfolio project.

Seating Capacity This is, in my opinion, the trickiest question. You know that they have 15 tables and 60 seats, so there are roughly four chairs per table. An observation about that right off the bat is that if we assume the tables are all the same size, they are missing out on real estate to solo diners and couples who come in and do not use all the seats. So, you'd want to investigate the data to see how many people are served by each order that is coming through.

If you view the data, you'll see that the majority of orders are only for one or two pizzas, which confirms my suspicion that they may be underutilizing their space. The winner of the challenge, Gerard Duggan, put onto his dashboard a recommendation that the pizza shop introduce counter service (high-top seats along the counter) and/or two-seated tables for this reason. You can find his dashboard and write-up on his Maven Analytics portfolio here: `https://mavenanalytics.io/project/1412`.

> *Gerard Duggan is one of the best dashboard builders I've ever seen. He's very active in the Maven Analytics challenges. He will often post (free) content describing the process he went through to create his winning dashboards, and it's very informative. I highly recommend taking a look at his profile and related links. You can find some helpful content about the Pizza Challenge by following the link to his dashboard, or you can go right to his blog here:* `https://dg-analysis.com/blog`.

Once you decide on a length of time that someone would be sitting to eat their pizza after ordering, you can calculate how the shop is doing on seating capacity throughout the day. This could be done in a few ways. You could go back to either the line chart or the heatmap, which could display the information well.

Another option would be to create a bar chart with a reference line on it. The bars could show the number of seats needed, and the reference line could be fixed at the number of seats available. This ignores the idea that not every seat can be used based on table layout, but you do not need to be perfect with every single analysis and this is a great start.

Final Thoughts   This challenge put out by Maven Analytics is fun, and it's an approachable project for a new analyst's portfolio. Whatever challenge level you choose, be sure to keep track of and summarize your processes, not just your findings. This project is a good opportunity to showcase your ability to think about your end users' needs and analyze data with the intention of making business recommendations.

SQL Project Creation Advice

No data portfolio is complete without a SQL project—but it is much harder to figure out what a SQL portfolio project should look like. A Tableau or Power BI project is very clear. You can post a picture of the dashboard and provide a link for anyone to interact with the dashboard. No questions there. But SQL? Here's some questions I had:

- What should the output of a SQL project be? A report? A single line?
- Should I be editing tables as I go along, or just querying tables and getting results in a new table?
- How do I showcase my work? Is anyone going to read through a list of queries?

I have never hired data analysts, so I cannot speak to exactly what they would be looking for. However, I can tell you the advice I got from analytics managers and what worked for me in my portfolio.

A SQL portfolio project is likely going to serve one (or both) of the following purposes:

- Data exploration
- Data cleaning

A data exploration project is one where you are asking questions of the data and your queries lead you to answers. An example of this is asking, "Who was the second most profitable sales representative in March?" or "Which ingredient of mine is the most expensive?" You may even be asking for a small table of results, such as "What was the average number of customers per day that came to the store last year, grouped by week?"

On the other hand, a data cleaning project is focused on getting the data to a state where it is ready to be used to build reports or queried for data exploration. Data cleaning projects tend to be more advanced than data exploration projects. Of course, you could do a SQL project that starts with data cleaning and then progresses into data exploration!

Alex The Analyst has example SQL exploration and cleaning projects on his YouTube channel, which I think are excellent examples of what a SQL project could and should look like. Both contain a series of queries, one after the other, with comments at the top to explain the purpose of each. He also stored a file with the queries for each project on his GitHub page, which could be a good example for you to see what his sample project looks like. You can find his channel by searching **Alex The Analyst** or going to www .youtube.com/@AlexTheAnalyst. His GitHub SQL portfolio page is at https://github.com/AlexTheAnalyst/PortfolioProjects/ tree/main.

So, let's take the Maven pizza project as a sample SQL project that you could complete. Instead of using Tableau to answer the business's questions about their sales and performance, you could use SQL to query the data. Then, you could come up with a summary or even a slide deck of your findings from the project, which you would present to Maven Pizza once you finished.

However, you're not presenting to Maven Pizza, right? They are not a real store. So how do you get this information into your portfolio so that a hiring manager could see what you have done? It took me a while to figure out a method that worked for me.

I suggest saving all your queries (and the comments associated with them!) in a document as you go along. Once you've finished, enter a bulleted list at the top of the document that includes every function you ran during your analysis. Here is an example:

Queries used:

- SUM
- CASE WHEN
- GROUP BY
- SORT BY
- INNER JOIN
- LEFT JOIN
- A query with three CTEs
- Subqueries
- The LIKE Operator
- RANK

Then, start a GitHub repository for that project and include a readme file. Upload the file with all your queries to the repository. Then, open the readme file and add project details, showcasing what you've done. Keep it brief and informative, and be sure to include the bulleted list of functions you used in the readme file. Then, if this is a project you're showcasing in your portfolio or your résumé, you can link it right to the main page of the repository so that the first thing a hiring manager sees is the project you accomplished and the functions that you have proved you know how to use.

If you are feeling unfamiliar with the terms *repository* and *readme*, I explain them in more detail in Chapter 6, in the section "Where Do I Publish and Store My Work?"

Any of the case studies in this chapter would make good SQL portfolio projects. I recommend choosing SQL projects that contain multiple original tables so that you can practice and showcase using JOINs.

From the Portfolio to the Job Search

I hope this section has excited you and inspired you to jump into building your data analytics portfolio. The way I see it, your data analytics portfolio is the real start of being a data analyst! For at least the first few years of your data career, your portfolio is the place to learn and showcase your skills.

This chapter has given you many options for getting started on projects, depending on the level of support you're looking for. You can use this information to help you decide where to go next. This can mean looking for more guided projects or using the free resources I've pointed out to you to keep doing projects.

Once you have at least one solid project in SQL and Tableau and/or Power BI, it is definitely time to start looking for jobs. Hopefully you have already started making connections and friends on LinkedIn before reaching the point of having an application-ready portfolio.

Job searching is your next big project. It has a bigger learning curve than any of the analytical tools, in my opinion! In Part III, I'll shed some light on what the job search process looked like for me, and give you all the tips and advice that I was given . . . or learned the hard way.

Before we move on from portfolios, I want to encourage you to see this as a starting point. Just because you have a few good projects in each skill and you start job searching does not mean you should stop doing projects. It is important to stay fresh with your skills while you are applying.

As I write this book, the job market is *very* competitive. There have been a lot of layoffs, and the economy is in a weird place. Many people are having a hard time finding data jobs. If the market is challenging when you're searching as well, think about what might help you stand out as a candidate.

Having a portfolio is one important way to stand out as a candidate, but many other people will have one, too! If you feel comfortable in your data skills using the beginner-friendly data sources we've talked about before, then it is time to think about doing unique projects. This might include finding real data on Kaggle and drawing insights from it, or finding data in your own life that you can analyze.

I know, this advice is very vague, unlike my previous advice. The nature of finding unique projects that will help you stand out means that I cannot recommend them to you! I can advise you to look on Kaggle or see if there is someone's data you could volunteer to analyze, but this will look different for everyone.

If you follow the roadmap I've laid out, you'll be in a strong position. Start by learning the skills and building a portfolio using approachable, beginner-friendly data. Then start applying to jobs and working on yourself as a candidate. Then you can decide on what steps to take to level up your portfolio (or yourself as a candidate) once you see what it's like to apply to jobs and go through interviews.

Getting in the Mindset for Projects

Something that took me a little bit to realize when I decided to get into data was that doing deep work on a data project/learning activity requires me to focus in a different way than any other thing in my life.

A year and a half into learning data analytics and becoming a data analyst, I can finally say I know just the things I need to do to get in the zone to work on a project. But it took some trial and error and very distracted days to figure it out. Everyone's process for getting into the zone is different, but I hope that hearing mine can help you think about yours.

Before I can even consider getting into the zone and single-mindedly focusing on the project at hand, I have to do a few things to get myself set up. I find the requirements-gathering portion of a project to be a mentally exhausting process, and I'm constantly switching back and forth between so many frames of mind and tabs that I cannot "flow." So, the first things that I need to do are identify the project, identify the dataset, and decide what tools I'm going to use. I also need to think about the project and outline a general structure that I'm going to take action on. This means considering what business questions I'm trying to answer, and looking at the data and deciding how I'm going to answer them.

One of my favorite tools for outlining and whiteboarding is the (free) website Figma at `www.figma.com`. At the start of every project, I start a Figma document where I plan how I'm going to answer the business questions. This includes outlining the general structure of the dashboards I'll use, and placing either a mock-up of things like bar charts or just a text note of what is going to go where.

If I'm working on a personal project, I can start this right away. If I'm working with a client, I start with at least one scoping and planning meeting with them before I can go to this step.

Once all that is set up, then I know I'm ready to try to enter the zone. My secret weapon is music. I have a pair of over-the-ear, noise-canceling headphones. Once I put those on and sit at my desk with a glass of water, I might not emerge from my tunnel of focus for the next four hours. I have to be careful to set alarms when I cook food while doing this, because I have burned several meals in the oven from not paying attention.

I've heard a lot of people give the advice that if you just learn data analytics for 30 minutes a day, then that is 3.5 hours a week. They say that the trick to learning data analytics is just consistency. I agree with the fact that consistency is the key, but I cannot work in 30-minute increments. By the time I get settled in and catch myself back up to speed with what I was working on, I have maybe 10–15 minutes to truly focus before my mind wanders because I know I have planned something else to do next.

I prefer to take an entire afternoon or two a week to work on learning and projects if I don't have much time. But when I was learning data analytics I was putting in at least 20 hours every week! However, if you get overwhelmed by the idea of three- to four-hour sessions, maybe the 30-minute increments idea will work for you.

If I know that I'm going to be working on a project where I want to stay in the zone and focus on only that, I need to eliminate all other distractions and get my body ready. Usually this looks like making sure that I take a nice walk, eat some food, and get a nice big glass of water for my desk—which I usually end up forgetting about anyway until I finish!

You may or may not work the same way I do. But many data professionals I know have talked about this concept of "the zone" or a "flow state." Once you start working on projects, or even while you're still learning and taking courses, I strongly encourage you to try experimenting with what types of things are going to get you into a flow state.

Do you need to clean your space so that it's not messy before you can focus? Do you focus better when you're in a cool space and not feeling too hot? Do you need to go for a run or do some push-ups before starting a project to expend some energy? Will having some kind of handheld fidget at your desk be helpful?

I also encourage you to try out different sensory environments. Do you prefer to be cozy with a blanket or sit upright in a hard chair? Do you like to have music playing, or would you prefer for your work environment to be totally silent? I listen to music, but my mentor told me he often listens to podcasts and talk shows while he designs dashboards!

PART

III

The Hard Part

8 | Starting Your Job Search

What's Here

- How do I know when I am ready to start my job search?
- Where and how should I look for jobs?
- Job titles to search for
- Where to find salary information
- What is the data analyst's career progression?

The thought of searching for a data analyst job was the most intimidating part of my transition. I had no idea what to expect, except that I would be putting myself out there to face rejection! In this chapter I will share with you all the questions I had (and ones I get from my followers), along with my experience with each.

How Do I Know When I Am Ready to Start My Job Search?

I often hear people answer this question with the advice, "Before you are ready." The thing you need to know about job searching in tech is that if it is your first tech job search, it is probably going to take longer than you'd expect. So, many people will give the advice that you should start as early as you can, because there are lessons we all have to learn at the start of our search.

I'm not sure if I agree with this advice, but I do think there is merit to it. The thing is, if you start job searching before you are "ready," then you are likely going to encounter even more rejections than you would otherwise. That can be really discouraging. So, if you are going to start job searching and applying before all of the "boxes" are ticked, I think that's fine! You just need to be prepared to go through a learning curve.

So, how do you know you are ready? Every person and situation is different, but here are the things I would put in place before sending my first application (but feel free to start looking at job descriptions as early as you want!):

- A résumé that has been updated and tailored using tech-focused resources (not the same résumé you've been using for the last five years)
- A solid portfolio (with the two projects per skill on your résumé)
- Practice talking (out loud!) about each of the skills listed on your résumé
- Experience (in projects) using SQL, Excel, and a BI tool (like Tableau or Power BI)
- Practice answering (out loud!) common behavioral interview questions

Although you can start applying to jobs before accomplishing/practicing all of these, I recommend focusing on accomplishing everything on the list before devoting your time and energy to applying to jobs. This will help prevent job-search burnout as well.

As of this writing, I've been thinking about my next job search. I have loved being a Tableau consultant, but I'd been seeing signs internally at my company that it might soon be time for me to move on. As I finished writing the previous part of this book (Part II, "Portfolios"), I got laid off.

I will speak more about my layoff later in this book, but as you read the chapters in Part III, you'll see the way I talk about my job change. For the first two parts of this book, I was speaking from the perspective of being an employed Tableau consultant. From this point forward, you'll be hearing about my own experiences job searching—past and present—as I navigate my second job search while speaking about my first.

Where and How Should I Look for Jobs?

The first, and easiest, way to start job searching is to browse the job boards. We'll talk about networking later in this chapter, but let's begin with the job boards. When I was job searching for the first time, I only looked on LinkedIn. However, that is not the only place to look! Here are some job boards (as of June 2023):

- LinkedIn
- Indeed
- Glassdoor
- Wellfound
- Built In
- Talent.com
- ZipRecruiter

LinkedIn is an easy and quick choice for job searching, and I found fewer "garbage postings" on there than I did on Indeed. However, you have to pay to use LinkedIn's job features as an employer, so small businesses and start-ups often opt to use other job boards or just post the job right to their website.

When I say "garbage postings," I mean jobs that either are not real or are not even remotely appropriate for the "entry-level data analyst" category. Fake job postings will generally contain grammatical and spelling errors, and they may try to lure you in with unrealistically high salaries. The other ones are job postings like an "entry-level data analyst" position that requires five years of experience as an analyst, two years of experience with machine learning, one year of JavaScript experience . . . things like that. You'll learn to immediately mentally screen out those types of postings—they are essentially spam.

Searching Posts

A little hack I discovered about searching for jobs on LinkedIn that led me to two interviews was using LinkedIn's search function, not within the Jobs part of the app. If you go up into the regular search bar, you can search a term like **hiring data analyst**. Then, filter it down to **posts** and only results in the past week.

You might find people who are hiring right now, who posted about the job on their own profile. This is an interesting way to get an in with the job poster, instead of just applying to the same ad as everyone else. That's how you can catch those jobs that never get posted to LinkedIn officially.

Job Titles

Unfortunately, there are many different job titles that fall under the "data analyst" job category. If you only search for **data analyst**, you'll be missing many jobs. Here is a selection of the titles I applied for when job searching:

- Data analyst
- Business analyst
- Data insights specialist
- Data quality analyst
- Analyst, data visualization
- Analyst, data insights
- Junior business intelligence associate (they took one look at my portfolio and told me I was overqualified)
- Digital analyst
- Healthcare analyst
- Consultant, healthcare analytics
- Associate analyst (the lowest-paying jobs I interviewed for, alongside the junior position mentioned earlier)
- Statistics analyst
- Payor data analyst
- Data consultant
- Product data analyst
- Python developer/data analyst (Looking back, anything that is an entry-level position with Python in the title, especially Python developer, is likely *not* an entry-level data analytics role. It might also indicate a company that has no idea what they're really looking for and is just copy and pasting.)

Depending on the industry, you might see a mix and match of terms with the words "data" or "analyst." It is somewhat tedious and frustrating that there are so many titles out there, but there are many different areas of business in which data analysts can be needed.

Where Can I Find Salary Information?

What salary can you expect to make as an entry-level data analyst and beyond? Unfortunately, I cannot answer that for you. It is dynamic, location dependent, and relies on so many other factors. But there are places where you can look up this information for yourself. Here are my favorites:

- Glassdoor, a source for not only salary information but also company reviews.
- Fishbowl, a social media platform for connecting with other professionals, which also contains salary information.
- Levels FYI, a website that collects salary data from most of the top companies. It is referring to how many companies "level" their candidates, which can be junior/senior, or "analyst level II." These levels determine your compensation "band," or range.

The issue with these sites is that data roles can have a large salary range. I have known entry-level data analysts in the United States in 2022 who started at $55,000 a year and another who started at $95,000! That is a massive range. You will see this reflected on many of these sites as well. Most people I know started around $65,000–$75,000 (USD).

I can tell you that when I was searching for my first job in data in 2022, the roles I was applying for all fell within the range that I listed here. However, the majority of them were at the bottom end of the range, and it was very unusual to see a position that was truly entry level that was offering the top of that range. If you find a salary range on the Internet that seems large, you can expect that many roles will fall into the bottom half of the salary range.

What Is the Data Analyst Career Progression?

So far I've talked about data analytics from the perspective of what it looks like to be an entry-level data analyst. But how about what comes next? If you launch a data career, what can you expect your roadmap to look like in the future?

The beautiful thing about working in tech in general—and analytics is no exception—is that it's always growing and evolving. Earlier in this chapter I talked about how curiosity and a love of learning is a valuable part of the data analyst mindset. There are so many ways you can make a career in data.

The only thing I can say for sure is that you can't get into data analytics and expect that it's always going to stay the same. As you move up the chain of data analytics, the expectations for you in your role will evolve. Additionally, the tools themselves will always be changing and evolving. I heard a story recently about someone who got into a senior data analyst role just by getting really good at Excel. When they decided to try to get another role, they couldn't. They refused to learn SQL, and when they tried to find a senior data analyst job that didn't require any SQL (or Python!), they couldn't find one.

Since every industry needs their data analyzed, and data is such a fast-growing career, the possibilities are almost endless. Here are some options/job titles for the future career path you could take once you get into data:

- Data quality analyst:
  - Develop data quality standards and perform audits and data quality assessments to identify and resolve issues.
- Senior data analyst:
  - Analyze complex datasets and identify trends to help drive business decisions.
  - Collaborate with team members to develop data-driven strategies and recommendations.
- Senior research analyst:
  - Conduct in-depth research and analysis on industry trends, competitors, and market conditions.
  - Present findings to inform strategic decision-making.
- Senior financial analyst:
  - Analyze financial data and develop forecasts to guide business decisions.
  - Evaluate investment opportunities and provide recommendations.

- Analytics manager:
  - Lead a team of analysts to gather, analyze, and interpret data.
  - Ensure data accuracy and provide insights to inform decision-making.
- Director of analytics:
  - Oversee the analytics department and develop data-driven strategies.
  - Collaborate with executive leadership to drive data-centric business growth.

Analyst-adjacent roles are jobs you may be able to transition to after being a data analyst, as either a promotion or a lateral move to a similar career. All of these paths would allow you to take the skills that you gained and sharpened as a data analyst and apply them to a new, non-data analyst role.

- Data scientist:
  - Apply advanced statistical and machine learning techniques to analyze data.
  - Develop predictive models and algorithms to solve business problems.
- Data engineer:
  - Design, build, and maintain data pipelines and infrastructure.
  - Ensure data is available and accessible for analysis by other team members.
- Analytics engineer:
  - Develop and maintain tools and systems for data analysis.
  - Support data analysts and scientists with technical expertise.
- Chief data officer:
  - Oversee data management, governance, and strategy across the organization.
  - Ensure data quality, security, and compliance with regulations.
- Data project manager:
  - Plan, execute, and close data-focused projects while managing timelines, resources, and stakeholders.
  - Coordinate with cross-functional teams, including data analysts, engineers, and scientists, to achieve project goals and deliver data-driven solutions.

- Project manager:
  - Plan, execute, and close projects while managing timelines, resources, and stakeholders.
  - Coordinate with cross-functional teams to achieve project goals and deliverables.
- Product manager:
  - Identify customer needs and collaborate with technical teams to develop and improve analytics products.
  - Translate customer feedback into actionable product improvements, ensuring a seamless user experience and driving project success.
- Data governance specialist:
  - Establish and maintain data governance policies and procedures.
  - Ensure data is handled securely and in compliance with legal and regulatory requirements.
- Data quality engineer:
  - Design and implement data validation processes and systems.
  - Monitor data quality and address any inconsistencies or issues that arise.
- Data steward:
  - Act as a liaison between data users and data management teams.
  - Ensure data is organized, accurate, and readily available for analysis.
- Data evangelist:
  - Promote the value and importance of data-driven decision-making within the organization.
  - Provide training and resources to help team members embrace data analytics.
- Head of data analytics:
  - Lead the data analytics department and drive data-focused initiatives within the organization.
  - Oversee the data analytics team, ensuring alignment with the organization's strategic goals and fostering a data-driven culture.

As you can see, there is no one path in data. There are so many directions you can take your career once you get your foot in the door. It will come down to personal preference, the people you meet along the way, and luck!

The most common paths I have seen from my network are as follows, in order of popularity:

- Data analyst > Analytics manager
- Data analyst > Data scientist
- Data analyst > Thinks they want to go into data science > actually ends up going into data engineering

As you move up the chain, you'll eventually need to decide if you want to remain in individual contributor (IC) roles or if you want to move into management. If you move into management, you will move away from hands-on technical work and spend more time training and overseeing the strategy and direction.

You'll have plenty of time to make those decisions in the future—first you need to get your first job! In the next chapter we'll go over the building blocks of every job search: résumés, networking, and using LinkedIn. Learning to job search may feel like an annoying detour from the interesting data analytics work you want to be doing, but it is an essential part of having a tech career.

9

Résumé Building and Setting Your Public Image

What's Here

- How do I write a résumé?
- Where can I find salary information?
- How do I optimize my LinkedIn?
- Can you tell me how to network?

For most data jobs, your résumé is your only chance to make a good enough impression on the hiring team to get the chance to talk to a real person. So it is important!

The Applicant Tracking System (ATS) is often the tool that employers use to scan your résumé to see if you have the skills and experience they are looking for. The ATS may screen out applicants who do not meet their requirements. You will see all kinds of "ATS hacks" all over the Internet if you look for advice on writing a good résumé.

One of the popular "hacks" is to copy the entire job description and paste it into your résumé at the bottom. Then make the text all white and turn it to a size 0. According to this "hack," the system will pick up on every single keyword that it is looking for and automatically highlight you as a star candidate.

However, I have seen multiple HR professionals respond to this hack and call it not only bad, but stupid. Many of those systems will make those words normal sized and black, and display them in the PDF of your application. That is embarrassing.

As you can see, despite what social-media gurus might tell you about "ATS hacks," the most important thing is that you have a well-written résumé that clearly communicates who you are as a candidate. And if the "hack" for looking like a good candidate is to have your résumé contain keywords from the job description, then take the time to legitimately get the keywords from the job description into your résumé!

How Do I Write a Résumé?

I am not a résumé expert. It is, in fact, one of my least favorite parts of job searching! That being said, I recommend seeking out resources created by HR professionals, recruiters, and hiring managers to assist you in writing your résumé. For example, Greg Langstaff is my favorite creator on LinkedIn and TikTok (@Greglangstaff) for résumé information, and he has a great selection of templates. Paden Janney (www.linkedin.com/in/padenjanney) is a career coach I've spoken with, and I've been surprised more than once about job searching knowledge that she has shared.

I'll share with you a collection of tips that have been helpful and informative to me in writing my résumé, in both my first job search and my most recent. You can also find samples of my résumés at the end of this chapter: my first draft (Figure 9.1), the final state of my résumé when I got my first job (Figure 9.2), and my new résumé now that I have been a data analyst for about a year (Figure 9.3).

If you would like to see vetted samples of data analyst résumés, one of my favorite job search tools, Teal, has a section on their website (www.tealhq.com/resume-examples) that includes sample résumés for many different career paths, including data analytics.

Length

As an entry-level data analyst, you'll most likely have little to no work experience that is directly related to the positions you are applying for. If you do

Annie Nelson

myemail@gmail.com
###-###-####
LinkedIn
Portfolio

PROFESSIONAL SUMMARY

Former educator and leader with excellent interpersonal skills and the ability to manage multiple tasks at a time. Skilled at understanding the needs of key stake holders and using that to communicate complex information in an individualized manner. Self-taught data analyst with the demonstrated ability to continue learning more.

SKILLS

- ✓ Excel/Sheets
- ✓ Tableau
- ✓ SQL
- ✓ Leadership
- ✓ Presentations
- ✓ Self-directed learning
- ✓ Communication
- ✓ Research
- ✓ Organization
- ✓ Teaching to diverse learning styles
- ✓ Empathic listening
- ✓ Building group culture
- ✓ Familiarity with Python, R and Git at an introductory level

ACADEMIC EXPERIENCE

MS, Occupational Therapy- ___ college   **Graduating August 2022**

Leadership roles: Student government president, member of the honor society, and co-founder of the diversity chapter on campus. Mentor and assistant in graduate program's research course. Led a team of 5 to complete a mixed methods (quantitative and qualitative) study that is in consideration for publication.

BA Psychology, Geography Minor- University at _____   **2017**

HIGHLIGHTED ACCOMPLISHMENTS

- **TikTok**: Created a community of over 22,000 followers on TikTok in 3 months, by creating content about my process of learning data analytics- exemplifying my ability to connect with my audience.
- **Paid Contracting** (In Progress): In May, I have taken on my first paid project assisting a startup with optimizing their dashboard to ensure user friendliness.
- **100 Days of Code** (In progress): Completing a self-directed course focused on learning Python. Developing a portfolio of 100 Python projects (self-coded), demonstrating hands-on abilities.
- **Google Certificates**: In 1 month obtained the Google Data Analytics certificate. Including: SQL, Tableau, Spreadsheets, and R. *Portfolio: https://anniesanalytics.wixsite.com/annie-nelson*
- **Discord**: Created and collaboratively manage a Discord channel for Data Analysts with 800+ members.

PROFESSIONAL EXPERIENCE

Self-Taught Data Analyst   **2022**

In just three months, self-taught core data analytics skills including SQL, Tableau, and Spreadsheets. Over the following two months, additionally gained an entry level familiarity with Python, R, and Git. Built a website showcasing a diverse portfolio demonstrating data skills- and then presented many of these skills in an approachable way on Tik Tok and LinkedIn to over 20 thousand followers.

Educator, Professional Caregiver   **2017-2022**

- **Preschool teacher**: Co-taught classes of up to 20 children; designing lesson plans, communicating with parents, and maintaining safety while playing with children in a fun and developmentally appropriate way.
- **Nanny**: While managing a dynamic schedule working between several families, connected individually with children of different ages to provide a fun, safe, and connected experience.
- **Field Director**- Summer 2019: Assisted the director in implementing a summer program for 100+ children ages 2-10 with 20 staff. Spearheaded the creation of a comprehensive curriculum that is still being used.

Figure 9.1 The first draft of my data analytics resume.

have an academic background, it might be in subjects that are unrelated to data. This was the position I found myself in when I began my job search.

Your résumé should be brief and (human) scannable. Instead of containing an overview of *all* your prior experiences, it should be the "highlight reel" of your history. It is very likely that this can be done with one page—and one page only. Many recruiters have told me that if your résumé

Annie Nelson   Data Analyst

| location | ###-###-#### | AnniesEmailnotreally@gmail.com | Portfolio | LinkedIn |

PROFESSIONAL SUMMARY

Former educator and leader with excellent interpersonal skills and the ability to manage multiple tasks at a time. Skilled at understanding the needs of key stake holders and using that to communicate complex information in an individualized manner. Data analyst that has used SQL, Python, R, and Excel to create a growing professional portfolio.

KEY SKILLS

✓ Excel/Sheets	✓ Leadership	✓ Communication	✓ Teaching to diverse learning styles
✓ Tableau	✓ Presentations	✓ Research	✓ Empathic listening
✓ SQL	✓ Self-directed learning	✓ Organization	✓ Building group culture
✓ Familiarity with Python, R and Git at an introductory level			

HIGHLIGHTED ACCOMPLISHMENTS

- **TikTok**: Created a community of over 22,000 followers on TikTok in 3 months, by creating content about my process of learning data analytics- exemplifying my ability to connect with my audience.
- **Paid Contracting** (In Progress): Redesigned and increased user-friendliness of a company's client dashboard. Created Tableau visualizations from large datasets and wrote tooltips to highlight key data to stakeholders.
- **100 Days of Code** (In progress): Completing a self-directed course focused on learning Python. Developing a portfolio of 100 Python projects (self-coded), demonstrating hands-on abilities.
- **Google Certificates**: In 1 month, obtained the Google Data Analytics certificate. Including: SQL, Tableau, Spreadsheets, and R. **Portfolio**: https://anniesanalytics.wixsite.com/annie-nelson
- **Discord**: Created and collaboratively manage a Discord channel for Data Analysts with 1000+ members.

ACADEMIC EXPERIENCE

MS, Occupational Therapy- _____ College   **Graduating August 2022**

Leadership roles: Student government president, member of the honor society, and co-founder of the diversity chapter on campus. Mentor and assistant in graduate program's research course. Led a team of 5 to complete a mixed methods (quantitative and qualitative) study that is in consideration for publication.

BA Psychology, Geography Minor- University _____   **2017**

PROFESSIONAL EXPERIENCE

Self-Taught Data Analyst   **2022**
In just three months, self-taught core data analytics skills including SQL, Tableau, and Spreadsheets. Over the following two months, additionally gained an entry level familiarity with Python, R, and Git. Built a website showcasing a diverse portfolio demonstrating data skills- and then presented many of these skills in an approachable way on Tik Tok and LinkedIn to an audience of 23,000+. See my portfolio for my intermediate SQL skills!

Healthcare Worker- Student   **January 2022-July 2022**
Presently working in a student capacity as an occupational therapist in two separate healthcare settings which cover the full lifespan. Collaboratively managing caseloads of over 20 patients. Conducting moderate complexity evaluations, designing intervention plans, and experiencing medical documentation of services.

Educator, Professional Caregiver   **2017-2022**
- **Preschool teacher**: Co-taught classes of up to 20 children; designing lesson plans, communicating with parents, and maintaining safety while playing with children in a fun and developmentally appropriate way.
- **Nanny**: While managing a dynamic schedule working between several families, connected individually with children of different ages to provide a fun, safe, and connected experience.
- **Field Director**- Summer 2019: Assisted the director in implementing a summer program for 100+ children ages 2-10 with 20 staff. Spearheaded the creation of a comprehensive curriculum that is still being used.

Figure 9.2   The resume I submitted to my first job as a data analyst.

goes into a second page, unless you have an exciting history and list of accomplishments, it means you have included too much information. If you include too much information, then the critical information that you want the interviewer to read may get missed.

Annie Nelson   Data Analyst | Tableau Consultant

| Location | | ###-###-#### | | email | | Portfolio | | LinkedIn |

PROFESSIONAL SUMMARY

I'm a curious lover of data that brings my background in psychology and education to my role as a consultant and data analyst. I also teach my online community of 55k+ about data analytics and literacy in my free time.

KEY SKILLS

✓ Tableau Desktop/Online	✓ Introductory Python	✓ Chat-GPT
✓ Complex SQL	✓ Alteryx	✓ Consulting
✓ Excel	✓ Figma	✓ Data Visualization

PROFESSIONAL EXPERIENCE

Data Analyst/ Tableau Consultant   July 2022-June 2023

Zuar: location   (Fully Remote)

Delivered **bespoke dashboards** which drove client success through effective project scoping to optimize executive's **cross-functional workflow** and put my client's data back into their own hands.

- Worked with **dozens of clients** across a diversity of industries to **deliver** and **provide training** on dashboards to match their **analytical maturity** and data needs.
- Enabled data driven decision making by updating **siloed** reporting and **variable metric definition** with **5+** businesses. This was accomplished by working with executives to create trusted definitions of **key metrics** which form the basis of **cross-functional** reports.
- Actively participated in project **scoping,** ensuring alignment with client **workflow** requirements, and delivering **sustainable solutions.**
- Developed proficiency in **complex SQL** for **data modeling, governance**, and **ETL** tasks to bring data from client's databases into their projects including multi-table joins, window functions, CTE's, and filters.
- Utilized **Python** for **documentation automation** and data **cleaning**, which saved **20+** hours per project.
- Some client wins include creating a revenue workbook that tracks ~**$#** in previously lost revenue and enacts a tracking system to monitor **$#/month** in **at risk revenue**; and independently designing a client's **public facing product** in Tableau and Figma which recently sold to their first customers for **$#** each.

HIGHLIGHTED PROJECTS AND ACCOMPLISHMENTS

- o Leveraging a strong personal brand with over **55k** followers on LinkedIn and TikTok, I've successfully made data analytics **accessible** and **engaging for a global audience**. Through educational content, work insights, and advice, I've become a **trusted voice** in the field. I create **multi-media** analytics content, including **video,** posts, and **authoring a book** about learning data analytics, which is soon to be published with **Wiley.**
- o Check out this custom SQL (de-identified) which I wrote in Tableau to get a customer's data into the right shape for a Sunburst on their dashboard.
- o Scoping a new project in Tableau involves formatting a customer's needs and workflow into an analytical flow that makes sense and can be easily used. Here is a project I made to simplify the process of scoping, which pairs with this file which we use as a basis for whiteboarding.

ACADEMIC EXPERIENCE / CERTIFICATIONS

Tableau Certified Desktop Specialist – issued by Tableau	2023
MS, Occupational Therapy- University	2022

Leadership roles: Student government president, member of the honor society, and founder of a diversity chapter for the program. Also mentored research students and authored a research paper.

BA Psychology, Geography Minor- University	2017

Figure 9.3   My new resume, now that I have been a data analyst for about a year.

Technical Skills

At the top of your résumé, list your relevant skills for the role. In my first draft I felt like I needed to pack my skills section, so I included both soft and hard skills that could be relevant to the role.

However, I have heard from many experts since then that you should list only the *technical* skills that you are proficient in, not soft skills. It is up to your experience and interview skills and conversation to demonstrate skill proficiencies such as communication skills, public speaking, or attention to detail.

For example, my résumé as an entry-level data analyst contained SQL, Excel, and Tableau, but I took out skills such as "self-directed learning" and made sure instead to bring that up when I interviewed.

Relevant History

When you create your résumé, it may be tempting to list all the previous roles and accomplishments that you are proud of from your past. I get that. I adored the family that I nannied for and was proud to include that on my résumé. The problem here, however, is that your résumé needs to be written for the job you *want,* not the job you *had.*

When I had to cut a lot of my childcare experience out of my résumé to make room for a projects section, I was heartbroken! It was surprisingly emotional to leave that experience off my résumé as if it never happened. But once I had deleted it and added a Projects and Accomplishments section, I realized that I had made the right choice.

You do not have enough space on your résumé to easily make connections between your previous experiences and the role you are applying for, but your interviews will give you the chance to verbally make those parallels. For example, my training as an occupational therapist helped me get good at connecting with clients and helping them accomplish what is meaningful to them, but I was not going to use a résumé bullet to explain that.

However, there may be clever ways that you can relate your prior work experience to the role you are applying for. If you were a manager at Starbucks, you likely had to manage inventory and use spreadsheets to track your orders so that you could make sure you never ran out of stock. That sounds a lot like using data and Excel to make informed business decisions!

Formatting

When I first started my job search, I thought it would be a cool idea to create a résumé using R or Tableau so that it would be a beautiful (and possibly interactive) résumé that showed off my technical skills. I even gave the R résumé a try and thought the results looked sleek!

I can now say with confidence that I do not recommend that approach. I have talked with over 100 recruiters and hiring managers about the subject and every single one of them have told me that they do not spend much time on anyone's résumé. They do not want to be dealing with sorting through some polished résumé. They want a standard, scannable format that is easy to read.

Here's the prevailing advice I've heard around this:

- Use color sparingly; this is not an art project.
- Do *not* include graphics, including your headshot.
- One-column résumés are preferred (the alternative is a résumé that is separated into two columns: one for work history and the other for skills and contact information)

Leave some whitespace for information to breathe. A "busy" page that is filled with information makes your résumé harder to read and it's much more likely the person reading it will check out altogether and miss the important information. Leaving actual white, blank space on the page makes it easier to read and draws attention to what is important. Another benefit to keeping your résumé simple and avoiding any additions is that it leaves you more space to pack in valuable information about yourself as a candidate while leaving room for whitespace.

Use Metrics

One of the most common pieces of résumé advice I hear from professionals is to make sure that you include metrics in your résumé—for example, "Created a sales dashboard that saved 4 hours of work per week in data gathering and refreshing tasks." Four hours is the metric in this case.

The problem with this is that as a career changer, you may not have any directly relevant experience that is worth showing metrics for. A career coach may be able to help you manipulate your words and experiences for a résumé (it is their job, after all!), but I just did not see how "nannied for up to 4 children at a time, ages 1–8 years old" could be a valuable addition to my résumé, no matter how you spin it.

My approach was to deprioritize my previous experiences and instead focus on the span of time when I had been learning data analytics. When I freed up space by deleting all of my résumé bullets from my work as a nanny and minimizing my graduate school experiences, it gave me the space to list the courses I had taken to expand on my data projects and accomplishments.

I want to reiterate that you and/or a career coach may be able to find better ways to write bullet points from your prior experiences and include them in your résumé; it was just not the approach that worked for me.

How Do I Optimize My LinkedIn?

So, what's all the hype with this idea of "optimizing your LinkedIn"? To translate this to normal language, it means editing your LinkedIn profile so that anyone who comes to it will get a clear picture that you are a data analyst worth hiring. Additionally, "optimizing" refers to how you are tailoring your profile to follow some guidelines on keywords and how you showcase your experience so that anyone using LinkedIn Recruiter will be able to find your profile when they search—and will like what they see.

This concept was overwhelming to me, so I decided to take it in little steps. I worked on my bio one day, my work experiences the next. This made it more approachable. When I was job searching, my main resource for figuring out how to optimize my LinkedIn, besides some random videos I came across on TikTok, was other data analysts' profiles. There is no shame in copying the formatting of someone else's page if you think they have done a good job.

I still haven't found a lot of great resources on LinkedIn optimization. I know that Teal, which I've mentioned before, tends to put out good content on the subject. I haven't found any definitive guides. LinkedIn prioritizes creators who are creating job-search-related content, so my best recommendation for finding good free resources is to search for the topic on LinkedIn and follow creators who have good advice on the subject.

I do happen to have a few followers on LinkedIn, and regularly have recruiters reaching out to me about my profile. So I can pass on the advice that I've learned, mainly from seeing random posts on the subject and taking mental notes after seeing other people's pages.

History

Your work history/experience section is a key place that anyone who is interested in hiring you is going to examine. It's essentially a place to include an extension of your résumé. Some of the bullet points you left off your résumé to make it shorter can make it into your longer experience section on LinkedIn. However, like your résumé, your experience section is *a high-light reel* and *not the whole movie*.

Lifeguarding at the town pool for five years 10 years ago is not a valuable addition to your experience section. My approach to my experience section, as someone with no relevant data experience, was to focus on showcasing that I'd held a professional job with diverse responsibilities. I chose to list only the last couple of years' worth of positions, because I had also been in graduate school at the time.

Then, I created my own "Annie's Analytics" page on LinkedIn and set that as my "current employer" from the time I started learning data analytics (February 2022), to the present. I listed it as "freelancing" and specified that I was learning at the time. This gave me a chance to touch on the courses I had taken and to list my projects and "experience" as a data analyst.

If you are able to find projects to do for people in your life—even if you don't charge—you can put that in your experience section. My intention was that if recruiters came to look at my page, the first experience they would see listed is data analytics. Even if it is just learning data analytics, I saw that as more likely to catch their attention than having nannying or occupational therapy listed as my most recent experience.

When you add work experience to your profile, you get to also add a description and the skills you used. I've looked at a lot of experienced analysts' LinkedIn pages and they are always formatted like a résumé—an overview of the role consisting of a couple of sentences, with action-based bullet points listing their skills and accomplishments.

Since you are not as limited by space here, you can include more bullet points that are relevant to the position you are going for. It's even okay to include a few bullets for jobs that are not related to data—if you can list skills and accomplishments that you could tie into data when you get into your interview.

Here's an example: I included some bullets about my experience as a nanny, which showcased how I could handle a fast-paced environment with competing priorities. I also had to manage the interests of multiple stakeholders—three-year-olds, five-year-olds, and their parents all tend to have different ideas of how we should spend our time.

I did not explicitly tie nannying to managing stakeholders in my LinkedIn bullet points, but when I got to my interviews I knew that it was a subject I would bring up if I got the chance. This can apply to a wide variety of professions.

Connections

There is a misconception that having as many connections as possible on LinkedIn is going to get you a job faster. I can see how people would think it would be linear—if they can just connect with enough people, then one of them will look at their profile and decide to hire them. I had a vague idea this might be possible when I started on LinkedIn. However, I can tell you that 99 percent of the time, that is just not going to happen. Hiring managers are not trawling through random profiles on LinkedIn looking for an applicant—entry-level data analyst roles get hundreds of applicants.

There is no magic number when it comes to connections, and more is not necessarily better. However, I've heard that recruiters like to see that you have at least several dozen connections (one recruiter said 100 or more), because it shows that you are active, interested, and a real person.

The most important thing to know is that quality > quantity when it comes to connections. There is something called "Social Saturdays" on LinkedIn. The premise is that you engage with their Social Saturday post—commenting about who you are and what job you are looking for. Then you connect with everyone else who commented on the post, completely at random. The goal is to get as many new connections as possible.

I think the person who started this was well intentioned, but it is simply a bad idea. If you are trying to become a data analyst and you connect with florists, paralegals, social media managers, and any other profession you can think of, those connections will likely become nothing more than just a number. If they post, you'll scroll past it. If you post, they'll scroll past it. You do not have common interests!

If someone scrolls past your post without engaging with it, then the algorithm will think, "Okay, this post is not interesting," and it will show it to fewer people. So, it hurts both you and the person that you have connected with randomly to do this, because you are both connected to someone who is going to scroll past your post without engaging. So, in my opinion, most Social Saturday posts out there are just engagement machines—posts that creators post with the intention of getting a lot of people to comment and engage, which helps them (and not you).

The important part of this is that those connections are not going to help you get connected with anyone meaningful. Instead of focusing on a volume of connections, you should be looking to connect with people who share interests with you.

LinkedIn has this feature where it tells you how distantly connected you are with someone. So "1st Connections" are people you are connected with. But then "2nd Connections" are people you are not connected with but who are connected with someone you are connected with. Finally "3rd+ Connections" are people with whom you share no mutual connections.

If you have quality first connections, then you get the benefit of their network. When I was job searching the first time around, I saw a post someone had made announcing that they were hiring an entry-level data analyst. I only saw this post because a second connection of mine had posted it, and then a first connection had commented on it, and so it showed up in my feed.

Another benefit to second connections is that sometimes it allows you to message someone you otherwise would not. Depending on how someone sets up their profile, you can only message them if you are first or second connections, and the option does not exist at all for third+ connections. This is relevant because if someone posts a job and you want to send a message to them about your interest in the role (after you apply!), being able to do so might help your job search.

Instead of spending your time randomly connecting with florists and paralegals, you should research specific areas of data in which you are interested in working, find people talking about subjects that interest you, and try to connect with them.

Many people who are not content creators screen every connection request they get. Many will not accept your request if they do not know you and you do not add a personalized message to the request (this is something LinkedIn allows). So, when you're connecting with people of interest, be sure to attach a note letting them know that you saw in their profile or a post of theirs that you share a common interest in _____ and that you would love to connect.

People send me personalized connection requests all the time that I can tell they asked AI to write for them. I accept all connection requests anyway, so I find it a little irritating that they could not take the time to personalize it themselves. Here is an example of a connection request I asked ChatGPT to write after pasting in the text of a recent post of mine (I did not send this request, this is just an example of what AI would come up with):

Subject: Enjoyed Your Recent Tableau Tip Tuesday Post!

Hi, Annie,

I hope this message finds you well. I came across your recent post on #TableauTipTuesday and found it particularly enlightening! The zoom-in feature for calculated fields is indeed a game hanger, and it's one of those little things that could make a substantial difference in our daily analytical work. I can see how this will certainly save me from some eyestrain!

It was refreshing to read your shared insights, and I appreciated the casual tone in which you communicated those practical tips. It is apparent from your post that you have a deep understanding of Tableau, and I'd love to keep learning from your experience.

With that in mind, I thought it would be great to connect here on LinkedIn so I could stay updated with your future posts and perhaps even exchange a few thoughts on data analysis and visualization tools.

Looking forward to staying in touch and continuing to learn from your tips and insights!

Best,

[Your Name]

This connection request is overly verbose, and there is no need to ever add hashtags (or @ signs to tag me in the message to myself). I would cut this down to look like this:

Hi, Annie, I saw a Tableau Tip Tuesday post of yours. I never knew you could zoom in on calculated field boxes! I love using Tableau, and after checking your profile I can see that you talk about data, analytics, and Tableau, so I would love to connect so I can stay updated on more tips like this!

I don't sign my name at the end of messages because my name and entire profile are attached to my messages. Here's an actual connection message I sent the other day:

> Hi, Helen, I listened to your episode of Kyle Winterbottom's Data Driven podcast and I loved hearing your story. The way you articulated data strategy and finding a single source of truth resonated a lot with me—that's the direction I'm trying to bring my career.
>
> So I'm happy to get connected so I can follow along with your story! I know that podcast was a few years back now.

I let her know how I found her, expressed a common interest, and then told her that I would like to be connected with her. Simple, friendly, not asking for anything. She accepted and wrote back a short, positive response.

Headline

Your headline is the little blurb that goes underneath your name anywhere you comment or show up on LinkedIn as well as underneath your photo on your profile. The most common mistake is people calling themselves an "aspiring data analyst" when they're searching for jobs.

If you were an employer and someone applied for a job at your company and they told you they are an aspiring data analyst, would that excite you about their candidacy? Or would you be more interested in hiring someone who *is* a data analyst? I think the second.

I get it—you feel like an imposter calling yourself a data analyst before you get a job doing it. I felt that way too. However, that is not how LinkedIn works. Honestly, you can call yourself just about anything you want. I see all kinds of headlines. Generally, you need to put in the headline the job you *want*, not the one you have.

If you still feel unsure about it, let me make one more point. There is no threshold for being a data analyst. It does not require a degree or that you pass a certain test. Have you used Excel to analyze data? Have you used SQL to gain insights from a dataset? Have you created a dashboard? If you answered yes to any of these, then congratulations, you *are* a data analyst. You have analyzed data, using tools that data analysts use to analyze data. Do not let imposter syndrome hold you back.

Now that we got that out of the way, your headline should not only say "data analyst." It is the place where you can get your top keywords in so that even without going to your profile people can get an idea of who you are and what you do. On LinkedIn you use the pipe operator (|) to separate ideas. You put the job you want first, and then add some magic.

Here is my current headline: "Analytics Consultant | Data Analyst | Break Into Tech Creator | Data Storyteller | Tableau Lover." I am using this prime real estate to catch the attention of my target audiences, and for me there are two. Let's break it down.

Analytics Consultant   I am saying, "Hey! I am a data analyst that you can hire to consult for you! And also, I have the experience of working with multiple different companies, which is kind of impressive."

Data Analyst   My primary audience on LinkedIn is people who are data analysts, or who want to become data analysts, so having "data analyst" in there is key to reaching new friends, employers, and people wanting to become a data analyst.

Break Into Tech Creator   I've covered my main bases with employers; now I want to make it clear to anyone who sees my comments or posts that I create content specifically for people trying to become data analysts, especially career changers.

Data Storyteller   This part of the headline goes back to letting other data analysts and employers know about my skills in data. I want to differentiate myself as someone who can help you tell the story of your data, especially in a dashboard.

Tableau Lover   I'm not a huge fan of this line—I think it is a little tacky. However, it is a deliberate addition to my headline. I've made a bit of a name for myself in the Tableau community, and I have strong Tableau skills. I needed to make sure Tableau was mentioned in my headline—I could not leave that keyword out of my headline.

Profile Photo

Your profile photo is kind of like the cover of your book. For better or for worse, people have a gut response to your profile based on your profile photo. You do not need to be in a fancy suit or expensive blouse in your photo, although 10 years ago that was probably the norm. You can be a bit more casual than that, but you do still want to look sharp. Here are some tips:

- Your profile should show your head and shoulders. If the photo is just your face, that is too zoomed in; if you can see below the bottom of a quarter-zip top or so, it is too zoomed out.
- Good lighting! Having a profile photo in good lighting makes a huge difference in how you are perceived.
- It doesn't hurt to smile, but no need to push yourself to look like you are laughing.
- Keep the background simple—you are the focus, not the background.

I've seen some people recently posting about how they were able to upload a regular photo of themselves to an online AI photo generator and it produced some smart and completely realistic-looking headshots for them (and a few goofy ones!). If you do not have access to a photographer or you struggle to make a good facial expression in your photos, consider researching something like that to help you.

Can You Tell Me How to Network?

When you hear "networking," it might make you cringe. I know that until recently it was a subject that I tried to avoid. Despite being a content creator with a good number of followers, I did almost no networking in my first job search. I was too intimidated by it—and simply did not know how. All of the advice I had seen about networking up until then was so forward—it required me to directly message people I didn't know and ask them to give me their time and help out of the blue. I did not feel comfortable doing that.

I know that approach does work for some, but it's not the only way! Now that I am job searching for the second time after a year as a data analyst, I've been exclusively networking—and I do not feel gross about it at all. If I was sending out random messages to people I did not have a personal connection with, asking them for help, I assure you I would feel gross about it.

What Is Networking (and What Is It Not)?

So, what is the purpose of networking, on and off LinkedIn? It has quite a few benefits! Let's start by getting one thing out of the way—the definition of networking. To me, networking means making connections and having conversations with people in the world of data about shared interests. It can be done at in-person events, in Discord groups, or on social media like LinkedIn. Discord is an online social forum platform.

You'll also hear creators talking about online networking in the form of reaching out to hiring managers or strangers on the Internet and asking them for a job or a referral. I do not see that as networking—networking implies that you are making real connections with people around a shared subject, not asking for their time or a job.

Here are some things that I see a lot of new data analysts do that they think will help but usually don't:

- Joining a Discord group and then never engaging in it
- Sending a blind message to a creator on LinkedIn with your résumé attached (or a short bio) and asking if they have "any roles open in their organization"
- Messaging someone you do not know who works as a data analyst and asking them to help you get a job

There are no shortcuts to building a network and getting a job. Low-value messages and comments will get low-value results. True networking is building connections with other people based on shared interests, without the ask that they will get you a job or spend their free time helping you.

I find that there is a bit of a gray zone between true networking and simply reaching out to people and asking for something. Sometimes it can be a benefit to reach out to people and ask them to have a conversation with you, which still categorizes as asking for their time. I'll leave it up to you to decide where the line is. In the rest of this section I'll pass along my advice about making connections and reaching out to new people.

At the most basic level, networking has the benefit of helping you make friends with people who share interests similar to yours. Especially if you intend to work remotely, this is no small thing. These connections can help you make friends, learn new things, advance your career, and yes, hopefully it can help you get a job as well.

As an entry-level data analyst, you likely do not have any existing connections in the industry. That's okay! We all start from somewhere. As I mentioned in the "Connections" section, the smart way to do it is to find people who are doing or talking about what you are interested in, and to send them a message. If they are posting content regularly, the best way to start is by striking up a conversation on the comments of their posts about the subject of the post *before sending them a message*. If someone gets to know you by talking to you through the comments on their own posts, they're much more likely to welcome a message in their inbox in the future to continue the conversation.

However, you do not need to be networking only with people who create content regularly. This next part is where I struggled as a new data analyst, but I'm gaining more confidence and comfort as I get more practice.

I also want to point you to a resource written by a friend of mine, Michael Dillon. He is one of my favorite people to get networking advice from, and he published an e-book dedicated entirely to networking. I found it to be excellent material for entry-level data analysts. Check it out here: `https://michaeldillon.gumroad.com/l/infinite_upside`.

Networking and Messaging on LinkedIn

A networking tactic that I've heard repeatedly works well for people who are brave enough to do it is to research an area of focus or industry that you're interested in, maybe a specific company, and look up people who are doing just that. It might be sustainability analysts, or healthcare data analysts, or even someone working at a specific financial company you're interested in working for. Connect with them on LinkedIn and take advantage of the personalized connection note to send them a message.

In your message, express that you are new to data analytics, but you know that you would like to specialize in the area of _____. You saw from their profile that they have [#] of years in that position and you'd love to connect and ask them a few questions if they have time. Then, if they accept, you either need to be prepared to ask them a few quick and easy-to-answer questions via their inbox or ask for a 15-minute "coffee chat."

This will not work every time; it likely will not even work half of the time. I've heard from multiple people that they tried this and only one out of every 15 people responded, but that still meant that they got to set up a few coffee chats and learn more about becoming a data analyst in their area of interest.

In these messages and meetings, they aren't asking for a job, a referral, or a résumé review. They aren't asking the other person to do any work for them. They're simply asking if they can ask them a few questions about how they got into their job, what tools they use on a regular basis, and what it is like to do what they do.

The thing about this strategy, however, is that I know a few people who have done this and then a month or two later when a junior role opened at that person's organization, the person the job seeker had connected with reached out to the job seeker and offered to refer them to the role. It makes sense to me that this would work; if I had an organic conversation with someone who seemed genuinely interested in what I do every day for work (without expecting anything in return), then if a position opened up I'd feel good about referring them to the team.

This is not a sure strategy to bet on, because many people will never even be on a team that has a junior role open up, even if they do like you. However, it is popular advice, and I've seen it work for some people.

Messaging Jobs Directly

Some people might call reaching out directly to jobs "networking." I tend to call it messaging. Regardless, it's important to discuss how to message recruiters and hiring managers. Messaging can take two forms. The first one is sending a message to a recruiter who has a role open that you'd like to apply to. This is as easy as applying to the job and then sending a message to the recruiter that you have just applied for the role and are looking forward to speaking with them.

I've tried this a few times, although I can't say that I am the best at it or have had the best results. The best advice I've seen on how to do a good job sending a message like that is to keep it short, express your interest, and put in a bit about why you would be a good fit for the role.

For example, let's say I had just applied for a financial data analyst position that called for strong interpersonal skills. I might have said, "Hello, I am a data analyst with experience using SQL and Tableau, and I just recently completed a financial report in SQL and Tableau, which is featured on my page. I just applied for the data analyst role that you are hiring for and wanted to drop you a note to express my interest in the position. My background in psychology has given me strong interpersonal skills that I think would make me a great fit for the team. Looking forward to hearing from you."

I used the job description and my personal history to curate a personalized message to the recruiter/hiring manager, to hopefully help me stand out from the possibly hundreds of other applicants. As with the last point I made, this does not always work! But you only need one job.

If this is something you're interested in learning more about, I suggest you do some research on it. I did use this tactic when I was job searching my first time around with some limited success, but by the time I realized that this was a possibility I had already started getting traction from my other applications and I was spending much less time looking at and applying to jobs. I haven't used it once this time around, but I will if I do not get a job in the next few months!

The second option for messaging recruiters and hiring managers is one I haven't tried myself, but I've heard a few people successfully getting jobs from using it. So, I will give you an overview with the warning that I haven't tried it myself. If you'd like to try it, more research will likely be needed. This approach is to find recruiters and hiring managers who might be hiring in the areas in which you'd like to get a job and reaching out to them.

For example, let's say you were interested in becoming a financial data analyst because you have a background in banking. What you could do is check out banks and other financial institutions you may be interested in, and look through their employees on LinkedIn. What you're looking for is recruiters who specialize in early career and/or data, or managers of analytics. You will want to be sure to personalize your message, as I described in the "Connections" section.

In the message, clearly and concisely communicate that you have a banking/financial background, you are a new data analyst, and you'd love to work for [insert their institution]. Then you could ask if they have any roles currently open or opening in the future for early career data analysts for which you could apply.

I get a lot of messages like this in my inbox from people who clearly have not looked at my profile. I know that *you* would never send a message to someone blindly without doing your homework on them and personalizing it. Be aware that hiring managers may be suspicious of your message because they also get many messages from people who do not care about their organization at all—they just want a job and are blasting out as many messages as they can in the hopes that one sticks.

A less direct version is to ask hiring managers what kind of things they would be looking for in a candidate. This is similar to the advice I gave earlier about general networking, but it is more job focused. Here's an example:

> Hi [name], I am a new data analyst and I have a strong interest in get-ting a job as a financial data analyst at a company like [their company]. I see that you are a manager of analytics, and I was hoping I could ask you about what I can do to stand out as a candidate. Are there any specific tools or hard or soft skills that you look for when hiring new data analysts? Thank you in advance!

I've used a modified version of this recently. One of my friends intro-duced me to the COO of a small consulting organization that I'd love to work for someday, but I need more experience. I reached out to the COO a few weeks later and asked if she could offer tips for setting myself up to be a strong candidate when I began looking for a new consulting position at around my one-year mark of being a consultant/data analyst.

She very kindly responded and offered to have a half-hour coffee chat the following week. At the start of the call, she asked me about my back-ground, gave me some great advice on navigating some challenges at my current role, and helped me understand what she is looking for when she hires senior consultants and analysts. She helped me understand the things I need to do in the next few years to get myself to the point of being a strong candidate.

I did not go into that phone call looking for a job right now, but she told me that she'd like to stay in touch and maybe in a year or two we could revisit that conversation. That's the kind of long-term networking that I've heard many people on LinkedIn talking about. I hadn't tried it myself until I realized recently (a little over six months into being a data analyst) that I should.

Networking Events

LinkedIn is not the only place you can network. You can also go to events, either in person or virtual. I see all kinds of virtual events popping up in data analytics such as free conferences, virtual happy hours, webinars, and even some events specifically designed for helping new analysts get jobs. These are good ways to meet people who share your interests.

Last but not least, in-person networking is something that I completely underestimated until I went to the Tableau Conference, which is now hosted by Salesforce, earlier this year. In-person networking was not appealing to me when I was job searching because it involved travel, I might have to pay an entrance fee, and I'd feel like an imposter hanging out with people who already had jobs in data!

When I went to the Tableau Conference in Las Vegas, I had been a data analyst for nine months. I had the intention of going to sessions and doing some networking. I ended up losing my voice by the end of the week from talking so much, so loudly, at so many networking events in the dry air. I had such a good time meeting new people and networking that I even missed some of the sessions I had planned to go to.

I realized that people who like data enjoy hanging out with each other and talking about their shared interests. When I talked with new people, they seemed genuinely interested in having a good conversation regardless of my level or title. If you go to an in-person networking event, such as a conference or a (free) Tableau user group, the people there are going to welcome you. If you come with a desire to learn and make new friends, they'll be happy to share their community and tips with you.

This strategy may not lead to a job right away, as a career fair might, but it will help you accelerate the process of making connections with like-minded people much more than if you were talking with the same people online through messages or even Zoom. I strongly recommend that you look for data meet-ups in your area using LinkedIn, Google, or even the app MeetUp.

I know that networking is intimidating to most people except for maybe the most social extroverts. It can be uncomfortable and intimidating to think about putting yourself out there, asking for help, and/or putting yourself into a position to be rejected. However, having the courage to reach out and get outside your comfort zone can help you make friends, learn things you'd never have access to otherwise, and lead to connections that can advance your career.

Interviewing

It is a lot of work to get yourself out there and network, work on your LinkedIn, and edit and rewrite your résumé multiple times. By the time you get the hang of it, you'll be just about ready to take a break! But hopefully this is when you'll start scheduling interviews for jobs.

The next chapter dives into interviews. I'll explain to you the different stages as I've come to understand them, and what you can expect at each. Interviewing can sometimes be a six-step process, so understanding what is to come and preparing for it ahead of time is the best way to be successful.

On one of my posts about preparing for interviews recently a commentor asked, "Don't you think that telling people what happens in interviews ahead of time is kind of a bad idea? If people know what to expect and are practicing and rehearsing their answers ahead of time, doesn't that defeat the purpose of assessing them?"

My answer was no. Interviewing for any job is stressful, and knowing what to expect and getting the chance to practice your answers ahead of time gives you the opportunity to show the interviewer who you really are, instead of fumbling your words or drawing a blank because of the pressure.

Bonus Tip: An Idea for Your First LinkedIn Post

If you're anything like me, when you decide to start posting on LinkedIn, you might find yourself staring at the screen, drawing a blank. What could you say that would be valuable? As I was writing this book I read my friend Michael Dillon's e-book about networking, and he had a great idea in there that he gave me permission to steal. You can use your takeaways from this book as a post!

When you finish this book (or get to a good stopping point), sit down and think about what your key takeaways were. Was it comforting to hear someone else's story and see what it felt like to become a data analyst? Was the portfolio section particularly helpful? I can guarantee you, there are people out there who would like to hear your thoughts.

Collect your thoughts with one to five key takeaways you had from this book or the roadmap that you end up creating for yourself. Then, turn that into a LinkedIn post! Talk about your thoughts and/or experiences in the post. The post should be about you, not just the book. At the end, use just a few relevant hashtags, such as #dataanalytics, #careerchange, or #dataportfolio.

This will break the ice on your LinkedIn presence and give you a networking opportunity right away. I often see posts from people who are at the beginning of their data journeys. If they take time to write out their roadmaps or list insightful takeaways from a book or course, other data analysts who are aspiring as well will often see it and comment on it. I know multiple people who have made friends just from seeing and commenting on other people's posts like this.

If you'd like, you can also tag me in the post. If you are following me or we are connected, all you need to do is write @Annie Nelson and my profile should come up in a drop-down menu. Once you select it, you can tag me, and when I see it, I can comment on it to help boost the reach of the post (and cheer you on!).

Even if you are a total beginner to data, you can add value to the conversations on LinkedIn by sharing your key takeaways and/or roadmap.

10 | Stages of Data Interviews

What's Here

- Why do tech interviews take so long?
- Can you tell me about the different interview stages?
- "How should I . . . ?": How I handled some common how-tos
- What are your favorite resources?

Congratulations, you just got your first call back to begin interviewing for a data position! But wait—what comes next?

That's how I felt when I started interviewing for roles in data. I'd heard about some different stages I might encounter, like technical interviews. But I still had no idea what to expect. It was all this mysterious process that somehow can take months.

This chapter is dedicated to "everything data interviews" so that you know what to expect and can prepare yourself for success.

Why Do Interviews Take So Long?

Around the same time I seriously considered searching for my first job in data, I heard the advice, "Tech interviews can take months." I had no idea what that meant. You couldn't be interviewing every day during that period of time, right? Would they just take a long time to get back to you? Are we talking about multiple companies or a single company taking that long?

That was a year ago, and I get it now. They *do* take a long time. Here are some of the reasons:

- Interviews are multistep processes. They will often go three or more rounds!
- Companies can take a week or more to decide if they want to move you to the next step.
- You will likely face a surprising number of rejections (unless you know to expect it).
- It takes time to learn to be a good candidate (interviews, résumés, and discussing your portfolio).

From the time I started job searching to when I accepted my job, it was almost three months. And those three months made me question everything about what I was doing and why. I did not enjoy job searching. In fact, having such a bad experience job searching is one of the reasons I decided to keep creating content after I did get my job—so that hopefully it would be better for the people who stumbled across my page.

Can You Tell Me More about the Interview Stages?

If you have never interviewed for a tech role, you may be familiar with an interview process that consists of one meeting, maybe a hands-on portion—for instance, like a preschool teacher meeting some of the kids they could be working with. The proof that you are a good fit for the role comes from your prior work experience, possibly combined with references or a degree. However, if you try to transition into data, most of that will not matter. The proof of your candidacy will be in how you interview.

The following are the stages tech interviews generally go through, though not necessarily in this order:

- Phone screen (will always come first)
- Meeting the hiring manager (is interchangeable with the phone screen)
- Behavioral interview

- Technical interview
- Panel interview
- Culture fit
- Follow-up (will always come last)

Before we get into the interview types, here is an important piece of advice that I still offer to my friends who are job searching for their second roles in data: always ask about "next steps." When you get to the end of an interview, it can be a relief to have gotten through it. Your head is likely buzzing from pent-up stress and anxiety. Thinking clearly can be difficult.

I can say from experience that the worst thing is finishing an interview and then a few days later wondering what is supposed to happen next. "Was I supposed to follow up with them?" or "When can I expect a callback? If they haven't called me back yet, does that mean they never will?" are common questions that many people have wrestled with. Or, even worse, I've had a few friends say that they scheduled an interview, and when they logged into the interview they were surprised to learn it would be a technical interview! Nobody had warned them ahead of time.

So, take it from me. Always close the interview by asking about next steps. When can you expect to hear back? What happens after this? This might feel pushy, but it is standard practice. Now, let's dig into what happens at each of these interview stages.

Phone Screen

This is the company's first point of contact with you, besides your application. If you're talking to a larger company, for the phone screen you'll likely be contacted by a recruiter. At smaller companies you may do a phone screen with the hiring manager for the role. The phone screen is a quick check-in at a high level to see if you are a good fit for the role. Here are some common features of *most* phone screens, but remember, every company is different:

- About 5–15 minutes long.
- *Usually* cameras off, even while on Zoom.
- General questions about your background and what might make you a good fit for the role.

- Much of the time, the recruiter has noticed you have a portfolio from the link on your résumé but has not even opened it.
- Recruiters are often late, but log in five minutes early to set a good tone.
- A phone screen typically starts with the person interviewing you giving you some background on the company and what the role involves.
- The person you're talking to may not know the specifics of the day-to-day for the role, or even someone on the team you would be working with, especially if you're talking to a recruiter.
- It is a good time to ask general questions about what the company is looking for with the role but not a good time to ask for specifics.
- The main focus of this call is for them to get a sense of who you are and check off some boxes specific to the role (such as "can use SQL" or "has used Tableau").

The phone screen is the most "chill" step of the process. Once you do a couple, you'll get used to them and your nerves will not be so bad. To prepare for a phone screen, you should do the following:

- Practice your "elevator pitch" (short bio about you).
- Know the job description (this is where a service that saves and tracks those job descriptions, like Teal, can be so helpful).
- Have your résumé in front of you.
- Practice talking briefly about your skills in anything you list on your résumé (think 15-second blurbs).

Sometimes recruiters will call you out of the blue for a phone screen, but typically you'll get an email to schedule it. When you are still early in the process of applying to jobs, pay careful attention to what they ask you on the phone screen. Many people do not make it past the phone screen for the first few weeks at least, and so this is your best time to collect data about what kinds of things companies are looking for and how they are reacting to you as a candidate.

One question I can picture you having is, "How do I know if the meeting is a phone screen or another type of interview?" Although this "phone screen" language may be new to you, every single time I've been asked to schedule a phone screen, the person setting up the interview has called it a phone screen. So, they should tell you.

Meeting the Hiring Manager

This interview can take a few different forms. Sometimes a company will skip a phone screen and go right to this step. Typically smaller companies will move right to meeting with the hiring manager, whereas larger companies who work with recruiters will often start with a phone screen.

If your interview process begins with a meeting with the hiring manager (not a phone screen), you can still expect to have overview conversations to start out with. The hiring manager will tell you about the company and the role. Then you'll tell them a bit about yourself and your background. They'll also give you time for questions and maybe have a few questions for you.

When you're meeting a hiring manager instead of a recruiter, one difference is that the hiring manager likely knows how to do the job they're interviewing you for. A recruiter, on the other hand, is probably not a data person. So, you can expect that a hiring manager would have a more insightful understanding of your skill level when you answer questions about your experience with various tools.

In my experience, it was very hit or miss what hiring managers were looking for at this stage. At some companies they were looking for someone who had a year or so of experience with the tools that position required, and it did not matter how personable I was. Other times, it seemed as if they were looking for someone with the capacity to learn who would be a good fit for the team overall. Those went much better for me.

I've heard a few cases of people getting jobs just from one interview with the hiring manager, where they spent about an hour on the call getting to know each other. In each of those cases, that person also had a portfolio that the hiring manager was able to look at and see their skills. So it is possible that the interview process could end here—but that's unlikely. The majority of people I've talked to say that this is just the first meeting with the team, and it sets them up for what's next.

My advice for succeeding at this step is the same as with the previous one, but with more gravity. Instead of just reading and knowing the job description, you should also have looked at the company's website and their mission statement. Another piece of advice is to come prepared with questions. Generally, there is time for questions at the end of an interview like this, and the questions you ask are an important indicator of your fit for and interest in the role. I'll talk about formulating insightful questions later in the section, "How to Come Up With Good Questions."

Behavioral Interview

The behavioral interview tends to be either loved or hated by data analysts, depending on how comfortable they are with public speaking. If you Google "common interview questions," then you'll find the subject matter of many behavioral interviews. This is where you'll be asked to "Tell me about a time you made a mistake at work" or "Describe the last project you worked on that truly excited you."

Volumes of great information are available about behavioral interview questions. I am not a recruiter or someone who enjoys job seeking, so later in this chapter I'll point you to other resources for practicing for behavioral interviews, such as using ChatGPT to help you with your job search. Remember that the goal of your interviewer in this part of the interview process is to understand how you'll respond to stressors and projects should you get hired at their company.

When you think about answering behavioral questions, always keep in mind that they are adapting your answers to their company, experiences, and team. So, the more you can draw a straight line between the answers you are giving about yourself and the requirements for the role you are hoping to fill, the better your chances are at standing out as a good candidate.

Technical Interview

The technical interview is known to strike the most fear into the hearts of aspiring analysts. I know that I was a ball of stress before each of mine. Technical interviews can take on many different formats. Sometimes a company sends you a link to a private quiz on a website such as HackerRank, where you answer some SQL questions and run your results to see what happens when you write different queries. Others will be with a service that keeps track of every keystroke you make so they can see you think your way through the problem.

Sometimes, a technical interview is a live coding exercise where you're given a simple dataset and then given some questions and asked to write the SQL queries while on the call with an interviewer. For the one interview that I did like this, they did not even have me run the queries and did not care about exact syntax; they just wanted to see how I thought through it.

Some companies will have you do a take-home assignment that includes Tableau and Excel; I've even heard of some companies asking candidates to put together a PowerPoint to present their findings. I had one take-home Tableau test: I was given data and four hours to put together a Tableau dashboard. As you may be guessing, technical interviews are not only often the most stressful part of interviewing but may also be the most time and energy consuming.

Not every company will ask for a technical interview. The company that hired me for my first job did not ask for one, because they just looked at my Tableau public profile and we talked about a project I had posted on there. It is important that you ask your contact person at the company what to expect at each step, because you'll want to be prepared and in the right headspace if you have a technical interview coming your way.

Another variable in this equation is that the difficulty of technical interviews can range from straightforward to intentionally difficult. My favorite resources for preparing for SQL interviews (aside from doing projects) are the sites DataLemur and HackerRank (https://datalemur.com and www.hackerrank.com). I also think that using an AI website such as ChatGPT could be an excellent way to practice your technical skills—I'll talk more about that later in this chapter.

I have spoken with some 20 senior analysts and hiring managers to get their input on what companies are looking for during technical interviews. I've gotten two main responses. Sometimes companies are just looking to see what level you are with the skills listed on your résumé. However, the overwhelming sentiment from these experts I talked to, and from my own interviews, is that they aren't expecting you to be a technical rockstar. Instead, they're looking to see how you think and how you approach a problem.

As I've said before, being a data analyst is so much more than knowing how to write a complex SQL statement. Data analysis requires being able to break down complex problems, approach them logically, and think creatively.

Technical interviews, especially the trickier ones, are a good chance for your potential employer to see how you would tackle problems that you'd encounter in that position.

I had one technical interview that was so difficult that, in an hour, I could not come up with the correct solution for any of the four questions they asked me. Looking back, I think the answers might have had something to do with LAG and LEAD functions, but that's not the point. The point is that when I got into that interview it was like my brain became static. I saw questions I wasn't sure how to answer, and everything in my brain came grinding to a halt.

I was allowed to use Google and other sources during the interview, so I was searching around somewhat desperately for functions that would help. What I should have done was taken a deep breath, taken a step back, and thought through the problems logically. I could've broken them into steps, and tested one thing at a time. Then when I went to Google, I would've known exactly what I was trying to accomplish. But I didn't do that. It was not fun.

I'm not sure what the landscape of technical interviews will look like now that ChatGPT and other AI tools have been released. When I was interviewing, all of my technical interviews were "open book." It makes sense, on the job you'll be able to use Google, so why not in the interview? However, I can imagine that each company is going to have to come up with their own stance if they want to hire entry-level analysts who can write SQL but need AI's help to do so.

I did end up getting a call back to move to the next round for that very difficult technical interview I just described. When I mentioned my surprise to my interviewer, they said that they had been hired just a few months prior and had also felt stumped by the technical interview. He said that the company didn't expect me to arrive at the correct answer—they just wanted to see how I would approach the problem.

If I can leave you with one piece of advice for technical interviews, it is to do your best to show your work and talk through your thought process. The interview is probably just as much about what you come up with as it is about *how* you came up with it. Technical skills can be taught, but the ability to think a certain way is much harder to teach.

Panel Interview

The panel interview typically comes toward the end of the interview process. By the time you reach the panel interview (if the company asks you to do one), they have likely already decided that you would be a good candidate and want to use this opportunity to see how you would fit into the role. It is often a combination of the technical and behavioral interviews, and the company's best peek into how you would perform as a candidate. I question this logic because interviewing in front of multiple people is a unique stressor that can be very different from on-the-job work, but I don't make the rules.

The panel interview will generally take one of two forms. It can be a more intense version of the behavioral interview, where you meet with multiple interviewers at a time or back to back, and they ask you behavioral-style questions and give you the opportunity to ask questions. You are on display here even while asking questions; they want to see how you converse with the team, think about the role, and talk about your background.

The other style, which I think is more of a true "panel interview," is to bring a technical component into it. You're presenting your work to one or multiple interviewers. Some companies will give you a take-home technical assessment and have you present that; others will ask you to present work you have already done.

When interviewing for my first job in data, I was asked to present work I had already done, and my interviewer (who became my boss and friend) was clear that he did not want me to be doing unpaid work on behalf of the company just for an interview. He even told me that one of the dashboards that we had just spoken about in the half-hour-long interview we'd just had would be perfect for me to present.

Not all companies will be so progressive. It seems that there is a general sense, especially in the corporate world, that it is a privilege for you to be interviewing for a role. Creating work just for the interview seems to be a well-accepted way to ensure that candidates are completing original work in an acceptable time frame.

The panel interview for my first job in data was, admittedly, for a role as a Tableau consultant. So presenting a dashboard I made to a group of people who were pretending to be my end users was an appropriate exercise for determining whether I would succeed in the role. In that interview I presented to about six people, and most of them did take time to ask me a kind and insightful question at the end.

I recently interviewed for a mid-level role that had a panel as part of the interview process. The panel was also a presentation of a dashboard. However, for this one I'd been given a dataset without a time limit and asked to make it into a dashboard, but they said they did not want me to spend more than six hours total on the project. I asked if I could get back to them the following week because I was pretty busy with work, and they said that was fine.

I took time over the weekend to work on the project, and then when I finished I sent them my materials and we scheduled a time for me to present the dashboard. When I got to the panel presentation, I was presenting to only one person, but the entire meeting was recorded. I spent about 10–15 minutes presenting my work, and then the interviewer took at least 20 minutes to ask me questions about the project and how I went about creating it.

As you can see, panel interviews come in many flavors. However, they all serve as a final test of a candidate to get the most realistic view possible into what kind of employee and coworker they will be.

Here is some advice for panel interviews:

- Relax. Take some deep breaths before you log on.
- I like to put on silly music and dance to release some stress right before a panel interview.
- Keep a glass of water nearby. Your mouth may dry up from stress! It's happened to me.
- You are interviewing them, too. When you ask questions, think about whether you would *enjoy* working on that team.
- Try to make it conversational! Even taking a pause and checking that everything makes sense to your audience gives them the chance to stay checked in and get in a relevant point if they have one.
- Keep it simple. Being able to explain complex subjects in a clear and approachable way is a desirable skill for a data analyst to have.

Culture Fit

It is not too common to hear someone say they got scheduled for a "culture fit" interview, but it is, in some way, usually a part of the interview process. The idea behind the culture fit interview is that the company wants to get a sense of how you would operate within the interpersonal fabric of the team. Will you get along smoothly with the team, or are the "vibes off"? This is an unscientific way to describe it, but I've heard so many times that the point of this interview is to assess things like "vibes." The more formal language is probably "interpersonal fit."

This part of the process might happen during a panel interview or in the process of meeting with the hiring manager. Sometimes you'll be given the chance to talk to members of the team you would be joining, to ask them questions about what the job and the team is like. This is also a "culture fit," and they'll likely be asked afterward about their impressions of how you would fit with the team.

Now, I cannot say that I think that this idea of a "culture fit" is equitable. If a workplace's culture is dominated by a majority group—let's say, for example, able-bodied, straight white men—then if you do not belong to that group then you may not pass the culture fit, even if you can handle all the other aspects of the job.

There is a huge chance that neurodivergent, LGBTQ+, disabled, or other minority candidates who are absolutely capable of doing the job are going to have a harder time shining in a "culture fit" situation. I am not a hiring manager and, again, I do not make the rules. So there is nothing I can do about this (at least at this point in my career), but it feels wrong to tell you about the culture fit interview and not mention that it has a large potential to be discriminatory.

Although team cohesion is important and it can be problematic to hire a candidate who is unable or unwilling to work with the rest of the team and organization, it is up to each organization to be inclusive and welcoming of diversity—and that isn't always the case. I do not have any advice for passing a culture fit interview, because it is highly situational how teams work together and what they might be looking for. However, it is important to know that this is one of the considerations during the interview process.

Follow-up

After you've gone through an interview process consisting of two to six steps, and that has taken weeks or even months, then what? Wouldn't it just be great if you could ace your final interview and get offered the job right on the spot? That may happen, but it is usually a waiting game. After your final interview, be sure to ask when you can expect to hear back . . . and then you wait.

After your final interview, your potential employer will need time to get a team together and discuss your interviews. Other candidates may be interviewing at the same time, which could delay the decision even more. Then, the company needs to decide on the benefits and salary they will offer you and finalize the details of the role.

In my experience, when getting ready to offer you a role for an entry-level data analyst position, companies are often considering how *little* they can pay you and still have it be a good offer. I bring this up because it is up to you to define your worth, not them! Many people new to data feel defeated by a low salary offer and think that it defines them. But remember, you are working with a business, and it is in their best interest to keep their salary costs low. Your worth is more than a salary.

Companies generally take about a week or so to make a decision. One company completely ghosted me when it appeared they were going to offer me a job; I never even got a rejection! Other times I have been offered a job, it has happened within a few days. As I have mentioned elsewhere, I have been job searching for a new data job recently. I have received two offers (which I have turned down), so I have received a total of four job offers since I started my data journey last year, and all of them have come within three working days of my last interview with that company.

If a company takes more than a few days to extend an offer, do not lose hope! Like I said before, they may have other candidates they are waiting on. I prefer working with small companies, so my quick job offers have come because there was little to no other competition for the role. My friends who have accepted roles at larger companies have told me they waited a week or more for a decision.

How I Handled Some Common How-Tos

While I moved through the process of job searching, I came upon two questions that I've heard echoed by many other job seekers. Both of these questions are common subjects of discussion for content creators in the recruiting and career seeking space, so I know it must be universal problem! The questions are:

- How do I answer, "Tell me about yourself"?
- How do I come up with good questions to ask at the end of an interview?

These two subjects are an important part of acing your job search in most industries, not just data. I struggled with the "Tell me about yourself" question initially, because none of my history was "relevant" to the roles I was interviewing for. On the other hand, until recently I didn't know how to ask good questions or, more important, the "right" questions at the end of an interview. It took working with many businesses, talking to managers and executives, and understanding what it is like to work in the "corporate" world for me to get a handle on this.

I want to preface this discussion by stating that every interviewer will be looking for something slightly different. When it comes to career advice, you'll hear *so many* different opinions. I encourage you to seek out resources that dedicate their professional life to helping job seekers, and resources that have been in the position of hiring candidates (preferably analysts) many times before. What I'm going to tell you next is just *my* interpretation of how to answer these questions and the approach that has been success-ful for *me*.

Tell Me about Yourself   When an interviewer asks you to tell them about yourself, they don't want to hear your life story. A better interpreta-tion of this question would be along the lines of "Give me a relatively brief summary about your relevant past experience, what you are doing right now (as it relates to this role), and what you are looking to do in the future (should you get this job)."

I am a literal person, so it helped me to figure out a formula for answer-ing this question. I've seen a couple of different opinions on this, but this is the formula I came up with:

- Give a short recap of the things that I have done in the last few years that brought me up to the point of deciding to get into data, men-tioning my degrees and professional work experience.
- Explain my progress in learning data analytics, which includes men-tioning that I took a course or two and have since built up a portfolio of projects in each skill (mention each skill).
- Discuss the direction I would like my career to go and what I am looking for in my first data job.

For the first part of this, I knew that I did not have any "directly relevant" experience to discuss, which was initially intimidating to me. However, I learned to roll with it and give a good overview. If I was applying for a healthcare-related role, I could mention my healthcare background and have it be relevant. I also discovered that talking to consulting managers about my previous experience as a nanny went well, because they resonated with the idea that looking after someone's children is a bit like working with clients' data.

Really, any previous role could be relevant to data in some way. Previous professional experience could show organization, attention to detail, business acumen, interpersonal skills, critical thinking skills . . . it could be anything. When hiring entry-level analysts, managers are looking for a collection of interpersonal skills aside from technical capabilities, so this is the time when you can set yourself up to show off your soft skills.

Next up is talking about the present. Here is where you'll introduce yourself as a data analyst. Employers do not tend to care much about courses and their related certifications, so there is no need to focus on the "education" part of it. I found it easiest to talk about what I was doing at the moment as a data analyst by mentioning that I took some courses, and then transitioned into completing projects.

I had only started learning data analytics a few months prior, which could have been seen as a weakness. So I would bring it up in the context of "in just four months I learned SQL and Tableau, and some Python, and then I went on to build a portfolio in those skills, which can be found on my website." For employers who were truly looking for entry-level candidates with the high potential to learn, this was an impressive way to open and led to good conversation.

The final part of this statement is the wrap-up that I saw as the opportunity to give the interviewer a chance to see me as an employee at that company. I thought that it would be crazy to have a five-year plan laid out just as I decided to switch careers, so instead I focused on the type of role that I was looking for and used that statement to show that I could be the type of person they were looking for.

Here is an example of my response to this question—my "elevator pitch" as some call it:

> Thanks for asking. So, for the last few years I have been working
> as a professional nanny, and I am actually just finishing my master's
> degree in occupational therapy. That's not data, you may have
> noticed! At the start of this year I enrolled in a course to learn

data analytics just for fun and realized that I loved it. So I kept learning and taught myself SQL, Tableau, and some Python. I already had experience using Excel for research in graduate school.

Over the last few months I have been really enjoying learning data analytics. I love that I get to apply critical thinking and logic to data and see it come to life. I have been working on a portfolio website, which I linked to in my résumé. I have completed multiple projects in SQL and Tableau, and even a few using R and Python. However, SQL and Tableau are the areas that I am strongest in, and I would be happy to show you a project of mine if you would like.

I ended up loving data so much that I decided to switch careers, and so I started looking for jobs as an analyst. I am looking for a role where I get to be hands-on with data tools every day, but I also get the chance to use all of the interpersonal skills I have built over the years in working with stakeholders and other team members. I would like to grow into a career in data, and so I am looking forward to the opportunity to keep growing and learning in my first role.

Some people have told me that their elevator pitch is shorter than that, and they simply list the facts in a very professional manner. Storytelling is a gift of mine, however, and so using it to answer that question was a good fit for me. I often found that hiring managers were interested to hear my story! Telling them my background, my career change, and highlighting why I had done it (my love of data) got their attention in a good way.

It is important that you practice your answer to "Tell me about yourself" and consider tailoring it to the job that you have applied for. This way, it comes out smoothly. Remember, they do not care about your dogs or your baking hobby. This question is, "Tell me your professional story."

How to Come Up with Good Questions For the entire duration of my job search, I had no idea what I was supposed to say when asked, "Do you have any questions for me?" I did not know much about the data world, so I felt like I did not have much to ask there. They had always given me a good amount of information about the job and the company, so I did not have anything I was curious about on that subject either.

At some point in my search, somebody told me that asking good questions is important and is likely one of the metrics by which the interviewer will be evaluating you. Good questions indicate that you are knowledgeable and serious about the role. So, I started looking around for "good questions to ask at the end of an interview." I found all kinds of questions, attached to people telling their audience how deeply impressed these questions left their interviewer.

One of them was, "Ask the interviewer if they have any reservations about you as a candidate. Then it will give you the chance to address them and to know how you stand as a candidate. When I ask interviewers this, they are always impressed with me." So, I thought I would give it a try—it flopped.

I do not remember the exact answer I got, but I'm pretty sure it was something along the lines of, "Uhhhh, no concerns really, this is going well." A few weeks later, I got a rejection. But what was the problem? Was this a bad question? No! In the right context, it would have been a good question. But I did not fully understand the "why" behind asking it, so instead of deploying it at a contextually correct moment, I used it like a prop and it failed.

One of my favorite creators in the career space is Daniel Space. He is an experienced HR professional and always tells it like it is. He has talked about the "asking the right questions" concept several times. He maintains that the questions you ask during an interview could be the deciding factor that gets you a job over the other candidates, but any list of "Top 5 questions to ask during interviews" that states that these are the best questions is "bull" his word.

The reason for this is that the questions you ask in interviews should be natural and organic to the interview, not preplanned from a list. According to Daniel, the best types of questions to ask are going to do two things at once:

- Inquire about something that you are genuinely curious about.
- Demonstrate your value.

If you ask about things you are genuinely curious about, it shows that you have an interest in the role. At the same time, it also demonstrates a familiarity you have with the topic the question is about, which has inherent professional value. For example, in a recent interview I asked, "Can you tell me more about how you connect to data? Will I need to be writing SQL or doing any transformations in a database, or will I typically just be connecting right to a database to pull data right into Tableau for analysis?" This demonstrated not only my curiosity, but also that I understand that data often needs to be cleaned and transformed before being connected with Tableau.

Showing familiarity does not have to be limited to technical skills! You might ask a question about career progression and skills development while in the role, which has been informed by your experience in healthcare, where you attended continuing education classes at least twice a year. This shows a familiarity with being a professional and holding yourself to a certain set of standards.

Daniel continued on this topic to break these valuable questions into two categories:

- Connection-based questions
- Humble-brag questions

So what does he mean by that? Well, to start, a connection-based question is like the example I just gave. It shows the person who is interviewing you that you are competent, familiar, and comfortable with something important to the job, whether it be team dynamics, a job responsibility, a system that you interact with, a process you would oversee, or simply the day-to-day operations of the role. Table 10.1 shows examples of some of the different domains.

A humble-brag question is similar, and I see a lot of overlap between the two. The difference with the humble-brag question is that not only are you showing familiarity and competence with the role, but you understand the problems you face in the role at such a high and competent level.

You are less likely to happen upon situations for humble-brag questions as a brand-new analyst, because you probably lack the in-depth understanding of analytics to be able to ask a question that demonstrates your clear, unique knowledge and competency.

Table 10.1   Breaking down what interview questions communicate to the interviewer.

Competency	Example	Rationale
Team Dynamics	On this team, what is the process for collaborating and supporting each other through roadblocks? Is there any kind of a team Slack channel or meeting in place for collaboration, or are individuals working independently?	This demonstrates that you are familiar and comfortable with working with a team and helps you understand how siloed, or "on your own," you might be in this role. *This question would likely not be a good fit for a role where you know they are expecting you to work independently, without collaboration or support.*
Job Duties	Would I be responsible for creating or maintaining the data pipeline to bring data into the visualization tool, or will it already be prepared for me to connect to with simply a set of credentials?	This demonstrates familiarity with using visualization tools and connecting them to a database, or connection types other than Excel. It also helps you determine whether you'll be writing SQL and working in a database, or whether someone else will be writing SQL and you'll just be building visualizations.
System	Do you use Salesforce data in this role? If so, do you have a Salesforce administrator who understands the data model and would support me?	This likely would be most relevant to a sales-related role; Salesforce is a common platform that sales teams use to track leads and deals. It shows that you have at least some familiarity with Salesforce, which can be a tricky system to navigate from a data standpoint.

Competency	Example	Rationale
Process	What is this team's process for quality control? Do analysts perform reviews of each other's work, or will I be working with a manager to double-check my queries and the accuracy of my data? Or is there another way?	This tells the interviewer that you understand that working with data is not a linear process, and that checking your data's accuracy is an important part of being a data analyst. It also gives you a sense of the process of checking your work, which can be intimidating.
Day-to-Day	Is there an expectation that I will be working on a certain schedule, such as 9-5 EST daily? Or is the focus on attending meetings and accomplishing projects on a reasonable timeline?	Asking about the day-to-day is likely an area about which you won't struggle to ask questions! We have all experienced the day-to-day life of *some* job. These questions are focused mostly around information gathering, but could also display your familiarity with working in a professional environment.

I can give you an example of a question that I asked recently in an interview that, upon hearing an answer, was a quick signal to me that the role was lower level than I was looking for. I asked:

I want to make sure I understand here. It sounds like you are getting your data for these reports from [four different data sources]. These platforms are really different, and so even if Tableau had the right connectors for piping in all this data (it does not), you would have to do some serious transformation and exploration before you could analyze this data together and produce a valid report. In this role, would I be in charge of using SQL and potentially Snowflake, Alteryx, dbt, or Python to preprocess the data, or would a data engineer be handling this step before the data gets to me?

My interviewer, a director of analytics, fumbled on this answer. It was clearly a more complex question than they anticipated. I learned that the data engineers do all of the preprocessing work, and the only data modeling I'd be doing would be in Tableau. My interviewer also added, "I mean, of course, you would be performing calculations in Tableau." This signaled to me that this position would not provide the kind of career progression I was looking for.

The next day the interviewer called to offer me the job. He expressed to me that from our interview he could tell my level of experience and that I would be a perfect fit for the role. He knew that I was looking at other roles and so he wanted to express his urgency in hiring me as a candidate. I wound up turning down the position because I was fortunately able to do so. The point of this story is to demonstrate how asking a question you are genuinely curious about can also signal to your interviewer that you are a skilled and valuable candidate.

If you go through all of your entry-level interviews simply asking connection-based questions and never get the chance to ask a humble-brag question, that is okay! Remember, interviewers are looking for entry-level candidates who can learn and think critically, not for a high level of technical competency.

Resources

There are many, many creators and resources out there for job seekers. In the age of social media, these will be always changing and evolving! I can give you advice on my favorite resources right now, and I imagine that all their existing content will still be available for years to come. But you should also do your own research and search LinkedIn and whatever other social platforms you use to find HR specialists, career coaches, and recruiters who post free information.

At the end of this chapter, I'll provide you with my favorite resource: ChatGPT. But first, let's go over some of my favorite career-focused resources and content creators.

Teal

When I decided to take the leap and try to get a job in data, I decided I was going to be organized about it and keep track of my application data.

I made a Google Drive folder with a spreadsheet and document template, ready to track and save the jobs I was applying to. I was also doing that so on the off-chance they took down the job posting while I was in the interview process, I'd always have access to the job description.

I quickly realized that upkeep of the spreadsheet was just one extra step that I did not mentally have the energy for. Within the first dozen jobs, my aspirations to track everything started to fall apart. Unfortunately, it took me until just about the end of my job search to discover Teal. Teal is a free service that can do exactly what I hoped to do with my Google Drive folder, but way better and with more features.

The most immediately relevant thing Teal offers is a job tracker—right from the page where you see the job description listed, you can save the job to your job tracker. Once jobs are saved to your job tracker, not only can you track your progress through the application process—such as "applied" and "interviewing"—but it will also analyze the job posting for you.

It highlights keywords and helps draw your attention to things you might want to target in your résumé, cover letter, and interviews. If the employer takes down that job posting, you can still access it in Teal.

Teal also can help you with writing résumés and cover letters. It has integrated AI into its platform, and it can help you write smart résumé bullets and a professional summary, give feedback on your résumé, and even outline a smart and tidy cover letter for you. Teal is mostly powered by ads, but you can also sign up for a paid version to get rid of the ads and have access to some enhanced features to help with résumé writing and related features.

I have talked with multiple members of the team at Teal, and I can say that they truly do share a mission of helping job seekers. Teal is not just another company out there looking to make a quick buck. It includes as much as it can for free while still keeping the lights on! I am not sponsored by Teal in any way—I just respect what it does and have personally used its tool to help with my job search. I only wish I'd found it sooner.

I imagine that there are other job trackers out there aside from Teal's; this is just the one I know and love.

Maven Analytics

I've mentioned Maven Analytics before in other portions of this book, but they are worth mentioning again here! For the team at Maven Analytics, helping people get jobs in data is more than a job; it is a passion. I've talked about analytics-focused offerings from Maven previously, but I want to highlight their job searching resources here.

Maven is consistently updating their course catalog, so the courses I refer to here might change or have different names. However, they are committed to continuing to offer courses to support people with job searching, so no matter when you read this there should still be something in their catalog to help. Two courses that are currently available and can give you a boost on your job search are "Thinking Like an Analyst" and "Launching Your Data Career." The first course is where you can get a good idea of the types of thinking interviewers will be looking for.

Their "Launching Your Data Career" course covers writing your résumé, optimizing your LinkedIn, networking, applying for jobs, acing the interviews, and finally a "career launch checklist"—so, all of the things you need to learn how to do in order to have a successful job search! The course is offered as part of their monthly subscription. I took this course toward the end of my job search, and even though I had already learned a thing or two about the search, I made some changes to what I was doing by the time I finished. Another resource I wish I had started with!

Content Creators/Small Businesses

My favorite way to get information about acing the job search is from social media. There's just something about not feeling as if you are taking a class or a lecture but instead getting the information via storytelling and a social story on TikTok or LinkedIn that seems effortless and more interesting to me.

Here are my favorites:

Greg Langstaff   Not only does Greg have excellent content, but he offers résumé templates. I used one of his paid templates as inspiration for creating my own, and I still use that layout today. Find him @greglangstaff on most social media platforms.

Daniel Space   Daniel Space is my number-one top voice on LinkedIn and TikTok for job search advice. He has been in HR and recruiting for a long time, and he will tell it to you straight. Find him at @dan_from_hr on TikTok.

Teal Staff Pages   Teal has its own social media pages. They like to share lots of excellent career and job search advice, alongside marketing (of course). Additionally, the founder (David Fano) and head of brand and content (currently Lia Zneimer) both post a lot of excellent job-search-related content to their own pages. If you Google **Teal job search tool**, they will come up, or on LinkedIn you can look up **Teal** for the page (their logo is teal-and-white-colored) or **David Fano Teal** or **Lia Zneimer Teal**.

LinkedIn Top Voices Do you want to know who the top creators are on LinkedIn who are creating content about job searching? Every year on LinkedIn, they release lists of "LinkedIn's Top Voices." You can Google this list for the most up-to-date version of the top voices.

Working with Data Creators

As someone who creates content in the data analytics space, I naturally pay attention to the people who do the same. It seems that there is a growing popularity for analytics content creators to be offering courses or career coaching services as a side hustle. Some even leave data analytics to become content creators, course instructors, or career coaches. I want to give my two cents.

If you're going to work with a content creator to help with your data career transition, I urge you to look past the number of followers they have before handing over your money. Many people have found some level of success in data analytics and then realized that they could turn around and monetize that. Talking about how "easy" it is to become a data analyst, especially if you can mention a six-figure salary, is a quick and dirty way to get a lot of followers. Everyone wants to hear that it is easy and that the pay is high.

I think there is such an abundance of free information out there about getting into data analytics that you don't need to pay someone for career coaching services. Just be willing to put in the work of scrolling, reading, and watching all the content that is available to you. I've done my best to give you a clear roadmap and resources so that you don't need someone else to put those pieces together for you.

However, if you get to your job search and you are truly stuck and want to work with someone one on one or access more support, here's what I advise you to look for:

- Someone who is a senior analyst or higher—this means they actually have a variety of skills and experiences to pull from.

- An experienced HR professional (or similar) who has a deep experience base to pull from to advise you on interviews, résumés, and more.
- Someone who has *actually hired data analysts* or, if it is an HR professional, someone who has hired *many* candidates for various roles. If you work with someone who has never hired new candidates before, then they are only able to tell you about their experiences. This is worth reading about, but in my opinion it is not worth paying for one-on-one services when there are people out there who have hired candidates.

Using AI

ChatGPT had not come out yet when I was searching for my first job in data, but I am currently on the hunt again (one year later), and there are all kinds of AI tools available that can help. And they only seem to be getting better with time!

The next chapter is dedicated to helping you prepare for every step of your job-search journey. Using AI will help you obtain personalized feedback as well as the opportunity to practice your answers, all without hiring a career coach. Career coaches are incredible options if you can afford them, but this book is focused on doing things the free or cheap way.

11 | How to Use ChatGPT to Aid Your Job Search

What's Here

- Writing your résumé
- Writing cover letters
- Practicing for each step of data interviews
- Writing follow-up emails

You have an incredibly valuable tool in your toolbox that I did not have when I was getting into data: artificial intelligence (AI). With the rise of ChatGPT and other similar technologies, the ability to gain information and get good feedback on your job search process has never been more accessible. This chapter explains how to use ChatGPT to help you land a job in data.

Writing a Résumé

If you use Teal or other services that can help you write your résumé, they already come with AI built in. Teal, for example, can suggest résumé bullets, help you with your skills section, and help you write a professional summary.

185

When I was rewriting my résumé a few months ago to get ready to job search again, I decided to test out how I could use ChatGPT. I'd already used Teal's résumé-building service, but I wanted to see what else I could do. I used the following prompt:

> Here is my résumé. It is your job to act as a hiring manager for a mid-level data analyst position. You are here to give me feedback on my résumé—to let me know what makes me stand out, what is irrelevant, and what needs more attention. Due to the text limitations of this prompt, please ignore the formatting and just give feedback on the content.

Writing Cover Letters

My advice for writing a cover letter is the same as it was for the résumé section. For cover letters, give as many tailored details in your prompt as possible. Include the job description, your relevant background, and information about the company, such as their mission statement and values. This should give you a good starting point for the cover letter, but be sure you look it over and consider adding some personalization. If you copy and paste straight from your AI tool of choice, it may be obvious that it was not written by you. Showing some level of personalization can make it clear that you wrote the cover letter. I'm genuinely not sure if anyone even reads cover letters, but if you're going to take the time to submit one, you might as well make it seem like it is coming from you.

Practicing for Interviews

You'll find many resources on the Internet about practicing for data interviews, but if you want feedback on your answers, you'll have to pay for it—unless you use AI! In the following sections, I'll suggest templates and ideas for how you can dialogue with AI to practice answering interview questions. I recommend you use a speech-to-text function so that you can speak your answers, just as you would in a real interview.

Phone Screen

Most interview processes start with a phone screen. That means it's important for you to get comfortable with your answer to "Tell me about yourself," so you have it ready to go if you get an unexpected phone call from a recruiter. Remember, it's your story, so this feedback is just something to take into consideration, For example, here's how ChatGPT responded to my elevator pitch. First, my prompt:

I am interviewing for data analytics positions. This will be my first job in tech. Every interview process starts with a phone screen. In the phone screen it is important to have a good "elevator pitch" to respond to "Tell me about yourself." Here is the elevator pitch I have come up with for myself. I think it does a good job of talking about my past, present, and future goals in the context of my professional self. I want it to be conversational and story-like, because that is a good fit for my personality.

Do you have any feedback for me on it? Please play the role of a recruiter who is not a data analyst but who is looking for the perfect candidate to fill a data role they have open.

And here's ChatGPT's response:

Your elevator pitch is quite engaging and clearly communicates your journey and your passion for data analytics. You do an excellent job of storytelling, which is important for making a memorable impression. Here are a few points of feedback from the perspective of a recruiter:

Brevity: While storytelling is an excellent way to share your journey, the pitch is slightly long. A recruiter might be interviewing many candidates in a day and might not have the time to listen to lengthy introductions. Keep the storytelling, but try to condense some of the details.

Relevance: The mention of your background as a nanny and occupational therapist may be cut short or rephrased to highlight any skills or qualities relevant to data analytics that you developed during these experiences. For instance, did these roles require you to be detail-oriented, problem-solve, or communicate effectively? If yes, then bring that up.

Skills Highlight: You've done a great job mentioning your technical skills. However, try to also highlight your soft skills. For instance, you mentioned wanting to use interpersonal skills developed over the years. Expand on this—how have you used these skills in the past, and how will they help you in this role?

Future Goals: While you touched on your future goals, being more specific about where you see your career going and how this job will help you get there might make your pitch more compelling.

Adaptability: Make sure to adapt your pitch to the specific role you're applying for. You're already aware of this, but it's worth reinforcing. Understand the job description and responsibilities, and ensure your pitch reflects your ability to meet these requirements.

Here's a revised version of your pitch based on these points:

Thanks for asking. My journey to data analytics has been quite unconventional. After years of working as a nanny and studying occupational therapy, I discovered my passion for data analytics. This unexpected interest began as a hobby but quickly became a career aspiration.

In my previous roles, I developed a keen eye for detail and excellent problem-solving skills. These abilities, coupled with my newly acquired technical skills in SQL, Tableau, Python, and Excel, have prepared me well for a role in data analytics.

I've enjoyed putting these skills into practice while building my portfolio, which includes multiple projects using SQL and Tableau. I'm particularly confident in these areas and would be happy to discuss my projects in more detail.

I'm excited about the prospect of combining my technical and interpersonal skills in my first data analytics role. I'm particularly interested in roles that allow for hands-on work with data and collaboration with various stakeholders. I see this as a stepping stone to a long-term career in data, where I can continue to learn and grow. I'm eager to bring my unique background and passion for data to my next role.

Remember, this is your story, so feel free to modify and personalize this as much as you need!

While I do generally agree with the points that ChatGPT made, I think it made me sound a little too "stuffy." If I had gotten this feedback while I was job searching for the first time, however, I would've compared my response with ChatGPT's feedback to shorten it.

Technical Interview

In the previous chapter I listed some excellent locations for practicing for technical interviews. For the purposes of coming up with and answering technical questions I recommend those sites as your first stop. Here's an example query that you could ask of AI to help you get started:

> Can you help me think of common technical questions that I might encounter when interviewing for entry-level data analyst positions? They may be questions about SQL itself or SQL questions, like about joins, or simple SQL queries.

As a follow-up question, you could ask the AI to create a sample data frame for you: "Can you give me a sample data frame about test scores that I could use to practice some SQL queries? Please make it 4 columns and 30 rows." This way you could practice answering technical questions right there and get feedback. Just remember, AI sometimes makes up answers! So take every answer with a grain of salt. I find that ChatGPT-4 is accurate at running SQL queries with a simple data frame like this one.

Although using a sample data frame to answer SQL questions using AI is a fun application of the tool, you should primarily stick to sites that have been designed for this purpose, like DataLemur. However, using AI is the only way I know to get feedback on your responses to narrative questions such as, "What is the difference between DROP, DELETE, and TRUNCATE commands in SQL?" Again, I recommend speaking your answers instead of typing to simulate a real interview.

Behavioral Interview

Behavioral interviews are pretty common in the world of job searching. So I asked ChatGPT to help me come up with some good behavioral interview questions. I was impressed to see that it did a good job of producing the types of questions I encountered in interviews. Here is the list ChatGPT came up with:

- **Can you describe a time when you made a mistake at work? How did you handle it?** The interviewer wants to understand your ability to admit mistakes and learn from them. It's important to demonstrate both accountability and problem-solving in your answer.
- **Tell me about a time when you had to deal with a difficult coworker or customer. How did you handle the situation?** This question is designed to assess your interpersonal skills and conflict resolution abilities.
- **Give an example of a goal you reached and tell me how you achieved it.** Here, the interviewer wants to understand your goal-setting process, your motivation, and your perseverance.
- **Describe a time when you had to juggle multiple responsibilities. How did you organize your time?** This question aims to assess your time management skills and your ability to prioritize tasks.
- **Tell me about a time when you took the initiative on a project or task at work.** The interviewer wants to gauge your proactivity and your ability to take charge when necessary.
- **Can you describe a situation where you had to make a difficult decision at work? What was the outcome?** This question is about your decision-making process and your ability to handle challenging situations.
- **Tell me about a time when you had to adapt to a significant change at work. How did you handle it?** This question aims to understand your adaptability and resilience in the face of change.
- **Describe a time when you had to persuade a colleague or manager to accept an idea that you knew they would not like.** The interviewer wants to assess your communication, negotiation, and persuasion skills.
- **Tell me about a time when you went above and beyond the requirements for a project or assignment.** This question is designed to assess your initiative, motivation, and dedication.
- **Can you share an example of a time when you received criticism? How did you respond?** This question is about your ability to accept feedback and make improvements.

Remember, in your responses, the interviewer is looking for concrete examples from your past experiences. Use the STAR method (Situation, Task, Action, Result) to structure your answers effectively.

It is amusing to me to see that the AI mentioned the STAR method in its response, because that's where I was going to go next with this chapter. I am comfortable in situations such as answering behavioral questions during an interview, so I did not spend much time looking at or thinking about the STAR method. However, I've spoken to many people who are uncomfortable in situations like that, and they said that the STAR method saved them from a lot of rambling, disorganized answers.

If you are unfamiliar with the STAR method, feel free to ask AI for examples! One idea for practicing behavioral questions and using the STAR method is to ask ChatGPT. For example, you could say the following:

> I am interviewing for an entry-level data analyst position. I am practicing for the behavioral interview—it is a behavioral interview only, not a technical interview. I do not have prior experience in data. It is your job to give me feedback on my answers to the question that is asked of me, and to let me know how well I applied the STAR method. My first question is "Can you describe a situation where you had to make a difficult decision at work? What was the outcome?" Here is my answer: [Input your answer here.]

I tested this out with several different questions, each of which took me a few minutes to write. ChatGPT was able to give me good feedback each time by giving me a summary of what I answered for each point of STAR and then providing two to three areas of improvement. ChatGPT is an excellent resource for job seeking, and it really shines here as a good place to help generate and practice questions and answers.

Writing Follow-Up Emails

A stressful part of the interview process that I rarely hear anyone talk about publicly (but I've talked to a lot of friends about it privately) is worrying about how and when to send a follow-up email after interviews. I don't recommend simply asking AI to write an email for you and sending that. However, it can help you get your thoughts out and provide ideas for a response.

If you're going to ask for feedback, be sure to be clear about your question. Include what stage you are in, how many days it has been since you interviewed, what day of the week it is, and any other relevant details.

I used ChatGPT to help me email a recruiter recently. I've been inter-viewing for a data analyst role that I am excited about, but I was not sure how long I'd have to wait after my final interview to hear a decision from the hiring team. I got a job offer from another company not long ago, but the offer came from my second-choice role. I asked them for a week to think about it, and then knew that I needed to email the recruiter from the company that was my first choice to let them know I received another offer and ask what the timeline might be for making a decision. I wanted to do this professionally and emphasize that they are my first choice and that I would *really* like to work there.

I was incredibly nervous to write this email because I do not want to somehow kick myself out of consideration by asking about it (which is improbable, but I'm still anxious about it), so I asked ChatGPT for help. I told it everything I've told you and asked it to help me write an email to the recruiter. Here's my prompt:

> Please help me Write to a recruiter that I got a job offer at another company, and I need to decide by next Tuesday EOD. However this position at [Company A] is my first choice. It is more aligned with my career goals and preferences. I have been very impressed with the team and company at [Company A] each step of the way - I love their open-source nature with their handbook, how they build asynchro-nous culture intentionally, and how I would be joining such a smart team. I particularly excited about this role because it excites me that I have deep SME and practical experience in leading a Tableau transfor-mation and would love to get to do that at [Company A], while also experiencing career development.

As you can see, it's not very polished! But it is specific. ChatGPT came up with a great response. I brought it into my email and made a couple of tweaks, and then sent it off.

Be Specific

As you can see, AI is an excellent companion for your job search journey. I particularly appreciate how I can just type my thoughts without worrying about spelling and grammar, and it still understands what I'm saying.

I have mentioned this before, but the last tip I will give you is to make sure you are specific about what you are asking. It's okay if you make typos, but if you aren't very clear and specific with what you are looking for, then you will not get a good response.

I think of AI as an intern with encyclopedic knowledge, but not great critical thinking skills. It can write code, give feedback on interviews, and help with grocery lists. But all of that depends on you giving it good input (questions).

12 | My Job Search

What's Here

- How I prepared to search
- Getting rejected (a lot)
- Changing my strategy
- Interview experiences
- Success!

The hardest part of my data journey was job searching. It's hard to convey to you in bits and pieces what the experience of job searching felt like, so this chapter is dedicated to the story of my job search. It was a roller coaster of emotions—usually negative. I often felt confused, burnt out, and "not good enough," and it made me genuinely consider giving up. If I'd known that it is hard on everyone else too, I would not have felt so discouraged! That's why I want to tell you my story.

"Open to Work?"

So first, let's set the scene. In April 2022, I had officially decided that I was going to try to get a full-time job as a data analyst. For the entire duration of my job search, I was still doing my field work for graduate school, which is essentially an unpaid internship. I was "working" at this internship, 40 hours a week, a half hour away, doing something that was emotionally and physically taxing. For the entire duration of my job data analytics job search, I was also doing this unpaid internship at an assisted living facility, which I found to be particularly emotionally draining.

I had decided to start my job search in May, and I was hoping that I would have a job by the end of June. I had no idea what to expect. I'd gotten most of my previous jobs through word of mouth. I had a résumé, but I'm not sure that anyone ever used it to actually make a hiring decision.

In May, I quietly switched myself to "open to work" on LinkedIn and shifted my focus from learning and projects to job searching. I started with refurbishing my résumé and figuring out what the heck "optimizing your LinkedIn" meant. That took me about a week, and I found myself randomly searching the Internet for resources until I located a few that spoke to me. If you'd like a refresher on optimizing your LinkedIn, return to Chapter 9, "Résumé Building and Setting Your Public Image," where I shared every-thing I've learned on the subject.

It all felt like a lot of busy work. Not only was I spending a lot of time on something that felt borderline meaningless, but I also had no idea whether I was doing a good job of it. I hadn't found many good examples of what it should look like. Although there were many good profiles on LinkedIn, I struggled to find résumé advice that could capture the situation of not having any relevant prior work/academic experience. "Include met-rics!" they said. The only metrics I had were "provided caregiving to up to four children at a time, from ages 1 to 8 years old." That *is* impressive, but not in the way they were looking for.

I was also uniquely nervous about the thought of job searching. Switch-ing my profile to the "open to work" setting on LinkedIn made me feel a little bit nauseous. Up until this point, everything that I had been doing had been for fun, and importantly, it had been *for me*. Sure, I had a TikTok and I was sharing my progress with people. However, I was learning data analytics and doing projects for fun, not to show off to others for their judgment or review.

Job searching on the other hand? Job searching meant being vulnerable. It meant putting myself out there and facing almost certain rejection. Switching myself to be open to work on LinkedIn felt like it was just inviting people to judge me and silently criticize. I was thankful that when I started learning data, I had made one LinkedIn profile for my data self and a separate one for my occupational therapist self. This meant that when I started job searching, nobody from my regular life could see what was happening.

I had heard that if you do a good job with optimizing your LinkedIn, recruiters will reach out to you about jobs. I was hopeful that I could get a job that way, because it seemed preferable to just applying to a job where you didn't have a warm introduction to anybody there.

Within my first day or two of switching my profile to "open to work," I got my first message from a recruiter. I still remember the scene. I was at the doctor's office, looking at an ugly patterned brown wall, sitting in an uncomfortable green chair. When I saw the message, a shot of excitement bolted through my entire body. I almost let out an audible squeal but restrained myself.

I do not remember exactly what the message said, to be honest. But it said something along the lines of "Hi Annie, I am recruiting for a data analyst role right now and saw your profile. I think that you could be a good fit; are you interested in hearing more?"

After consulting a couple of my data connections about it, I responded yes, that I was very interested. At that point, he sent me the job description and some more information about the company. The role would be a hybrid role based in New York City and would focus primarily on using Excel spreadsheets, with the possibility to upgrade their system to SQL in the future.

So it was official—my job search had begun. And my occupational therapy internship still had a month and a half left to go.

Beginning to Search

At the start of my job search, I was very idealistic. I wanted to work in a role, and preferably an industry, that was exciting to me. I talked and thought a lot about how important it was to me to be at a company with great culture, where they truly respect employees' work–life balance. Of course, I hoped to be making decent money as well.

In the first couple weeks of my job search, I mainly focused on leads from a few recruiters in my inbox and jobs that I'd heard about through my network on LinkedIn. However, I quickly realized that this approach was probably not going to get me a job. I was getting a couple of recruiters in my inbox each week, but many of them were not actually good options. I encountered messages for jobs that weren't even in data analytics, that were fully in person and over two hours away, recruiters sending me job postings that seem to be scams, and jobs that paid offensively low rates.

Here's an example of the scam job postings. A recruiter reached out to me about a role with a company called Coders Data. The role was fully remote, based out of Boston, but they seemed to have locations all over the United States. I was not suspicious of the initial posting, because I didn't know what to look for. However, when I got on the phone with the recruiter, I immediately started noticing red flags. It seemed that the recruiter was trying to sell me on something, rather than asking if I would be a good fit for a job.

After about 15 minutes of him rapid-fire talking at me, he told me that they have programs for brand-new analysts. If I wanted to apply for this job, he suggested that I go through an interview preparation course. It would cost $700, and I wouldn't have to pay it until after I got a job. It quickly became apparent to me that the job that the recruiter had reached out to me about did not even exist, and he was just trying to sell me their course. I imagine that there never would have been a job, even if I'd bought the course. Needless to say, I turned him down and blocked him. As a word of warning, you should never, ever *pay* a recruiter to do anything related to recruiting you.

To tie up the loose ends of that first recruiter, I ended up withdrawing myself from the interview process. Commuting to New York City would have been very expensive and energy consuming for me, and I really wanted to get a remote job. The salary for the position ended up being only $55,000 per year, and it appeared that my technical skills would go no further than using Excel. It wasn't a good option to launch into the world of data analytics at the time.

I learned during this process that there are some Excel-only entry-level roles out there, with salaries at the lowest end of the range for entry-level data analyst roles. I've known a couple of people who have accepted those roles early on in their job search. It meant that they did not have to job search for very long, which can be a huge benefit to some people.

Each of the people I know who accepted a role like that quickly decided that they wanted to start looking for their next job. They all expressed to me that they felt their data analytics skills, though new, were being completely underutilized. I am not passing judgment on these lower-paying Excel-based roles; I'm merely stating this observation here, because it would've been an interesting perspective for me to hear while I was searching.

After a few weeks of digging through mostly bad leads and feeling somewhat discouraged, I realized that I was probably going to have to start cold applying to jobs. I'd begun to loosen my criteria a little bit; maybe my first job would not be the best culture fit or the most interesting job. I was beginning to realize that getting into data is hard, and anything to get your foot in the door is a step forward.

I know now that your first job in data is often no more than a stepping stone. However, I still had high hopes for my cold application process. I figured that I would have to apply to a bunch of jobs, maybe 30 to 40, and then something would work out.

At this point I was also struggling to maintain any balance in my life. I was still participating in my internship for 40 hours a week, plus the commute, and all of my time outside of that was consumed with job searching. I was physically and emotionally strung out, my apartment was a mess, and so was my job search.

So, I set up a Google Drive folder to track my job search. I'd decided that I was going to keep track of every job I applied to with a spreadsheet and I would save the job description in a Google document. I was also doing that so I would always have access to the job description on the off-chance they took down the posting while I was in the interview process. As I mentioned in Chapter 10, "Stages of Data Interviews," I later discovered the advantages of using a job tracker, but at the start I was tracking jobs manually.

Applying to jobs, as it turns out, is actually a lot of work. I came to realize that it helps to be one of the first applicants to a job, because if you get to a job and 200 people have already applied to it, it is discouraging. As somebody with no experience in data analytics, I couldn't help but think that there was no way I could possibly compete with all 200 of the other candidates. But that meant I felt like I had to be on my phone, compulsively scrolling the job boards, all the time. It became all-consuming.

I also had to sort through a lot of junk. For every one job posting that looked encouraging, there were five other "entry-level" postings requiring five-plus years of experience, or a computer science degree, or an exhaustive list of tools that are better suited to data science or engineering.

Then when I did find jobs to apply to, I needed to do a lot of boring manual work. Some jobs had an "Easy Apply" feature, which lets you submit an application right from LinkedIn without having to put in too much information. For most jobs, however, I had to go to their website, enter my entire work history and résumé, upload my résumé, and write a cover letter.

For any job that asked for references right in the application, I honestly just closed out and didn't save the job. All of my references at this point in my life were from various childcare-related roles. I had not even told most of the people in my life that I'd decided to switch careers. I didn't feel comfortable calling up previous coworkers/supervisors and asking them to be a reference for me at a data analytics job. Fortunately, not many jobs ask for references.

Over the course of my job search, I probably applied to over 200 jobs. In that first couple of weeks, I probably applied to at least 75 jobs.

And you know what came of it? A whole lot of nothing. It felt like I was screaming into a void. The vast majority of jobs that I was applying to were not even emailing me back, let alone rejecting me. It was very discouraging.

Getting Reponses (and Rejections)

Despite my discouragement, a few companies did email me back about beginning the interview process. I came to learn that there are multiple steps to the job application process in tech; it's not just a conversation with a recruiter and/or a manager, and then a decision on whether or not you got the job. Most interview processes start with a phone screen.

My phone screens were generally about 5 to 15 minutes long, and they served as a chance for the recruiter to get a sense at a high level of whether I would be a good fit for the role. At this point in my job search, the phone screen was where pretty much every single one ended. I would get on the phone with the recruiter, they would ask me if I had any job experience using SQL or Tableau, I would be forced to say no, and that's where the conversation would end.

There was only one job that I had made headway with at this point, and it was actually the only job that I'd found thus far through LinkedIn. I'd seen a post that a company was hiring a data analyst, and I'd messaged them to express my interest.

I got far into the interview process for this job. The hiring manager was the one who did my initial phone screen, and although I was clearly inexperienced, I could tell that he liked me and that he could see that I was a good critical thinker. So, he moved me on to the next steps of the interview process.

The next steps of the interview process included a short technical interview, where the interviewer gave me access to some Excel files and asked me to talk him through how I would accomplish certain things with that data using SQL. I did not actually have to run the SQL queries; I just had to write them on a shared screen. What he was looking for in that interview was not that I had perfect syntax memorized but to see how I would approach the problem and how I would think about it.

The SQL part was fairly simple, such as finding the store with the most sales, a simple inner join of tables, finding the sum of sales, and maybe limiting to one record.

My final interview in the process was with the CEO of the company— it was a fairly small start-up. It's not uncommon to have an interview with an executive when you are interviewing at a startup.

By the time I got to that point in the process, I was very excited. I was impressed with everyone I'd spoken to at the company, and it seemed like they had a great culture. I was beginning to picture myself at that company and what my life would look like when I got a remote job working for them. I also did not have any other promising leads at the time, so all of my eggs were in one basket.

After that final interview with the CEO, I didn't hear back from them for several days. I was so anxious; I checked my email constantly. I had a pretty good feeling about it. I knew that the interviewers all had liked me, I had left a good impression, and they could see that I was a fast learner. After a couple days when I still hadn't heard anything, I decided to send an email to check how things were doing. About 20 minutes later the hiring manager who I had initially spoken with responded to my email, saying that they had decided they didn't have the capacity to bring on someone so junior at that time. He apologized and told me I had great potential but that it just wouldn't work for them.

I was devastated. I knew that the role was probably more advanced than the skill level where I was at the time, but that did not make me any less sad to be rejected. Not only had I been rejected from a company that I had mentally pictured myself working for quite happily, but that left me with no further prospects for a job. It was already June at this point; I had no leads. I had been job searching for a month, and all I felt like was a burned-out failure.

Pivoting

When I found out the bad news, I texted my friend Asa and told them that I was genuinely considering giving up. Who was I to think that I could just walk my way into a data analyst position with no experience? It seemed like every recruiter I talked to wanted experienced applicants. How was I supposed to get experience for an entry-level role without getting an entry-level role? I decided the data industry was impenetrable by somebody like me.

I also had not been outside in weeks. I was overtired, and I felt embarrassed to admit defeat. I had over 10,000 followers on TikTok at that point, so admitting defeat was not something I could easily do.

Asa very wisely texted me back that it seemed I had lost sight of why I originally decided to do this whole data analytics thing. I had not decided to become a data analyst because I wanted to be a job seeker—I had done it because I truly love working with data.

After spending an evening feeling sorry for myself, I got up the next morning determined to change my approach. If all I was hearing from recruiters was that they wanted me to have experience, then I needed to go out and get myself experience—even if it wasn't paid experience. I simply did not have enough work in my portfolio to say with confidence that I had experience in any of the tools.

I'd burned out quickly from job searching, and I needed to reconnect with my love of data. Working on some fun projects and maybe learning a few new fun skills would be just the remedy I needed. I re-budgeted my free time after I got home from the assisted living facility (my internship) to focus on projects instead of job searching.

I had also been hearing on LinkedIn about this thing called networking. People kept saying on LinkedIn that if you were active on LinkedIn, showing off your skills, and networking with people on there, it could lead you to a job. So I decided to focus on creating new skills, getting projects into my portfolio, and talking about them on LinkedIn.

Up until then, all of my LinkedIn content had been from the perspective of "Hey, I'm brand-new to data analytics and I'm just learning it for the first time!" I decided that it was time to start talking as if I had some level of authority on the subject, to demonstrate that I had experience using data analytics tools.

I also decided to take a Maven Analytics course in Tableau. I realized that I was able to upskill and learn to do new things in SQL on my own, but there was something about Tableau that I just was not understanding. I wanted to know how to get from that beginner level to projects that would impress somebody.

After taking a weekend off to go camping with my boyfriend and enjoy disconnecting, I started my pivot. For the rest of the month of June I stuck to my plan and focused on building my portfolio and talking about it. Right around then is when my job search started to change.

Once I started talking about being a data analyst on my page, the messages that I was getting from hiring managers and recruiters in my inbox in LinkedIn became much more productive. When I took that Tableau course I created a Tableau cheat sheet as a PDF and published it to LinkedIn. I also made a couple of posts about data topics like "How You Can Perform Data Cleaning in Tableau." These posts caught the attention of a few executives at smaller companies that used Tableau, and either they reached out to me directly or they had a recruiter for their company contact me.

Around then my responses to the cold applications that I sent in started to get better responses. Every time I did a phone screen, even if it didn't result in another interview, I thought about what the recruiter had asked me during the call. Every interview that I came out of, I noted the sort of things they were looking for. I then went back to my résumé and adjusted it so that those things were highlighted and easy to find.

By the end of June, I had so many interviews that I had to take a pause on applying to new jobs. One day I was so overwhelmed with what had happened at my internship that day, and the other interviews I had participated in that week, that I forgot about an interview. Complete no-call, no-show. An hour or so later I got an angry email from the recruiter telling me that they would be withdrawing my candidacy from the role.

So that was my official sign to focus on the jobs I was interviewing for already.

Interviewing

Although I was not nervous about the phone screens after the first few, I did get nervous about all the other interviews along the way. Chapter 10 examined the various types of interviews: behavioral interviews, technical interviews, and panels. Before every interview, except a phone screen, I found that my mouth would get dry. I'd get sweaty and sometimes even shaky. At some point along the way, I started doing this thing where before an interview I would put on some goofy, silly songs really loud and dance without reservation to get out some of my nervous energy. I am not a dancer.

Something that I learned during this interview process is that I do not ever want to have to come up with an answer to something for the first time while in an interview. For example, if somebody asked me about a SQL project of mine, I did not want that to be the first time I was talking about that project. Or if somebody asked me to tell them about a time when I experienced conflict at work, I did not want to have to think of an answer on the spot. I was already so nervous coming in to my interviews, and trying to think up entirely new answers was an incredibly heavy mental load. I usually did not have an answer that I felt happy about when I thought back on it later.

That was when I learned to start practicing all my answers ahead of time. I started looking up common interview questions on the Internet, especially for data analysts. On my drives to and from my internship every day, I'd practice my answers to common behavioral interview questions (out loud!). I would also practice discussing every one of my interesting projects, and how I did different things with the data, and the various tools that I used. I pretended I was on the phone with somebody and then worked through my answers to these questions.

Those practice phone calls were really helpful to me. I am a verbal processor, and the opportunity to verbally process my way through all of my answers boosted my ability to give good answers on the spot in my actual interviews. Some of my friends prefer to practice writing out their answers to these questions, because they process better that way than through talking. I strongly suggest finding your preferred method for practicing your interview answers.

Chapter 11, "How to Use ChatGPT to Aid Your Job Search," explained using the STAR method (Situation, Task, Action, Result) to structure your answers to questions about a situation you encountered. However, I didn't use STAR when I was practicing my behavioral interview questions, because I'm generally pretty good at answering behavioral questions about myself. So I won't talk about it at length here.

When I finished my internship on July 8, I was in the final stages of interviewing with a couple of companies. I had just finished a panel interview that was two hours long with a company based in Boston, and it seemed very promising. The recruiter said that I would be hearing back from them soon.

That panel interview consisted of a series of interviews, back to back. I would not even call it a panel. I met with four separate people in a row. They each asked me behavioral-style questions and gave me the opportunity to ask questions about the role of the company. I found that interview to be exhausting, and I didn't have enough questions prepared to make the interviews flow naturally.

Despite some troubles coming up with "good" questions, I felt the interview went well overall. I was interested in that role, but it was not my top choice. I hoped that they wouldn't decide too quickly so that I'd have enough time to finish my interviews with the other companies.

Well, that company ended up completely ghosting me. After all that work, I never even heard back from them.

The following week I spent the first few days camping with friends to celebrate finishing graduate school. When I came home from camping, I did two more panel interviews, one on Thursday and one on Friday.

The first panel interview was with a healthcare-related company, and it was an hour and a half long with four people from the company all at the same time. They took turns asking me different questions. Funnily enough, even though I had just gotten my master's degree in occupational therapy, I didn't want to work for a healthcare company. So the only thing that was challenging about that interview for me was that I was not super interested in that job. However, because I already had a background in healthcare, I knew that my best shot at getting into data analytics was at a healthcare company.

The panel interview on Friday was with my top company at the time. I was excited about the idea of working with that company, and I was incredibly impressed with the culture I'd seen displayed by the people I'd talked to already. It seems like they had a great, respectful culture and that I would have tremendous opportunity to grow there.

Naturally, I was nervous about that panel interview. In a previous interview the hiring manager had already looked at my Tableau Public portfolio with me and asked me some technical questions about how I'd created one of the dashboards on there. It was kind of like a soft technical interview. For the panel, I'd been instructed to present a project of mine as if they were the end users. It could be a project using any tool; however, the hiring manager had told me that the dashboard we had reviewed together during my previous interview would be a good fit for that panel interview. He had made it clear to me that he did not want me to create any new work for this panel interview; he did not believe in making people do unpaid work during an interview process. I have a lot of respect for that.

Once I started my work for this panel interview, my memory of the experience completely blacks out. I honestly do not remember most of that interview. I remember the meeting started three minutes late, and then I recall asking one question at the end of the interview. I also remember that during the interview, one of the interviewers had noticed something curious on the dashboard and asked about it. Looking back now, I had forgotten to synchronize an axis, so essentially, I had made a mistake. They were nice about it, but inside I screamed a little bit.

After the interview ended, they thanked me for my time and let me know that I would be hearing back from them the following week, since it was already Friday afternoon.

After the interview ended, I just sat in front of my computer staring blankly at the screen. I had so much emotion pent up inside of me prior to the interview, and now it was over, and I had no idea what was going to happen next.

I had two more technical interviews scheduled for the following week on Thursday and Friday. Both of those positions were interesting to me, but neither was my top choice. That weekend I went on a beach vacation with my parents, and I did my best to put the entire job search out of my mind. There was nothing that I could do over the weekend, except enjoy the beach.

Decision Day

Monday morning rolled around, and I woke up at 6:00, anxious to hear back about jobs. At about noon, the healthcare data company called me back and offered me a job. I still had not heard back from my top choice job yet.

The healthcare data company offered me a fully remote job, with the expectation that I would be working 9–5 every day. I have been targeting between $70,000–$80,000 for my first role, and they actually offered me a bit more than that. This made me feel incredibly anxious, but I got up my courage to thank them profusely and ask for three days to think about it. I told them that I needed to talk to my mom and consider the offer, and I asked them to send me an official offer letter so I could review everything. Part of me was afraid that they were going to rescind the offer if I did that, but so many people had told me that it is a very normal and realistic thing to ask for a couple of days to think about an offer.

At around 2:00 p.m. on Monday my top choice job finally emailed me back, but all they said was that they wanted me to schedule a meeting with the vice president whom I had done my initial phone screen with. I could not figure out if that was a good thing or a bad thing. If they were going to offer me the job, wouldn't they have just offered me the job? Did they want me to talk to the original person I talked to so they could reject me? I had no idea; all I knew that I was full of anxiety. We scheduled a call for 11:00 a.m. the next day.

Tuesday morning came, and again, I woke up at 6:00. Now I will note I am not a morning person, so this is very unusual for me. I managed to get a bit more sleep before eventually waking up and going down to the beach to stare out at the ocean and hope that they were going to offer me a job.

On July 19, 2022, my search came to an end. They offered me the job, and I immediately accepted. It was official, I had gotten a job as a data analyst! It was a full-time role at a company called Zuar. It is a consulting organization, but I was offered a full-time role with benefits, and I would be consulting on the company's behalf.

As soon as the call ended, I ran straight down to the beach to tell my parents. I moved out of my parents' house after college, so being able to share the news with them in person was special for me. I waited until I had signed the official job offer before emailing the other company that had offered me the job to politely decline, and to withdraw myself from the application process with the other two companies that I had technical interviews planned with that week.

I cannot express to you the immense level of relief I felt at being offered my top role, and at a company with a good culture, where they were paying me above average for an entry-level data analyst position! I tell people often that usually, the job search comes down to luck. I certainly feel like I got lucky.

I have also since gotten feedback that something that made me stand out as a candidate was my strong communication skills. The (now former) vice president at my company who found me on LinkedIn, and eventually hired me, told me that he could tell before he even met with me for the first time that I had the soft skills he was looking for. He could see by the way I articulated data concepts in my LinkedIn posts and responded to comments that I am a good communicator and a critical thinker. I have been told by many analytics managers that tech skills are easy to teach when someone has the right soft skills. But soft skills are not easily learned, no matter how great one's technical skills are.

After accepting my role, I was ready to start right away. We agreed that I would start on the following Monday, July 25. I would tell you that I spent the weekend preparing and eagerly awaiting starting my new job, but that would be a lie! While socializing and celebrating at the beach with my parents, I managed to pick up COVID-19. Three days before I started my new job, I got home from the beach and immediately got quite sick. I battled and slept my way through the weekend, crossing my fingers I would feel okay by Monday.

Since the job was remote, I was well enough to log in for my first day of work when Monday rolled around. I switched careers in large part so I could work remotely and reap the benefits of working from home. Then, my first week of work, I got to log in right from my own living room and take breaks during the day to lie down when I needed a break. Despite feeling very unwell for a week or so, I still look back fondly on those couple of weeks. The joy of successfully getting a remote, just plain awesome job could not be overshadowed by *anything,* not even COVID.

PART

IV
The Bonus Part

13 | After the Job Offer

For several days after I was offered the job, I was still in disbelief that it had actually happened. I couldn't believe that just one year ago I had no idea what data analytics was and was planning to go into occupational therapy, and here I was, overjoyed at accepting a role in tech. I felt lucky but also nervous that they would change their mind and take the job away! I had no idea what to expect when the job began. It would be my first time ever working remotely and I had a feeling I was going to love it, but I couldn't be sure yet!

Once you get a job, you'll probably want to jump in and start learning as fast as you can, as I did. Which is great! I also recommend you take some time to reflect on your journey and be proud of how far you have come. It took me a month or so before I was able to take the time and sit down and reflect on my many feelings about having taught myself a whole new career for less than $100.

Once I took some time to reflect on the prior six months, I realized that I was proud of myself for more than just learning data analytics—I was proud of myself for changing my life. Graduate school was a tough time for me, and I was depressed and angry for a lot of it, because I felt trapped by my program. Although I loved the field of occupational therapy, there were things about that career that still felt like a trap for me—like having to work in person every day and working within the healthcare system of the United States.

When I decided to switch to data analytics, it was because I saw a lifestyle that I wanted to be able to live and decided to go after it. Changing to data analytics involved more than just learning the skills to get into that new career; it was an act of taking charge of the rest of my life. It also was an identity change for me. I was no longer a "caregiver," which had been a huge part of my identity.

It took a lot of courage to change my life and my identity like that, and no matter what career you are coming from I know that it will be the same for you. Take some time to reflect on how far you've come and to be proud of yourself!

There is also something unique about realizing that you used the power of the Internet and your own brain to learn a whole new career. Once I realized that *I can learn,* and I can do it for almost free, I felt unstoppable. If I can teach myself a new career in data analytics, then what can't I learn?

It has opened a lot of mental doors for me. Since I got into data there have been several occasions when I've thought, "You know what, I bet I can just teach myself to do this!" One example of this is a bird box—a clear box I put in the window that has bird food in it—that I built for my window next to my desk at home. Now I have mourning doves and sparrows hanging out right next to my desk all day long. I first saw it online and decided, "You know what? I bet I could learn to make one."

Starting the Job

In the time between accepting your job and starting, you may feel like you should somehow be studying. I certainly did! However, I developed COVID a few days before starting my job, so I spent the weekend sleeping, coughing, and trying to get better. I'm glad that I didn't spend that time stressed, anxious, and trying to find something to study!

During your first week at a new job, especially as a first-time data analyst, you are not expected to be an expert! Anyone who hires an entry-level data analyst does it with the intention of training them. What your boss needs from you in your first week on the job is for you to show up ready to learn, without ego. My advice is that you fight any imposter syndrome that threatens to make its way in (more about that in the next section) and remind yourself that the company already saw your skills and abilities and decided to hire you; you are there for a reason and now it is time to focus on doing the best you can.

For most people, their first week on the job is spent getting to know their team structure, getting access to all the different technical systems, and learning the weekly cadence of meetings and responsibilities. There is often not much actual work that gets done in the first week, because all those other things take up a lot of time.

My first week on the job I spent a lot of time meeting with and shadowing my boss. He introduced me to the development plan he had for me over the next several months and showed me what the day-to-day of the job would look like. I was excited about the role—I could hardly wait to jump in and start learning. I could sense that my boss was thankful to have someone who was so positive and eager to learn.

Over the course of the first few weeks, I started getting projects to work on that gave my boss a better sense of my technical level, which gave him a more informed sense of what areas I would need the most development in, what my learning style was, and what I was strong in. I never felt like I was being judged or like there was some technical benchmark that I was expected to meet. It was just him doing his job as my boss to take the time to make sure he was scaling me for success.

Dealing with Imposter Syndrome

For the first six months of my job, there was some part of me that felt like I didn't deserve to be there and at any time they might change their mind and take my job away or cut my salary. That day didn't come, and instead my boss regularly congratulated me on my quick learning and progress. Despite what he said about how happy he was with my performance, I still had that lurking fear.

That was a form of *imposter syndrome*. I've spoken with countless other data analysts who also encountered imposter syndrome when they started their jobs, especially people who changed careers. It is common to feel like you are in over your head, like you somehow slipped past everyone without having the needed skills, or like your manager will change their mind at any moment and get rid of you.

Fortunately, hiring managers usually do a pretty good job, and they know what they are looking for in candidates. So, if they interviewed you—and many other people—and they chose you, then that means that you are the right fit for the job. You do need to continue to learn and grow over time, but that doesn't mean you have to be an expert right away. Give yourself permission to be new, because your employer should (and most likely will) as well.

Many hiring managers have been in data for so long that they have forgotten what it feels like to be new. When you have one-on-ones with your manager (which is common in tech), do not be afraid to bring up your feelings of anxiety or worry so that you can address them. You can even come up with a development plan for the future if that would help you feel more comfortable.

A common joke among tech workers is "If my boss could see the history of things I have to Google every day, I think they would fire me." It is universal—we all have to look things up!

Steps to Success

Some companies are more organized than others. In some roles you may have a clear understanding of your objectives, growth plan, and what success will look like in your first 60 to 90 days. Others will not be so structured, and it will be up to you to ask or figure that out.

Before starting my job, I was advised to ask about what success would look like in my first 60–90 days on the job. I liked this advice, and something I added to it is that it's important as a data analyst to understand how the work you do is directly tied to business objectives. Your success needs to be tied to the business's success.

In the first week at my first job, I asked my boss about what success would look like at month 1, month 3, and month 6. It gave me a clear understanding that the first month would be mostly dedicated to training; by month 3, I would be taking on my own customer projects; and at month 6 I would be operating mostly independently on consulting engagements, with support and oversight from my boss as needed. Some places have a formal process for this called a 30/60/90 (day) plan.

This gave me a clear understanding of what I was working toward, so I knew how to focus my attention. Since I worked at a small consulting organization, it was clear to me how the work I was doing was tied to the business objectives; the main form of income of my company came from consultants billing the hours of their client projects.

I have friends who are/were in more traditional data analyst roles, and I've heard that those are harder to tie to business objectives. Typically, entry-level data analysts are being asked to create reports that their boss has scoped and come up with—and it can feel many steps removed from actually supporting the bottom line of the business.

When I talk with senior data analysts, directors, and executives, they often emphasize the importance of understanding how your role ties to the larger goals of the business. This will make you a more valuable data analyst, which will in turn accelerate your career and make you more valuable to the team. When you start your role, it is the perfect time to ask questions and start familiarizing yourself with how the work that you'll be doing will directly contribute to the larger goals of the business.

What It's Like Working Remotely

I'd never had the pleasure of working remotely until I got a tech job. I knew I wanted to work from home, but I didn't know what it would be like. I have to tell you it has been one of the best things to ever happen to me. I love working remotely, and it has changed my life in more ways than one.

In my old jobs, I worked on a schedule (like 9 a.m.–5 p.m.). I got a scheduled lunch break every day, but other than that, I was tied to that schedule. There are some remote tech jobs that are not as flexible as what I have experienced, but my role was both remote and flexible.

Now my normal day is very flexible. I am not a morning person, and I almost never have morning meetings. So I haven't set an alarm for the past year; I just wake up when I am ready (usually around 8 or 9 a.m.). Then I will head over to my little office space and get started for the day.

I usually start by checking my Slack and email and getting a sense for my schedule. Then I will spend a few minutes planning out my work for the day and prioritizing. I like to start my mornings with easy development work, things like outlining dashboards or changing formatting. I save emails and meetings until the afternoon if possible.

Some people miss the sense of community you get from an in-office experience, and others have told me that it is much harder for them to be productive when they work from home. However, I do not have any of those issues! I enjoy working independently and being in control of my own schedule. My friends who also enjoy independence and autonomy have told me they thrive in a remote work environment.

I do think it is still possible to have a good workplace culture in an all-remote environment. A common way of fostering community in a remote environment is to have regularly scheduled "office hours" that are hosted by a manager as a time blocked off for analysts to ask questions and get assistance with roadblocks. My company did this for the first six months at my job until they decided to restructure, and upon reflection I'm so thankful for the six months I did get with office hours, because it kept me from feeling alone. It also kept me from getting into situations where I felt like I was just banging my head against the wall looking for a solution and never finding one.

I also had a one-on-one meeting with my manager scheduled weekly. These one-on-ones were a time for me to talk about my projects and development, ask questions, and get emotional support that I needed for my role. The concept of one-on-ones is common in remote work, especially for entry-level data analysts.

One of the benefits of having a flexible, remote job has been that I don't have to work standard hours. Although I do typically still end up working from 9 to 5, that is not always the case. I'll often go grocery shopping, to the gym, or out on walks during the day. I have been lucky enough to be at a company that was okay with me flexing my schedule however I wanted, as long as I was still making my meetings and getting my work done.

The flexibility of being able to go to the gym during the day and then just shift my work to the evening has been very freeing. It helps me avoid traffic and crowds, and it is especially helpful on days where I'm working on a difficult project and need to take a midday break before coming back to it. I would say that at least once a week I end up taking off for a few hours during the day, and then working from 5 to 8 p.m. to make up the time. Sometimes I will make up a few hours over the weekend instead of in the evenings.

It took me a while to become comfortable with the flexible schedule. I would ask my boss if it was okay to do the littlest things, like going on a walk or scheduling a half-hour appointment around lunch time. After a few months I became accustomed to this flexibility; now I just make sure to put things like appointments on my calendar and give my boss a heads-up about any commitments that are going to take more than a few hours out of the "standard" workday. The "standard" schedule is flexible, because my co-workers and customers live all over the country. I work on Eastern Standard Time (when I am not traveling), but I have multiple customers on the Pacific Coast and coworkers in every United States time zone.

Some Things About Tech That Surprised Me

I cannot speak for every company, but I noticed when I got into tech that some things that were new to me are common/expected. From 121s to setup stipends, here are the common things that surprised me.

121s

The 121 stands for "one-on-one" with your manager. This is typically a once-a-week or once-a-month meeting with a manager to check in on your progress, goals, and experiences. They are also called "one-on-ones" or "one to ones", which can be typed out as "1:1," "1x1," "121," or "1-1" (I usually title the meeting "Annie <> Manager- 1:1"). I'm sure other professions have them, but I hadn't yet encountered them as a standard practice before getting into tech.

I typically use the meeting time to mostly socialize with my manager with a work-related focus, because I am pretty communicative throughout the week about what is going on, and if I have a roadblock, I'll likely reach out before a formally scheduled meeting. However, even my own coworkers have told me that they do follow a more formal format with their one-on-ones, because that's how they prefer to do it.

Some of my friends have told me that they only get a monthly one-on-one with their boss, and it always feels rushed. They have also expressed that they do not get to communicate with their boss very often in general due to busyness. That worked fine for them because a lot of their job revolved around building slightly different versions of the same reports in Excel and SQL, so they didn't need regular contact with their bosses except to be assigned new work.

Home Office Stipend

It is common for remote tech jobs to offer a home office stipend. As of this writing, around $1,500 is a normal amount for this in the United States. This stipend can be used for purchasing a work laptop, headset, second monitor, or other home office supplies. Each company has its own way of doing this; they may send you a preloaded card to use or reimburse you for using your own. Some companies will require you to send your work laptop to them when your employment is over; others will let you keep it.

Alternatively, your company may send you a work laptop. There is almost no chance that a company would hire you as an entry-level data analyst and expect you to have your own expensive laptop with a good processor. At my first job, I was able to purchase my own and be reimbursed, and I chose a Dell Latitude with a core i7 processor. It has worked great!

Company Party / Offsites

Another phenomenon in the world of remote work is a companywide get-together. I was astonished to realize that even small companies will often host a yearly get-together and pay for employees' flights and hotels for the occasion. I have been in the world of tech for only one year now, and this past January we all got together in Texas at a resort for a few days to have our yearly kickoff.

Another example is *off-sites*. In-office jobs will typically have an off-site day where they get together for team-bonding activities and maybe have some presentations. Remote companies may have a virtual off-site, which is usually reserved for presentations about the company (potentially to announce a new strategic direction or company restructuring). Typically, on virtual off-site days you'll be encouraged to order lunch and expense it.

Meetings

There is a different set of etiquette rules for in-person meetings than there is for virtual meetings. The number-one rule for virtual meetings is to learn how to operate your mute button! One of the most common meeting interrupters is people who think they are muted and are not (and start talking to someone in the background over the presenter), or people who think they are unmuted and are not (and awkwardly miss their moment to speak).

Each company and team will set their own policies and expectations for on-camera versus off-camera work. When you start in a new role, it is always best to check with your team about these expectations. For example, in my meetings with clients I always have my camera on, in meetings with my team I usually have it on, but for all-hands staff meetings I never have it on.

I've noticed that sometimes when I'm taking part in on-camera meetings with executives they'll be multitasking during the meeting—you can see them clicking around and sending emails. It took a bit of time for me to get used to that—because everyone's camera is right in front of them, it is surprising to see someone multitasking and not paying attention right in front of your face on the screen.

One of the nice things about working remotely is that you don't have to dress up as nicely. It definitely takes some getting used to when you start tuning into meetings with a relatively nice shirt over your comfy sweatpants. Now that I have experienced meetings in sweatpants, it's hard to think about ever going back! In general, in-office meetings tend to call for a more formal dress code than virtual, but that is of course dependent on the situation.

Another surprising thing to me about meetings is how easy it is to schedule them. Many people will now have a calendar link at the bottom of their email signature, which you can access at any time to put a meeting on their calendar in times that they have specified as open for meetings. However, I caution you to always make sure these meetings end up on your calendar as well so you won't forget them. I have Slack and Outlook notifications turned on so that five minutes before every meeting I get a reminder; otherwise, I know I would forget and miss them!

When you are looking at someone's calendar to schedule a meeting, if it is internal and you can see what is on their calendar, take a look at how many back-to-back meetings they have right before that. Many people in tech complain about how sometimes they will get a full day of back-to-back meetings put on their calendar because there is space available—but it is exhausting to go from one to the next without any breaks. If you were in person, there would naturally be more of a break built in between meetings due to location changes, but virtual scheduling tools do not add that buffer.

Referrals

In the world of tech, getting a referral to a job is a surprisingly big deal—especially if you want to go for jobs at bigger/more well-known companies. It is true in every industry that having a friend on the inside to refer you is helpful when you're trying to get hired. The difference that I have seen with tech jobs is that referrals are more formal and can help you with the interview process in a special way.

If you're applying for a competitive, remote tech job with a decent salary, then the chances are high you are one of many applicants. Having a formal referral in the system can help take your application to the front of the pile to be considered, which may help you with getting through the interview process more quickly.

If the person referring you has either a good working relationship with or authority over the hiring manager, then in addition to expediting your application process, the referral has the added benefit of hopefully casting you in a favorable light with the hiring manager as they review your materials.

A friend of mine co-founded a company called Refer Me (www.refer.me), a website where you can give and get referrals to jobs. It is mainly focused on the world of software engineering, but it's still worth taking a look. My friend is a software engineer at a top company, and he has personally seen the power of referrals (in the very competitive world of software engineering, referrals are an even bigger deal than in data analytics), and he wanted to share that opportunity with others who, like him, do not come from a wealthy and well-connected background.

Layoffs

Unfortunately, in the tech world layoffs are a fairly common occurrence. I entered the industry at a weird time. It was after the COVID layoffs, and after the economic downturn after the post-COVID period of growth. So, around the time that I started looking for my first job in data, big companies started having layoffs.

Layoffs used to be a sign of failure, but now they are a savvy business decision. Some companies intentionally over-hire to show growth and chase various initiatives, knowing that when the economy takes a hit, they'll need to do a round or two of layoffs. Of course, not every company is like this! Most small businesses cannot afford to operate this way. But it hurts everyone when the market gets flooded with great talent from companies such as Google, because the domino effect is that they take the jobs that are available.

When I started my job, the first thing I did was set up a savings plan in case of layoff. I put away enough money to keep me going for many months if anything unexpected were to happen to my job. Only then was I able to think about other things (like student loans). Always be prepared for a layoff if you work in tech, especially if the economy is struggling.

I've heard hundreds of stories from people in the last year who worked for their company for years, sometimes over a decade, and their employment was cut off in an instant by a layoff. Many people had no idea it was coming, and they got completely locked out of all of their work-related systems at the moment they were laid off.

It is not a personal decision; many people who have been laid off are incredibly talented and were acing every performance review. It is just a business decision that is made without your input. As I was writing the third section of this book I was laid off, so the final chapter in this book will be dedicated to preparing for and recovering from a layoff.

When I was laid off, even though I was already searching for a new role to leave the company, in part because they didn't have enough work for me, I *still* struggled not to take it personally. Even if you are prepared for it, everyone who goes through a layoff needs a few days to manage the usually fairly emotional process.

Problem-Solving

Your most valuable skill as a data analyst is to solve problems. There is not a "right way" to solve problems. Each one will call for its own approach. Here's a tip I learned while I was in graduate school that I've seen echoed by my boss as well as many other analytics leaders: If you get stuck on something, be prepared to share three troubleshooting steps you took to solve it before going to your boss.

For example, let's say you need to join several tables together to make a report to send over to sales, but you cannot get the dates to aggregate to show monthly data per person correctly. Your first troubleshooting step might be keeping track of all the different solutions you can think of, including variations of GROUP BY. Next up might be a Google search and spending some time on Stack Overflow (a website where you can see questions that have already been asked by other people about code, and the answers to the questions). Finally, you might check similar reports that your coworkers have run in the past to see how they wrote the SQL.

In that process, you might find that you come to an answer and the problem is solved. If not, when you bring not only the problem you faced but also the solutions you tried to your boss, then they are better prepared to help you—and they can see that you are trying. This seems like a small tip, but I have heard it emphasized by so many people that it is still a worthwhile addition.

Travel

I cannot write about how to be a data analyst without including a section on travel while working remotely. In the past year, I've only spent about 65 percent of my time at home. The rest of the time has been spent traveling. I have been to New Zealand, Australia, Vermont, New York, North Carolina, Texas, and Nevada. By the end of the year I will add England, Canada, Tennessee, and Alabama to the list (at a minimum!).

One of the reasons I changed careers to become a data analyst was to give me the freedom to travel, and travel I have! Some of these travels have been alone, but much of it is to see my friends and family. I will often go for a week or two at a time, and so I work remotely. This means I don't have to take time off work; I just need to be smart about balancing my time spent working with socializing.

People have been telling me all year, "I would hate to have to work while I was on vacation," but the way I see it is that really, I am traveling, not vacationing. Since I do not want to have to quit my job each time I want to travel, my options are to either work remotely from home and *not* travel, or work remotely while traveling.

It was an incredibly powerful feeling to be standing on a beach, alone, in New Zealand after a month of solo travel, just one year after deciding I wanted to switch careers so that I could travel more.

To facilitate truly working while I travel, I've learned some tricks to help me out:

- I normally use a detached keyboard and vertical mouse on my computer at home, but I have a second mouse for travel, and I leave my keyboard at home when I fly.
- I bought a portable second monitor that attaches to the back of my computer with some magnets so I can have a second screen no matter where I am.
- When I started my job, they gave me a stipend to buy a laptop. I chose one that is small and lightweight, well suited for travel.

- I invented a silly little cable organizer using a microfiber cloth with some pipe cleaners (from a craft supply store) threaded through it that hold each cord individually, and then I can wrap it up so I never lose or tangle my many cords (see Figure 13.1).
- I have a nice noise-canceling headset so I can take calls from anywhere, including busy coffee shops.
- I tried a mouse with a trackball for working in cramped spaces where I would not have the space to use a normal mouse, but I ended up not using it.
- For my personal supplies, I got a suitcase that doubles as a closet organizer so I can just take the organizer out of the suitcase, hang it up, and all of my clothes are easily set up in "shelves."
- My travel kit is my work backpack with my laptop and computer supplies, my suitcase, a packable backpack rolled up inside the suitcase that I can use for adventures, and a thin cloth bag for laundry.

I like to travel cheaply, so I seek out hostels whenever I can. I was nervous about staying in hostels while also needing to get up early for work, but so far I haven't had any issues. I find that staying in hostels is a great deal for travel because they give me access to a kitchen (huge money saver while traveling), a comfortable common area with strong Wi-Fi, and a perfectly fine bed.

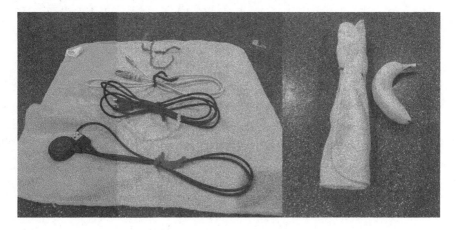

Figure 13.1 The microfiber cloth and pipe cleaner contraption I made for organizing my cables.

I have spent over 30 nights in hostels in the past year and experienced only one night with noisy neighbors. It was the night of the Super Bowl; I was in New Zealand, and my American neighbors were watching it in the shared sleeping space. Otherwise, staying in hostels has been a lovely way to meet people, and they offer an affordable space to get work done and explore the local area after work.

Data Has Changed My Life

Getting a remote job as a data analyst has changed my life. I am happier and healthier, I spend more time with my family and friends, and I've saved a lot of time and money by not having to commute. On Sundays I no longer get the "Sunday Scaries" where I dread having to work the following day, because I truly enjoy what I do.

I am so happy to say that I still enjoy my work as a data analyst, and feel true excitement and enthusiasm for continuing to learn and pursue my career. Although I do enjoy traveling and having a good work–life balance, I do spend a lot of free time online talking about data or upskilling to learn new skills and work on personal projects. Not everybody is going to love data as much as I do, but my data analyst friends and I routinely reflect on how happy we are to have jobs that we love, with a whole career of learning and progressing in front of us.

My friends and family have told me that although I have changed a lot since getting into data analytics, it feels like I have just peeled the layers of my personality back and they are seeing more of my true self than ever before. As I write this chapter I am closing in on the end of my second job search as a data analyst (which was easier than the first now that I have experience!), and I feel incredibly grateful to have found a career that I love, I am good at, and that affords me the kind of flexibility and freedom I want out of life.

I hope that by reading this book it can make your journey of getting into data analytics easier than it was for me, and at the end of it you too can find a job and lifestyle you love.

14 | Preparing for/ Recovering from a Layoff

I want to take a chapter to talk about something that you probably are not ready to think about yet—your *next* job search. There will come a day when you are ready. For me, it came sooner than I expected.

Don't Ignore Red Flags

About six months after I got my first data analyst job, I started to see some red flags. Although I loved being a consultant and the work I was doing, my company make decisions that changed the working environment—and not for the better. I felt "squeezed" by my company for all of February (my seventh month on the job); there was not enough work for me and my team to do, but they wanted us to be getting as much work as possible out of our clients.

Then, at the end of February they laid off some of my coworkers in customer success and operations. None of the data analysts were laid off, but I did not feel safe. I'd heard for months how companies had been laying off people left and right, even loyal, talented, hardworking employees. My company assured us that our jobs were safe and that they valued us as employees—and then turned around and encouraged my boss to help us find ways to upskill on our own time, that we did not get paid for, to learn more skills that would benefit the business (with no intention of giving us a raise).

It was at that moment that I decided I needed to prepare myself for the possibility of a layoff—or quitting. I could tell that my entire team was dissatisfied with the new direction of the company, and I worried that if senior consultants were laid off, then I would be left with work that I was not equipped to do—and I would have to decide whether to stay and figure it out on my own or leave.

The thought of job searching again after less than a year at my job made my stomach hurt. I do not feel any need to be overly "loyal" to any company—a job is a job. But I still worried about the optics of leaving my first role in less than a year (voluntarily or involuntarily). A popular topic among data influencers is that you can job-hop your way to a great salary in data analytics, but I was happy with my salary and was just looking for stability and a place to learn and be happy!

I also hated job searching the first time around. As you read in Chapter 12, "My Job Search," my experience was difficult and full of uncertainty, insecurity, and lots of wasted time. I didn't want to go through that again. However, I also knew that if I didn't prepare ahead of time and then got hit with a surprise layoff or a huge change in my job, it would be even worse.

So, I started to lay the groundwork and prepare myself for whatever may come. The first thing I did was look over all my projects and identify the best examples of my finest work as an analyst. Then, I took those projects and deidentified the work (I changed the names of tables and columns so that the original client could not be identified) and put them right into my portfolio. This was mostly complicated SQL I'd written for specific use cases. I'd created some long and complicated SQL queries to shape data in a certain way that I knew would be a great addition to my portfolio.

It was around that time that I started reflecting on and keeping track of my skills and accomplishments since starting my job, to get ready for updating my résumé. After a month of building up that document, I returned to Teal (the job search tool) along with my new "personal assistant" ChatGPT to update my résumé.

Resumes and Networking—Restarting the Job Search

Updating my résumé to reflect my new skills was much simpler (and less stressful) than creating it for the first time. It helped that I now had insight into the data industry, so I knew what kinds of things employers might be looking for. I was excited to realize that I had relevant experience, and so I could think about getting some impressive metrics into my résumé.

Since I am a content creator as well as a data analyst, I talk to a lot of people about their data careers. Around the time that I was working on my résumé, I started to pay attention to how my friends and peers were faring in their job searches. I wanted to know if people with a year or more of experience in data were able to quickly find a new job after getting laid off (or deciding to find a new job). What I started to hear, overwhelmingly, was that the job market was not great. There were many great candidates on the market post-layoffs and not many open jobs.

I also heard stories about how people were interviewing for jobs, only to find out later that the company decided not to hire anyone for the role after all. It appeared that applying for jobs was a possibility but not a quick or easy process.

I also saw a handful of stories from people who had gotten jobs through connections from LinkedIn or real life. Or they were connected with a recruiter who posted a job. Or a friend of theirs who knew they were on the hunt saw a job posting that they connected them with.

So, I decided to give networking a shot. My first move was to strike up a conversation with each of my data friends and casually mention that I might be job searching soon. I also took the opportunity to ask for tips and advice from people with more experience than me. Most people who have been in data analytics for more than a year or so have experience with job hopping or layoffs, so they had great tips. I was doing a livestreamed coffee chat series on LinkedIn and YouTube at the time, and if you check out my videos from March to May of 2023, I talked about the subject with more than one senior data analyst. You can find the videos here: `https://youtube .com/playlist?list=PL3wILOBlsv2vf8aAjTQXo017YntAXqrZc`.

Next, I signed up for the Tableau Conference. I'd been considering attending, because it seemed like a fun event and a good chance to hang out with like-minded people. I'd spent the past year using Tableau almost daily, so I knew that my best shot at getting a new job would probably come from leveraging my Tableau experience. Plus, I loved being a Tableau consultant and hoped to keep consulting if possible.

I'd been on the fence about attending because the price tag was steep. I would have to fly to Las Vegas, get accommodations for a week, and buy the conference ticket ($1,600). Eventually I decided that it was worth the price if it would land me a new job, but I don't think I would've gone otherwise.

I had a great time at the conference. I met about a dozen other consultants who were doing work similar to my own. They were all there with their companies—and their companies had paid for their tickets and accommodations. It seemed like the obvious move, especially the ones whose companies are partnered with Tableau.

Ironically, my company did not pay for my entrance to the conference, let alone anything else. Not only that, but normally I was given some professional development hours each week for learning, and when I submitted time logs for the specific sessions that I went to, they rejected every single one. I added that to the list of reasons why I needed to find a new job. A company that is not interested in the professional development of their employees is not a good fit for me.

Altogether I spent over $2,000 to attend the conference, not including meals. From the moment I stepped foot on the conference floor until the day I left, I was on the lookout for opportunities to network. Prior to the conference, to maximize my networking I had reached out to any connections I had who might be at the conference or know people there, so I was busy from day one.

By the time I left the conference, I had met my new employer. I just didn't know it yet. I had a great time; I learned a lot, and I met many interesting people. While I was there, I interviewed for two jobs and made connections with four small Tableau-focused consulting organizations. I'm so glad that I went, but I also got lucky in that I was able to go to the Tableau Conference as a Tableau consultant. Without experience in such a niche area of data analytics, it wouldn't have been a successful networking event.

I did not end up getting offered either of the positions I interviewed for while I was at the conference, but interestingly, my (now former) boss did. I interviewed for a consulting role that seemed awesome but out of my league. I had interviewed with the CEO of the company, and at the end of the interview I told him plainly that it was probably not a good fit for me but I knew the *perfect* person for the role. They connected on LinkedIn, and a month later my former boss started his new job. It gave him a salary bump, and he has thanked me at least five times because he is so happy at his new job.

An additional networking step I took before the conference was reaching out to some of the speakers of the sessions I was most excited to attend.

As a content creator, I know that I enjoy when my followers engage with my content and are excited about talking about the subjects that interest me. So I thought that the conference speakers might enjoy attendees of their sessions being excited to engage in their areas of expertise as well.

Some of the speakers I messaged did not respond to me, but some did, with interest! At the conference I talked to a few of the speakers after their sessions, and I was so glad that I had made a personal connection with them beforehand and was able to follow up on it in person. One of the people I reached out to was speaking at a Women in Data Strategy panel, the session I was the most excited to attend. After her session we spent at least 10 minutes talking before she asked about connecting on LinkedIn, which is when I revealed that I had reached out to her before the conference.

Her face lit up right away after I told her, and she said, "Oh, that was you? I loved that!" We ended up talking for another 5–10 minutes, and I could tell I left a positive impression on her. You'll hear more about this story soon! I did not think much of it at the time, but this interaction ended up becoming more significant than I could've guessed.

I'd stayed up well into the night with new friends and connections every night that week. After the conference, I came home and caught up on about a week's worth of sleep, and then I got to work. Being at the conference and attending all of the post-conference networking events and social hangouts made me realize how strong the Tableau community is. It is filled with people who are excited to share their passion about data with one another, on and offline. This ignited a fire in me to build my portfolio, including some good Tableau projects, and to be the best candidate I could be.

Updating My Portfolio

I spent the next month or so hard at work on my portfolio and portfolio website. I knew I would not be a strong candidate until I had a good portfolio to showcase how my skills had progressed. Coincidentally, that was the same period of time when I was working on writing Part II of this book, "The Scary Part."

Coincidentally, once I posted the work that I had done on my portfolio, one of my Tableau dashboards went "viral" on Tableau Public and attracted a lot of attention (thousands of views), which led to two different companies reaching out and offering me jobs based on what they'd seen in my projects and on my social media profiles. Those jobs ended up being not quite what I was looking for—I would've just been an order taker and limited to only using Tableau (not SQL or other analytics tools). I did not want to step down in responsibility, autonomy, and technical ability, so I thanked them but declined the jobs.

At around that time, the speaker at the conference with whom I had connected reached out to me. She said that she might be posting a data analyst job and she was wondering if I was interested. At the time I wasn't interested in leaving consulting, but when she explained the role to me and what she was trying to accomplish, it sounded like an interesting project and a great development opportunity, so I said yes.

As a summary, here are the things I did to prepare for being laid off:

- Update my portfolio.
- Keep track of my work accomplishments.
- Update my résumé.
- Stay open to connecting with people hiring for different roles.
- Upskill key data analytics skills for *me*, so that I can take those skills with me to the next job.

At the same time that I finished writing Part II, I got laid off. I was immensely thankful that my résumé and portfolio were ready to go and that I hadn't been caught completely off guard.

On the day I was laid off, I had an interview already scheduled with another Tableau consulting organization. That role did not end up being a fit for me, but I was thankful to have another possibility to occupy my brain on that strange day.

The Layoff

Although I was planning to leave my job already by that point, getting laid off was an odd experience. I made a TikTok video about what it was like to get laid off, and it has gotten over a million views. As it turned out, my experience with the layoff was common and resonated with a lot of people. Here's what it was like for me.

For a month I had a somewhat low pipeline, meaning my company was not making enough sales to fully support my role. I was suspicious that they might lay one of us off, but then I started working with a large new client. The following week, on Wednesday evening, my boss's boss put a "one-on-one sync" on my calendar. I was not having regular one-on-ones with her, so I was very suspicious. I texted my coworkers and my boss right away. Neither of my coworkers had gotten such a request on their calendar, but my boss assured me I had just gotten the big new client and so there was no way they were going to get rid of me.

The next morning, I was still highly suspicious of what was coming next, so I set up a video of myself on the call. When I joined the one-on-one call, the CEO of the company was also on the call. I knew then that it was over for me, so I just sat back in my chair and listened to what they had to say.

They explained to me that due to the lack of sales to support my consulting role, that would be my last day. While I was on the call I could see my Slack, Dropbox, and email all go blank—I was locked out. They said that it was not a choice made lightly or based on performance. They offered to provide referrals if needed, then gave me about two weeks' worth of severance and allowed me to stay on their health insurance through the following month (the end of July). After that I would need to choose if I wanted to get COBRA, which is a temporary coverage option that people from the United States can use to continue the same health care plan after losing their job—but you pay both your premium and your employer's premium, so it is more expensive.

I had some expensive medical appointments coming up, so I was relieved to be able to keep my health insurance. I felt somewhat sick to my stomach when I was logging on to the call because of the anxiety, but once it was over, I felt all the tension leave my body in a wave, and I just felt relieved to be done with it.

It felt odd to lose my job like that. It was incredibly depersonalizing—I had been working for this company for almost a year and during that time, I'd developed relationships with my customers and my coworkers. Plus, I was right in the middle of a few projects! They moved all my projects to my boss. (He was just as surprised as I was to hear about the layoff, and very unhappy about it. You know from my story earlier that he left the company shortly thereafter, thanks to the job I found for him.)

To have all of those relationships and projects just cut off in an instant was what felt so strange. It was especially strange to me because my company had asked us to be "all hands on deck" for months, and I'd felt pressure to work even outside of normal working hours to meet my weekly hours quota. I'd also been doing nonbillable work (work that I did not get paid for) to meet my customers' needs. When traveling in New Zealand, I'd changed and canceled plans in order to squeeze in extra hours—and I spent so much time worrying and being anxious on behalf of my company.

After all of that, when it came time, my employment ended instantly. No chance to say goodbye to my coworkers, or even think about wrapping up my projects. My employment was no more than a business decision. I think it is okay that my employment was (and always will be) just a business decision, but it is important for everyone to know that this is the case.

I'm so glad that I saw the writing on the wall months before and started to focus on upskilling for *my* sake. Instead of putting in extra time and upskilling on behalf of my company, I spent my time in the spring doing those things for me and for the sake of my career development. Then when I lost my job, I was able to take those skills, and portfolio projects, with me.

The company I worked for won a "best places to work" award in the winter shortly before making a lot of changes that made me think about leaving. When I started there, I truly felt committed to the company and believed that they cared about me and my teammates. This experience was able to give me the context I needed—it reminded me that a job is just a job, and my employment is just a business decision. If I hadn't learned this, I would've likely ended up in a situation where I overcommitted to a company and put in extra work that was for their benefit and not for mine.

I spent the first week after losing my job mostly lying in bed and writing Part III, "The Hard Part," of this book. I was not lounging in bed because I was depressed; I was just thoroughly enjoying getting an unexpected vacation and being able to fully relax. I also had a few different job interviews during that time, which helped keep me from constantly worrying about getting a new job.

During that week I reached out to the woman I had met while at the conference, let her know I was available, and expressed an interest in working with her. She'd told me the last time we'd spoken that she wouldn't know officially if she was posting the job for another month and a half. But after I reached out, I got a response that she had just made the decision that she would be posting that position and was interested in having me apply.

Over the next month, I got the opportunity to interview at several different companies. These interviews resulted from a combination of referrals from friends in my network (to whom I reached out at the start of the job search) and people I met at the conference.

These were all interesting roles, mostly in Tableau consulting, but I had actually decided by that point that I was most interested in the (nonconsulting) position with the woman whom I had gotten connected with at the conference. I realized that it would be a good chance for me to take a career step up and work in a long-term role solving problems that I wouldn't get the chance to solve if I was working in small 40–80-hour "buckets" of consulting hours. My customers would purchase a "bucket" of hours, and I would bill against that and stop when I ran out.

The connection I made at the conference ended up being the vice president of Data and Analytics at GitLab, and she was looking for a data analyst who had a background like mine and experience using Tableau. She messaged me the day the role was posted to invite me to apply—which I did promptly. I'd already heard of GitLab and only positive things about it. All my application materials were ready to go so I could apply right away when the role opened.

I knew that it was important for me to keep interviewing for other roles even though I felt like a strong candidate and had prioritized GitLab. The worst thing I could do to myself would be to get complacent and focus on the position at GitLab, only to have something happen and not be offered that role and be left with no options. That would have been incredibly discouraging.

Six interviews and over a month later, I was offered a data analyst position at GitLab! The story of how I found the role and subsequent interviews is a success story of networking. I never would've found that role if I hadn't gone to the Tableau Conference and put myself out there to network. Then, when I applied, I was able to do so with a referral from an executive!

Within the first few days of the role being posted, over a thousand people had clicked Apply on the posting on LinkedIn (I know this because LinkedIn made that data available for me to see). GitLab is a well known, fully remote company. The top of the salary range for the mid-level role was listed at a very competitive rate (over $130,000). Given this information, I can imagine that over a thousand applicants applied for this role.

When I looked at the job posting, I could tell that I would be a perfect fit for the role. I could see why my connection from the conference had reached out to me. The job posting was for someone with strong Tableau experience to help lead the way as GitLab transitioned from another visualization tool into Tableau to gain insights across all of GitLab (as opposed to being siloed to one department, such as a sales data analyst).

As a consultant, that's exactly the type of work I was doing. As I went down the bullet points of requirements in the job posting, I met almost every one. *But* I had only been a data analyst for one year, which isn't a terribly long time. The referral (from an executive) ensured I got the chance to get in and show off my skills.

In fact, about halfway through the interview process the recruiter called me to let me know that I had been leveled as a "junior," which is different from what the role was posted at (mid-level). I would have needed two years of experience to qualify for mid-level. She emphasized that everyone had been impressed with me and they wanted to continue interviewing me for the role. But I would only qualify for the "junior" pay band, which would not be what I had seen on the posting. The job title was just "data analyst"—the "junior" thing only came into play with salary. But it likely would've held me back from being able to show off my skills without a referral.

The interviews all went well. Instead of coming in unknown and feeling like I needed to prove myself, I had a little bit of a leg up. I knew I had a referral, and I was early, so they hadn't seen many other qualified candidates. This helped me approach my interviews with more confidence and just focus on selling myself.

When I interviewed for this role (and all the others that I was connected with this time around), I approached it as I would approach a consulting engagement. Instead of focusing on what the company could do for me, I thought of it as the first day of a new project, and I was gathering the information I needed to get started solving the problem that this role was looking to solve.

The six interview steps I went through in the GitLab interview process were a recruiter phone screen, meeting with the hiring manager (behavioral), a technical take-home plus a Zoom interview to review my answers, a meeting with a key stakeholder of the role, and an executive interview (with the executive I met at the conference). The length of this process is common for data analyst positions that are above entry-level.

I felt *much* less nervous about interviews the second time around. I had a year under my belt talking about my data analytics work and meeting with stakeholders. I also felt confident in my answers, knowing I had good experience solving problems with data (and getting paid to do it). It helped that I had started preparing six months prior; in that time I'd kept careful notes on my learning, challenges, and accomplishments, and boosted my portfolio. If I hadn't been thinking about the possibility of needing to job search again when I got laid off, I likely would've felt like I was scrambling to get myself prepared while also dealing with the sting of an unexpected rejection.

Adjusting for Your Situation

I was very privileged to be in a good position when I lost my job—many people are not so lucky. My advice for someone who has been laid off would be to take some time to themselves and enjoy a break between jobs if they are able to financially. It was healthy for me to take a few weeks to reflect on my employment and get some rest. However, I recognize that this advice would be insensitive to someone who immediately has to worry about their ability to pay their bills and get a new job the minute they get laid off.

Unfortunately, working in the tech industry means you should always be prepared for the possibility that you might get laid off. The tech industry is prone to layoffs—and many companies haven't learned how to tie their data analytics teams to revenue and business value yet, so as a cost-saving measure the data teams get cut when the company hits hard times.

Preparing for a layoff or even just keeping an eye open for your next step does not make you a disloyal employee. It is just an important part of putting yourself, and your career, first. Your job is your paycheck; your employment is a business decision on behalf of your employer, and you'll keep your job as long as you are still benefiting their business. They know that, and so it is important for you to understand and remind yourself of that as well.

Many people feel pressure from themselves or their employers to put in 110 percent at their jobs. And to what end? If you are in a salaried position, do you make more money when you sacrifice your holidays? When the company is struggling for money, are they going to remember the times you turned down going out to dinner with friends so you could work late? No.

Of course, hard work is essential to career progression. It could land you a promotion or bring you to your next great role. I am not advising you to slack off, or put in "the bare minimum" at work. What I'm encouraging you to do is to remember that no matter how great your job is, it is just a job. In my opinion, if you're going to go above and beyond to work hard, then make sure you're doing it for you and your career progression, not just for the benefit of your company.

I hope that hearing my story has been helpful to you. I know that hearing many other people's layoff stories over the last six months is the reason I was able to recognize when it was time to prepare for one happening to me.

Closing Thoughts

Well, there you have it. This is everything I know about becoming a data analyst alongside my own experiences, wrapped into one book. I appreciate you coming along for the ride. And if you are one of my friends and followers who have been with me for any part of this journey, thank you.

My hope is that you can use this book to help you make a plan and stick to it. You can learn all the technical skills you need to know to become a data analyst online, and you don't have to spend a lot of money! I'm just one of many people who have left burnout and their old career behind to jump into data.

Your roadmap will not be as linear as the four distinct parts of this book. You might start a LinkedIn at the beginning of the journey (which was covered in Part III), then start learning SQL (Part I), then do a project using SQL (Part II), share it to your budding network (Part III), and then go back to learning Tableau (Part I)!

While you are working on setting up your LinkedIn profile and making connections in the data space, I'd love to hear your key takeaways from this book and how it has helped you. Content creation is a labor of love for me, and when I hear how my words resonate and help others, it lets me know what subjects I should put more energy into talking about. Talking about this book in a post will help you make friends with other people who are learning right now, too.

When it comes your time to learn, share, and create projects, I hope you will remember my advice! Taking time to work on projects—starting with easier projects and working your way up—will pay off when it comes to job searching.

If your job search is not quick and easy, I hope you'll remember the struggles I had with mine. Getting a data analyst job can be challenging for even the best candidates, so you are not alone. I hope that the tips I've shared in this book, particularly Part III, will fuel your search to feel more organized and productive than I did.

Once you get a job in data analytics, it could change your life. Now that you've read my story, you know that it changed mine! Even if you don't land the perfect job right away, keep in mind that it is just step one of a brand-new career. Learn as much as you can, keep updating your portfolio with projects, and then when you're ready to go, you can leverage that experience to get a job more aligned with what you're looking for.

I've included a few appendices in this book as supplemental information that might help you:

- Appendix A: A checklist that can help you build your roadmap into data.
- Appendix B: Tableau tips that I learned as a Tableau consultant that will help you create better projects and build better dashboards.
- Appendix C: A short month-by-month breakdown of my journey to become a data analyst. It brings together the main concepts I talked about throughout this book and joins them into one narrative.

I hope you've enjoyed reading this book, but more important, I hope you love learning data analytics as much as I did and still do! It is a great joy to find an in-demand career that's both enjoyable and pays a good living wage. I wish you the best of luck in your job search, and I hope the resources I've identified as most helpful to me are helpful to you as well.

A
Data Analytics Roadmap Checklist

Do you have a hard time keeping track of all of the steps you need to take to become a data analyst? I took each of the steps outlined in my book and created this checklist for you. You can use this to help you plan your roadmap and keep track.

- Create a data analytics roadmap from start to hired.
  - Pick learning methods/courses ahead of time!
- Create a LinkedIn profile.
- Start posting and networking on LinkedIn with other analysts— *see Chapter 9 for ideas of what to post to get started!*
- Carve out a schedule/learning time.
- Start learning!
  - Excel
  - SQL
  - Tableau and/or Power BI
- Create and publish portfolio projects in these skills.
- Create a portfolio landing page.
- Optimize LinkedIn.
- Write your résumé.
- Review job descriptions.
- Apply for jobs.
  - Don't be afraid to make cold applications.
  - Reach out to recruiters and hiring managers.
  - Create content about your skills (get jobs to come to you!).

- Interview!
- Take a mental health break to manage the stress of job searching/any rejections.
- Negotiate offer letters.
- Start working as a data analyst!

Everything on this checklist is optional. I wrote it in roughly the order that I followed and suggest you follow, but everyone's path is different. Do what works for you—this is just a starting point.

B | Tableau Tips

I happen to be a Tableau consultant, so I didn't want to leave the portfolio section of this book without giving you some Tableau-specific portfolio-building advice—and Tableau advice in general.

To the entry-level data analyst, Tableau is often just a tool for doing visualizations of data—maybe some well-formatted bar charts and line charts put into a dashboard. That's a fine way to look at it, but I invite you to come behind the curtain with me and see how experienced Tableau professionals are leveraging the tool. This will guide you into creating a portfolio that helps you stand out above the rest.

What I Use Tableau For

I've had a dozen clients so far, and they come from different industries. They all have slightly different Tableau needs—from building an externally facing product that is the user interface for *their* customers, to internal reporting, to newsletter-embeddable reports. I've worked with nonprofits that are turning to Tableau as a way to share information between state agencies as well as with analysts who need to enable their internal customer support teams to be alerted to negative trends or individual customers that need attention.

The thing that all my clients have in common is that they needed dashboards that inspire and/or facilitate *action* from their end users. This is the most important distinction between "people who build reports that don't get used" and "people who can build impactful dashboards." So what is the difference? Let's unpack that.

Report Builders	Impactful Dashboard Builders
• Tries to build a dashboard that "does it all"—shows every column and possible metric in the data	• From planning to publishing, considers the end user's needs and purpose for the dashboard
• Is busy, with a lot of ink and information on screen	• Keeps it simple and intuitive
• Places charts at random	• Uses whitespace generously
• Does not apply visual best practices	• Is careful with color, uses color only to make a point
• Uses LOTS of color	• Facilitates action from end users
• Lacks analytical flow	• Has a clear purpose for every chart and the dashboard
• Lacks a clear purpose	
• Only supports the end-user action of looking at the dashboard	
• Requires the end user to export data or go somewhere else to investigate data findings	
• Uses the wrong chart type	

Notice I didn't say anything in there about the technical skills? While being able to understand complicated things such as LODs (level of detail calculations) in Tableau or functions like DAX in Power BI are both vital to the role, they aren't part of the conversation when we're talking about building powerful, effective dashboards that showcase your critical thinking skills.

The first hurdle to overcome when you are considering building effective dashboards is understanding that they are meant to be not an overview or a pretty picture, but a valuable data exploration tool. Sure, you have KPI (key performance indicators) dashboards that are typically more of an overview style, but I never build those as stand-alone dashboards. They always lead to the next dashboard, which is where analysis on the part of the end user happens.

So let's talk about how you can upgrade from "report builder" to "analytics tool builder."

The Why

The first thing you need to decide is "Why am I making this dashboard? What is its purpose?" If you can't come up with a clear purpose other than "It lets me see the data," then you likely don't have a clear enough purpose to create a dashboard.

Let's say you're creating a dashboard for the manager of a sales team. You might say, "Well, they need to get an overview of how their team performed last month." But that's an incomplete purpose. If you ask why, you might find the answer "Because they need to see when the numbers start trending down." Okay, that's getting somewhere now. But what are they going to need to do if the numbers start trending down? You might find that "they'll need to see if it is just one sales rep or all reps who are performing poorly."

Okay, so what happens as a result of one or the other? Well, if it is one employee, then they'll need more detailed information on that employee's timecard, leads, and other information relevant to what they're selling, before they check in with them. But if it's the entire team, then the manager will need to look at seasonal profit trends, potential product changes, and unforeseen production costs that may be impacting sales or profit. Now you know *why* it's worth spending the time to build the dashboard and why the end user would spend their time opening and using it.

Your purpose is "to enable a sales manager to monitor the performance of their team, and dig into the data when sales or profit are trending downward, so they can take the appropriate action to maintain the success of their team." That's much better. And now that you have a purpose, it will help you decide what does, and does *not,* go onto your dashboard(s).

The What

Now that you have a clear purpose in mind, consider what you're going to put on the dashboard. What questions are you asking of the data? What things does your end user need to know? What will they do with that information? At this stage I usually go into Figma and start to outline my dashboard. I call this step *wireframing.*

At this stage you're deciding which questions you want to ask of the data. Typically you ask one question per chart on the dashboard. If you're a beginner, you don't need to decide what kind of chart to use yet—you can just use a text box (or a written box if you are using pen and paper) to put this into the outline. I'll use "sticky notes" in Figma for this step; I like how the sticky notes feel informal and flexible.

Be careful to use your judgment at this step—it is just as important to decide what goes on your dashboard as it is to decide what doesn't. To return to our sales manager example, let's think about what's going into this dashboard. You need to know profit, sales, and potentially costs last month, and a way to compare them to other months and know the trend. You'll also likely want to know about related sales information, such as the number of leads or opportunities and the close rate.

What might you be tempted to put on the dashboard that is not relevant? Well, going back to the purpose, you want to know how your team is doing so that you can intervene if profits start to fall. Some things that might be interesting information but are best left for another dashboard include:

Sales Performance on Each Day of the Week   Although this might be relevant for staffing decisions, you likely aren't concerned about day-to-day profit fluctuations.
Delivery Time for Orders   If profit started to suffer, one step in your analysis might be to investigate operations and their impact on sales; however, that would make this dashboard too busy.
Sales Performance of Other Locations   Again, this would be relevant to a regional manager in *their* dashboard, but this manager is focused on their team and issues that need intervention.

When deciding on the "what," think of many different questions that you could ask of your data, and then keep only the ones that serve the purpose you've selected.

The How

Now you have a purpose and questions to answer. It's time to start thinking about visualizations! When you're deciding on the how, you need to answer two questions: (1) How am I going to display the answers that I find? (2) How am I going to organize the information?

To start answering question 1, it helps to know the possible options of different chart types that you can use to visualize data and which chart types are best suited to different situations. For example, a line chart is good for time-series data, but it shouldn't be used to visualize discrete (independent) categories of data. There are many great resources for this on the Internet; my favorite is a visualization by Tableau master Andy Kriebel. It is called "Visual Vocabulary" and has become a staple in the Tableau world. You can find it at `https://public.tableau.com/app/profile/andy.kriebel/viz/VisualVocabulary/VisualVocabulary`.

Here are general tips:

- BANs (big-ass-numbers) should go at the top or left of your dashboard, unless they are at the top or left of a container that they're directly relevant to.
- People in the analytics world seem to love to hate on pie charts. I think they are okay, but my advice is to consider turning them into a donut chart, and if there are more than three "slices," use a bar chart instead.
- I have mentioned this before, but if you are visualizing categorical data, do it with a bar chart, not a line chart.

The Where

Next up, you need to decide where to put these charts on the dashboard. This step is surprisingly important and incredibly vague when you're a beginner. I had no idea how to lay out a dashboard when I started—I was completely guessing. I've seen people promote "templates" that they use in Tableau when they make dashboards and had to hold my tongue. There are some general "rules" you should follow about layout. For each dashboard I create, I choose a layout that has purpose and analytical flow to it. Don't worry; I am about to explain analytical flow!

In English, we read from left to right and top to bottom. In most cases, this is the order in which your end users will view your dashboard. You want to build with this in mind so that users are following an analytical process as they work through the dashboard. There's a great article that I refer to every time I describe analytical flow and how to lay out a dashboard, which you can find here: `http://duelingdata.blogspot.com/2019/01/5-types-of-dashboards.html`. I see this as essential reading for any new dashboard builder.

My only criticism of that article is that the types of visualizations the author used in the dashboards were advanced. They are beautiful and eye-catching. However, when I used the article with my clients while we were trying to wireframe dashboards together and decide on the layout, they were distracted by the different chart types from one dashboard to the next, instead of absorbing the message of the analytical flow. So, I rebuilt the visualizations using simple data and charts, which I kept consistent through the various dashboards. This way, the person reading can focus on the message of analytical flow; check out the simplified chart types at `https://public.tableau.com/app/profile/anniesanalytics/viz/DuelingDashboards-Simplified/Granularity`.

The Why

Okay, okay, I already had a section on the "why." But I'm including it again at the bottom because it's important that you return to your "why" after you finish answering all the other questions. Especially when you are new to dashboard building, it's easy to get swept away by all the different types of visualizations and ways you could lay out your data, and then suddenly a chart that does not speak to your purpose ends up on the dashboard.

Final Checklist

Finally, let's go over some general visualization best practices:

- Be sparing with color. You want color to make a point and draw attention. It can't do that if there's too much color on your dashboard.
- If you have a bar chart of Sales, do not also color the bars by "sales." This is common and it's redundant. Think about keeping them all the same color, or using something else, such as Category, to color the bars.
- Minimize ink on screen. Simpler is better.
- Move labels and unnecessary/bonus information to your tooltips.
- Hide your axes and column/row headers whenever possible.
- Name your axes and titles wisely.
- If you're going to label your data, consider only labeling the min and max (or just max) instead of all values. Remember, that information is in your tooltips!
- Tooltips are a great place to add contextual information, such as a month-over-month comparison.

- Format your tooltips! Tableau will put information into the tooltips by default; it shows you're paying attention to the details to edit and upgrade the defaults.
- Use "tiled" containers, instead of having them "floating" on your dashboard. It takes some time to get used to arranging tiled containers, but it prevents objects on your dashboard from moving to places you don't want them and ruining your visualization when viewed on devices with different-sized screens.
- Whitespace is your friend. You can add "padding" to your containers to add separation between different charts.
- If you use a "dual axis" on your dashboard, don't forget to synchronize your axes. I made this mistake on the dashboard I presented in my technical interview for my first data job—a Tableau consultant role. Oops!
- You can use Figma to create sleek backgrounds or just to get images off the Internet and remove their backgrounds. I like to use The Noun Project to find icons.
- My favorite website for helping me pick a color palette is free—it's called Coolors.

C | My Data Analyst Journey

January

In January 2022 I was burnt out. I had six months of unpaid internships ahead of me, but since I was no longer a full-time graduate student and part- or full-time nanny, I had more time on my hands than I was used to. So, I started delivering for Instacart to help keep some cash flowing in—I was lucky to make $20 an hour on a good day.

I'd seen a lot of TikToks about side hustles and how lucrative the tech industry could be. I got the idea that if I could find a tech field that I could teach myself in a short amount of time, and do it remotely, I could replace Instacart with something I could do from home, at any time of day.

In the last week of January, I researched different jobs in tech and discovered data analytics. It seemed to me like part of data analytics was analyzing spreadsheets, and I saw some jobs on Indeed like "research assistant," which just involved analyzing their research spreadsheets. I had enough savings and free time that I decided to do an experiment and see if I could pick up a side hustle analyzing spreadsheets.

I Googled "how to become a data analyst" and the Google Certificates course in Data Analytics came up. They promised to teach you all the skills you need to become a data analyst, and you'd even get a certification at the end. I had heard enough to give it a shot, and I signed up for the free trial.

February

February was consumed with taking the course. When the weeklong free trial ended, I upgraded to the membership so that I could complete the course without a second thought. I found that I quickly fell in love with data analytics. I never intended to put much effort into learning anything besides Excel, but I quickly realized that SQL, Tableau, and R were all fascinating. I enjoyed the learning experience provided by the course, as well as the puzzle of working with data.

I finished the course right at the end of February, after spending at least 20 hours a week on learning. I carefully took notes on every module so that I could return to them later. I felt like I rushed through the course to a degree, because I wanted to finish it in under a month so I wouldn't have to spend $40 on another month.

In addition to the course, I started a small blog to document my learning experiences. I thought that it could be helpful to show to employers in the future to document my learning. I don't think any employers ever did or will read my blog, but you can check it out if you would like to read what I was thinking and learning from my perspective as I lived it: `https://anniesanalytics.wixsite.com/annie-nelson/blog`.

I also spent February building a small following on TikTok. I thought, "Hey, if this little experiment works, I bet people might like to know about it!" So, I started a TikTok account, thinking maybe a few hundred people would see my videos. By the end of the month, I was at 10,000 followers. Turns out, people were curious to see what would happen.

This part of the story is important because being on TikTok gave me exposure to a lot of people who were already in the data field. I realized due to all those interactions that there are many data analysts and people in the tech industry in general who make great salaries, work remotely, and don't have a degree in data analytics, computer science, or anything like that.

When I realized this subject I had quickly fallen in love with might have a low barrier to entry with a high career potential, that sparked my interest. However, I was still committed to occupational therapy. After all, I'd just spent over $80,000 on a master's degree!

March

March was my most directionless month of the learning journey. After finishing the course, I realized there were a lot of little things I had to do before looking for a data job, but I didn't have any one resource for what they all were or how to accomplish them. By the end of the month, I had:

- Completed two capstone projects at the end of the Google course that I could put in my portfolio.
- Built my own website using Wix (for free). It was not hard; I didn't have to do any coding. It was just time-consuming to decide on the aesthetics and elements. I started the website in February but made it presentable and styled in March.
- Put out a free GitHub file that was a collection of all the links and resources I'd found while taking the Google course, with links to many of my notes (which I hosted on my website). I still keep this file available at `https://anniesanalytics.wixsite.com/ annie-nelson/general-9`.
- Started a LinkedIn profile, which I treated basically as a résumé, and started making a few posts about what I was learning.
- Created a few basic portfolio projects on my own in Tableau and SQL using free data I found on the Internet. But I was so overwhelmed with where to get the data, which data to use, and then where to get started that I abandoned most of the project ideas I started.

I had begun to consider my options for the future at this point. On my TikTok I talked as if I was looking for a regular data analyst job, not just a side hustle. On the inside, I was conflicted. I genuinely wanted to become an occupational therapist and had worked so hard to do so. But I was looking around at other people in the profession and questioning whether it was the best choice.

When I thought about data analytics, I saw a profession that I found fascinating and exciting. I saw the possibility of remote work and a six-figure salary after a few months in the field. I love to travel, and so the idea of being able to work from anywhere was appealing. On the other hand, I looked at the therapists I was working with, and I saw a lifestyle that was less appealing.

When I looked at the life of a typical occupational therapist, I saw the challenges of existing in the American healthcare system. Often, therapists get treated poorly by their patients and their employers. One day when I was at my internship, the administration held a free lunch for all the nurses and healthcare staff, and scolded the physical and occupational therapists for showing up because they were not part of nursing. I was not ready to admit it to myself yet, let alone anyone in my life, but looking back I was ready to throw caution to the wind and pursue a career in data.

April

I was getting close to 20,000 followers on TikTok by the beginning of April, so I felt an obligation to everyone following me at that point to see my experiment through to the end. I started looking at data analyst job postings, and I saw Python listed in several of them. So, I spent a few weeks in April taking a lovely Python course. Although I enjoyed this course, I realized later that not a single recruiter or hiring manager was actually looking for Python skills.

In mid-April I went to visit some friends in Austin, Texas. While I was there, I was still plugging away at my Python course. The distance from home and my friends and family gave me the mental clarity I needed. I decided to go all in and get a full-time data analyst job while also still finishing my master's degree. I knew that if it didn't work, I had a perfectly good backup plan. I ignored how strange it was to be calling my master's degree a backup plan and carried on.

At the end of April, I began reaching out to some supportive friends from TikTok and LinkedIn and asked them to review my résumé. I'd started looking seriously at job postings and decided I would start applying to jobs in May. I put the last touches on my résumé, got my website ready to show to recruiters, and started asking my network what it would be like to apply to data jobs.

I also discovered something called "optimizing your LinkedIn." Apparently, if you do a good job setting up your LinkedIn profile, then recruiters and hiring managers will reach out to you and ask if you want to apply for jobs they have open. I say apparently, because at the time I was skeptical of this.

As it turns out, it was true. But it took me a few months to figure out how to make this approach work for me. I spent at least five hours researching creators on LinkedIn and other places on the Internet who were talking about "optimizing your LinkedIn" and trying to follow suit.

I didn't tell my friends or family (or anyone I knew besides my boyfriend) that I had decided to switch careers.

May

The job search began. I updated my résumé dozens of times throughout the month, seemingly to no avail. Despite sending out at least 50 job applications, I heard back from few companies, and most of the ones I did hear from ended in rejections (quickly). It turned into a month of rejections.

I didn't learn many new data skills because I was dedicating a few hours every day to applying to jobs and other job search–related items. It seemed as if every recruiter I did manage to talk to would quickly ask if I had any experience using SQL or Tableau professionally, to which I had to say no. I became so discouraged by the end of the month that I thought that my little experiment might end in failure, because nobody would hire me.

I'd also spent so much time on being a job seeker (plus my full-time internship, which was emotionally and physically exhausting) that I'd lost sight of my love for working with data. All the little tasks it took to look for a job in data had added up to a lot of time and effort. Working on my résumé, building a website, optimizing my LinkedIn, talking to recruiters—all of these things were not inherently fun for me, and I was tired.

At the end of the month, a friend of mine gently reminded me that I wanted to get into data because I love data, not because I love job seeking. So I decided that in June I would go back to my roots and change my strategy.

June

I sat down and thought about what all my interviewers had in common. I came to the conclusion that they all wanted to know if I could use Excel, SQL, or Tableau (which one depended on the role and company). So, I decided that if I could build out my portfolio with good projects to showcase my skills, then when they asked if I had experience, I could say yes.

I worked on a few projects in SQL and Tableau. I realized that, although I was finding upskilling in SQL on my own to be doable, I had hit this point in Tableau where I couldn't figure out what I needed to do to make my dashboards look better. So I signed up for a subscription with my now favorite course platform, Maven Analytics. I took a course in Tableau and immediately leveled up my Tableau skills and was able to create some cool projects.

I also took Maven's courses "Thinking Like an Analyst" and "Launching Your Data Career." It would've been better to take the "Thinking Like an

Analyst" course earlier in my journey, because it helped me understand that the key skills are actually the soft skills, like communication and problem solving. This helped me get a new perspective on my job interviews and prepared me to talk about my excellent critical thinking skills, instead of focusing on my lack of experience with the technical skills.

The "Launching Your Data Career" course taught me about portfolio building, optimizing my résumé and LinkedIn, and more about the data job search process. Although this would have been welcome information a month or two prior, it was a good time for me to take a look at all of this again and make more changes to my résumé and LinkedIn.

While I was taking the time to refocus on my data skills, I was still applying to jobs but not nearly as many. Instead, I started creating content on LinkedIn, talking about what I was learning and showcasing my new skills.

The combination of my new portfolio projects, everything I'd learned in the Maven courses, and everything I was doing on LinkedIn started to pay off quickly. Recruiters were sending me messages about jobs, and I even heard from a few hiring managers who told me an executive at their company had seen one of my posts on LinkedIn and asked them to reach out to me.

By the end of June, I was talking to so many companies that I had to stop applying for any new roles. I'd forgotten to add an interview to my calendar, and I'd had a stressful day at my internship—a patient with dementia, whom I adored, yelled at me. I was so swept away in the moment and emotionally exhausted from my three interviews the evening before that I forgot about the interview.

The interviewer sent a follow-up email chewing me out and told me I'd been rejected. The next day I put my search on hold and decided to focus on the leads I already had.

July

On July 8, I finished my internship and effectively graduated with my master's degree. I was interviewing seriously with four companies at the time and had about four more that I was in the beginning stages with. The following week I celebrated by buckling down on interviews. I knew that I was interviewing for a Tableau-heavy position, and so I put out my best Tableau project yet.

I'd already decided which role I was most interested in by the start of July, but I knew that I couldn't rely on getting that job. So I kept going with panel interviews and technical interviews at other companies. On July 18, I was offered a job at a company with a role that was interesting, but it was not my top choice. I knew I had one more interview/meeting the next day with my top choice, so I thanked them and asked for a few days to think about their offer. I was *very* nervous about everything at this point.

On July 19, I was offered a job at Zuar, a company based in Austin that provides data services to other businesses. I was offered a role as a fully remote Tableau consultant/data analyst, and I accepted immediately. I didn't even try to negotiate my salary or benefits—I felt too nervous. Additionally, this was my top company. I knew I would love it there. And they offered me a higher salary than I had originally been targeting in my job search.

I was at the Jersey shore with my parents that day, and so I ran straight down to the beach, elated, to tell them the good news. I don't live with them anymore, so it was a special moment to tell them in person. An hour later, I called two other companies and told them I would no longer be (virtually) attending my technical interviews the next day (90 minutes each!) because I'd accepted a role with another company. I also called the first company that offered me the role and thanked them and declined that job.

In just about six months I had gone from nanny/occupational therapist to data analyst (with a remote job). It still amazes me to look back at that time and think about everything I accomplished in such a short time. Since then, I have seen hundreds of other people do the same.

August–December

In 2022, I traveled more than I have in any other year of my life, except 2023. I spent time visiting my friends around the country and eventually around the world. Working remotely has completely changed the way I live my life.

I spent the first few months of my job learning how to do my job—and then I jumped in. 2022 was one of the best years of my entire life. I taught myself a new career that I loved, I finished graduate school (and passed the occupational therapy boards exam!), made a lot of new friends in data, got a job I was good at and enjoyed, and was able to travel all over the place.

I remember complaining to my boss in October 2022 that I had "peaked" and my life would only go downhill from there, because I didn't see how things could continue to be so awesome. So far, things have only remained awesome—despite some stress around changing jobs.

My learning journey did not end when I was hired. I've kept learning continuously since I started in data analytics. I love that I get to keep learning and growing. My boyfriend has told me that it feels as if I am a whole new person sometimes, because when I decided to become a data analyst it was more than just a career change. It was my way of stepping into a new lifestyle. I wouldn't change a single thing!

Acknowledgments

To me, this book is so much more than a book. It is the story of the last two years of my life, and it's also the story of how my life changed course drastically. How do you possibly find the words or the space to express your gratitude to the people who are part of that?

I don't know, but I can try.

Thank you to Nick and Asa, who, as far as I know, are the first two humans to ever truly see me as a data analyst.

Thank you to every person who commented, reposted, messaged, or otherwise came with me on my journey. Without the support and insights of kind strangers on the Internet, I never would've made it past my first course.

Thank you to Phil for enthusiastically welcoming me into the world of data analytics and being the best manager I could have asked for. Your friendship and support has cemented my love for data and accelerated my career.

Thank you to Cesar for seeing potential in me that even I couldn't see. Of all the people to randomly meet at a conference, I'm glad that I met you. Your insights into the industry are always exactly what I need.

Thank you to my content creator friends from whom I learn every day. Jess and Carly, having the support of other women ahead of me in this world is so valuable and I look up to each of you every day.

Thank you to Jim for seeing an author in me, and to Adaobi for making the editing process not only smooth, but enjoyable.

And then, of course, there are the people in my daily life without whom I never could have considered learning data analytics. Thank you to my parents for your unyielding support and willingness to accept all my random and sometimes surprising career choices. I owe so much to you.

And finally, to my Chris, thank you. Neither one of us predicted that someday you'd be trying to explain what a data analyst is at dinner parties, or that I would be asking you to cook dinner while I figured out that difficult line of code. Thank you for believing in me even in the hard times, and for being there to support me in so many new things in a row! From data analytics to contact creation to writing a book, you have rolled with all of it. You've been there through it all, and it wouldn't have happened without you.

About the Author

Annie Nelson is a full-time data analyst—with a master's degree in occupational therapy and many years of experience working with children. She has documented her unconventional journey to change careers and become a data analyst on TikTok and LinkedIn. Her posts are dedicated to sharing tips and tricks—as well as the real story behind what it's like to be a data analyst.

Thousands of people around the world have followed Annie's journey through the data space, and she has helped and inspired many to leave their previous jobs and make the leap into tech.

When she's not working or creating content, you can find Annie enjoying the freedom of remote work by traveling the world—or at least the United States. She is an avid rock climber and also enjoys hiking, skiing, and the occasional surfing session.

Index